Wainewright the Poisoner

Wainewright the Poisoner

THE CONFESSION OF
THOMAS GRIFFITHS WAINEWRIGHT

Andrew Motion

Alfred A. Knopf

New York

2000

Library of Congress Cataloging-in-Publication Data
Motion, Andrew.
Wainewright the poisoner / Andrew Motion.
p. cm.
Includes bibliographical references.
ISBN 0-375-40209-8
1. Wainewright, Thomas Griffiths, 1794–1847—Fiction. 2. Authors, English—19th
century—Fiction. 3. Art critics—Great Britain—Fiction. 4. Poisoners—Great
Britain—Fiction. 5. Convicts—Australia—Fiction. I. Title.
PR6063.O842 W35 2000
823'.914—dc21   99-089445

For Trezza Azzopardi

The fact of a man being a poisoner is nothing against his prose.
—OSCAR WILDE, "Pen, Pencil and Poison"

Oh self, self, self! Every man for himself, and no creature for me!
—CHARLES DICKENS, *Martin Chuzzlewit*

Contents

Contents

Illustrations

Illustrations

ACKNOWLEDGEMENTS

Archives Office of Tasmania, Hobart: 33, 35. Art Gallery of South Australia, Adelaide: 36, 37. British Museum, London, Department of Prints and Drawings: 1, 11. Henry Cary, *Memoir of the Rev Henry Francis Cary,* 1847: 24 (original portrait destroyed). Chiswick Public Library, London, Local Studies Department: 2. E. W. Cooke, *Fifty Plates of Shipping and Craft,* 1829: 30. Jonathan Curling, *Janus Weathercock, The Life of Thomas Griffiths Wainewright,* 1938: 9, 27, 39, 43 (location of original portraits unknown, possibly destroyed in WWII). Mary Evans Picture Library, London: 29. Greenwich Council, London, Local History Library: 3, 4. Paul Grinke, London: 18. Institut für Kunstwissenschaft, Zurich: 17. Mitchell Library, State Library of New South Wales: 34, 44. National Gallery of Australia, Canberra: 42. National Portrait Gallery, London: 6, 19, 20, 21, 25, 26. City of Nottingham Museums (Newstead Abbey): 7, 8. Private Collection: 13, 14, 15. Photo Bridgeman Art Library. London: 28. Scottish National Portrait Gallery, Edinburgh: 22. Alfred T. Story, *Life of John Linnell,* 1892: 5, 16 (location of original portraits unknown). *Survey of London* (vol. xxx, 1963): 28. Tasmanian Museum and Art Gallery, Hobart: 31, 32, 38, 40, 41. Victoria and Albert Museum, London: 12. *The Wasp* Journal of the 16th Foot, The Bedfordshire and Hertfordshire Regiment Association: 10. © Keith Wynn/London Metropolitan Archives: 23.

Acknowledgements

I could not have written this book without the help of the following libraries: the Allport Bequest Library, Hobart; the Bodleian Library, Oxford; the New York Public Library (Berg Collection); the British Library; the Chiswick Local History Library; the City of Westminster Archives; the Derbyshire Record Office; the Family Records Centre, London; the Greenwich Local History Library; the Hammersmith Local History Library; the Hertfordshire County Library; the London Metropolitan Archives; the Mitchell Library, Sydney; the National Art Library (Victoria & Albert Museum); the National Gallery, London; the National Portrait Gallery, London; the Norfolk County Library; the Public Record Office, London; the State Library of Tasmania; the Tasmanian Museum and Art Gallery, Hobart; the Tasmanian State Archive, Hobart; the Witt Library, London.

I am also indebted to the following: Anthony Bailey; John Beer; David Bindman; Juliet Brightmore; Chris Brooks; Max Browne; Martin Butlin; Stephen Calloway; Peter Conrad; Sarah Cupit; Diane Dunbar; Chris Fletcher; Sybilla Jane Flower; Lucy Frost; Des Griffin; Peter and Carolyn Hammond; David Hansen; Jean Haynes; Paul Hopkins; W. Nevin Hurst (Masterpiece Fine Art Gallery, Hobart); Lorraine Jenkyns; David Lawton; Hermione Lee; Roger Lonsdale; Tony Marshall; Jenna Mead; Philip Mead; Virginia Murray; Paul Paffen; Annette Peach; Cassandra Pybus; Lynne Smith; Lindsay Stainton; G. T. Stilwell; Jenny Thompson; David Weinglass; John White; Meriel Wilmot-Wright; Duncan Wu.

I am especially grateful to Jon Cook; Jan Dalley; Chuck Elliott; Nick Groom; Alan Hollinghurst; Nick Jose; Pat Kavanagh; Julian Loose; Christopher Reid; and Claire Roberts.

I would particularly like to thank Marc Vaulbert de Chantilly for the painstaking attention he has given to this book.

Foreword

Thomas Griffiths Wainewright (1794–1847) lived half his life close to the centre of the Romantic revolution, half in exile and disgrace. His grandfather-guardian was the founder of the *Monthly Review,* England's original "literary magazine"; he was educated by the great Classical scholar Charles Burney; he studied under two of the best-known artists of the day, John Linnell and Thomas Phillips; he painted Byron's portrait, and exhibited regularly at the Royal Academy during the early 1820s; he was good friends with Henry Fuseli, William Blake and Charles Lamb; he knew John Clare, William Hazlitt, Thomas de Quincey, Barry Cornwall and John Keats; he wrote art criticism for the *London Magazine* in its heyday; he was famously "amiable," "kind" and "good-hearted"—silver-tongued, and a tremendous dandy.

He was also an ingenious and unscrupulous criminal. In 1822 and 1823 he forged the deeds on a trust fund left to him by his grandfather, in order to finance his extravagant life in London. In 1828 his uncle died in suspicious circumstances, whereupon Wainewright inherited the handsome family home in Chiswick, Linden House. In 1829 his mother-in-law also died unexpectedly. The following year, Wainewright devised a complicated life-insurance scam which involved one of his wife's half-sisters, a young and healthy woman called Helen Abercromby. Helen died as soon as the policies were in place.

Wainewright fled to France after this third death, and lived there for five and a half shady years. During this time, rumours about his crimes spread promiscuously. When he was eventually arrested on a visit to London in 1837 and tried at the Old Bailey—not for murder, which could never be proved, but for forgery—his reputation was already in tatters. The sentence of the court branded him a despicable outcast: he was transported for life to Van Diemen's Land.

Most of Wainewright's friends had long since disowned him; now they began recalling his flamboyance as something sinister, and the facetiousness of his prose as hollow flippancy. His London paintings (which anyway he had never signed) were scattered and lost. His marvellous collections of prints, china and drawings were sold. His wife and son emigrated to America and never contacted him again. The fifty or so "convict works" he produced in Hobart after 1840 were disparaged or neglected.

In the process, many of the materials essential to his biography were destroyed. All but a handful of his letters have disappeared. He was rumoured to have kept a diary at one time: if he did, it has vanished. His story, instead of being properly investigated, was told and retold without any regard for its truth. Newspapers and magazines repeatedly used him as a byword for evil. Edward Bulwer-Lytton and Charles Dickens (who visited Wainewright in Newgate prison) both wove elaborate fictions around him; Oscar Wilde made him the subject of a brilliant and mischievous essay; and in this century, others have followed where they led—notably the Australian writer Hal Porter, whose novel *The Tilted Cross* adapts Wainewright's story.

This means that anyone wanting to write about Wainewright today would face formidable difficulties, if he or she were to use orthodox biographical methods. Not only is the overlay of legends very thick, but Wainewright falls out of the historical record so often, and for such long periods of time, it is impossible to construct the complete linear narrative of his life. Equally, the shortage of intimate papers makes it hard to hear the voice in which he spoke to himself and his closest friends.

None of this would matter very much, if Wainewright himself did not matter. But he does—not so much for his artistic achievements, as for his story. Sometimes this is for particular reasons. His contact with better-known contemporaries shines a bright light on their achievements, their personalities, their conscious aspirations, and their unconscious imperatives—especially their preoccupation with the self. In other ways, Wainewright's value is more general. His career dramatizes ideas that deeply concerned Wordsworth, Coleridge, Byron, Keats, de Quincey, Lamb, and many other Romantic writers and artists. By combining a life in culture with a life in crime, he embodies an extreme version of what they regarded as a general truth: that good and evil grow on the same stem.

This helps to explain why Wainewright became such a notorious figure for much of the nineteenth century—at once predictable and astonishing, appealing and appalling. In philosophical terms, it was just about possible for tolerant commentators (Alexander Gilchrist in his life of Blake, for instance, and Swinburne and Wilde) to keep the contradictions in balance. But when Wainewright's story was treated as a purely social thing, "astonishing" and "appalling" became the watchwords. Hence the fictional recreations, which were not interested in examining the facts of his story, but merely in hardening the impression of deep-dyed evil. Hence too the suppressions and disownings, which have made an orthodox biography so difficult.

In such a case, the long-term result is all too predictable: neglect. As the juggernaut of nineteenth-century studies has rolled forward, it has left Wainewright slumped in a dusty corner: a cardboard villain with artistic pretensions and a pair of fancy moustaches. And unless biographers are prepared to think differently about their work, he is likely to stay there, his whole personality over-simplified and demonized, his once vivid experience faded, his art ignored, his voice lost, his role in the lives of more famous contemporaries overlooked. But "think differently" how? Clearly, our responsibility to history includes a duty to report on forgotten lives—yet if the material simply isn't there, what can be done?

This book provides one possible answer. The bulk of it is a re-creation of that well-established nineteenth-century form, the confession, which purports to have been written by Wainewright in Van Diemen's Land shortly before his death in 1847. Although it often quotes or adapts his own words (taken mainly from his art criticism), and the words of his contemporaries, these could never be used to tell the whole story of his life. So the rest is my invention. Wherever appropriate, I have tried to ventriloquize his dandified, high-energy style—with the intention of capturing his charm as well as his callousness, his wit as well as his wantonness. More often (bearing in mind that the Confession is meant to be written at the end of his life, when he was broken and disillusioned), I have toned things down, and made him concentrate on telling "the truth." The example of his own prose that I kept most urgently in mind, and used as a kind of guide, was his ticket-of-leave appeal, written in Hobart in 1844, which appears on pages 240–2.

But this document was helpful to me in other ways as well. Although it seems to be reliable, it is in fact a ragbag of fair comments, evasions, and downright lies—which made me feel that when I "made Wainewright concentrate on telling 'the truth,'" I should not let him succeed too well if I was going to portray him accurately. Even though his major crimes were committed in England, he was still pretty devious after living as a convict for ten years in Van Diemen's Land—happy, as he always had been, to slip between different personalities.

In other words, the answer to the question "How reliable is the Confession?" is this: as reliably unreliable as Wainewright himself. In order that readers should not feel too disorientated by this, various things need to be emphasized. The great majority of scenes and encounters in the Confession, all the friendships, and all the main events, actually happened. Often (such as in chapter 9, when he organizes a dinner party for his fellow contributors to the *London Magazine*) I have used contemporary accounts, weaving them together with Wainewright's own words to make a consecutive narrative. (Chapter 9, for instance, uses extracts from Procter, Talfourd, Clare, Cary and others.) At other times, where no word from Wainewright survives (such as during his voyage to Van Diemen's Land, and the whole of his time on the chain gang), I have used other people's accounts of such experiences, and let myself add things that are typical and appropriate—for instance, the shooting of the albatross in chapter 18.

My "borrowed" words are a part of the orthodox biography that this book contains. A far larger part lies scattered through the many notes that appear at the end of each chapter. These notes are not designed to "correct" the Confession in any consistent way (though they do sometimes draw attention to the fact that it is not always completely honest). Rather, they provide the necessary background to characters and events, develop themes, and sometimes give mini-essays on subjects that were important to the Romantics in general and to Wainewright in particular.

So the book is an experiment. But while it contains a mixture of different forms—some imaginative, some factual—they all share a common purpose. They are dedicated to rescuing Wainewright from obscurity, and to bringing him back to life as a plausible and dynamic force. At the same time, they are designed to enjoy his achievements as an artist and critic, to explore his career as a criminal, and to investigate his self. The voice that I have given him is in some sense a confection, but it is nothing more nor less than the one I would have tried to characterize by more conventional means, had I decided to write a more familiar sort of biography. Exactly the same applies to my treatment of his personality.

This means that *Wainewright the Poisoner* goes public about matters that biography normally only implies. Readers are invited to accept its author at his word, but should always be prepared to take his honesty with a pinch of salt. I would have found it difficult—though perhaps not impossible—to have taken this line with someone who lived more importantly than Wainewright in the public mind. Philip Larkin, say, or John Keats. When I was writing about those two poets, I often found myself silently debating questions of biographical form, which I have more and more keenly wanted to ask aloud. Wainewright's Confession is meant to do just this, among other things, but in dramatic rather than theoretical ways.

Wainewright
the
Poisoner

I INTRODUCE MYSELF AND DISAPPEAR

Since nothing in life is certain (that is the only certain thing) I shall begin this Confession by insisting on what a less sceptical age would accept without question. It is the truth. Not the whole truth (for such a thing is impossible), and not the only truth (ditto), but not a lie.

I shall begin simply, as I mean to continue. *My name:* Thomas Griffiths Wainewright. Wainewright for my father; Griffiths for my mother, it being *her* father's name; Thomas for myself—that is, for doubt of myself, and of others, as we shall see. *My age:* Fifty-two years—forty-three spent among living minds, comprehending beauty; nine here, among dead things. *My address:* 8 Campbell Street, Hobart Town, Van Diemen's Land. *My occupation:* Painter; also, from now on, Author, as I used to be when I could argue with the best of them. In those days, I wrote for different reasons—for ornament and entertainment. Now I write for use, and to be plain. Let me put this another way, to ensure clarity in everything and at the beginning especially. Truth, like a strip of beaten gold, may be worked into a shape and remain the truth. We may have pleasure and still redeem ourselves.

One more thing—my *circumstances.* I am writing at a small honest table made of gumwood from the forest hereabouts (I mean, in the vicinity of Hobart Town), though which of the gum's infinite varieties I cannot say. I have my face to the window looking east. At my point in Campbell Street, which is closer to the harbour than those wild spaces where the road ends, the ground rises, offering a view which I have to admit is fine. Today, for instance, this late winter morning of 26 July 1846, I can look across a half-mile of scrub to the estuary, and watch the sea-tide running in against the current of the broad river Derwent. There is a clash of silver spear-points in the water. An immense warfare, silent from this distance, yet amidst the confusion it appears that the river must soon give way, and begin running backwards towards its source. The thought of such an unexpected thing makes my heart flutter, so that I can scarcely continue writing—only brood in silence for a moment on the difficulties of my own case.

Now I have stammered long enough. (I never did stammer; just a lisp, occasionally.) I shall begin. Not at the beginning, however, but at the centre, the fulcrum, where my existence hung between light and darkness.

The travesties of the trial were over, and their ruthless perfidy set in law. Like flotsam on a strong current, I was jostled down from the dock into a foul corridor, then immediately lower again to my more foul cell in Newgate. The companions I had left there earlier in the day—I cannot call them friends, although in the weeks gone by they had seen me more nakedly than anyone—my companions there: even they looked aghast at me. They had heard of my talk with the Governor; they knew I had come to terms. If my plea was guilty, I was to be shown mercy. All I had done was take what was mine. [1]

Now they heard that I was transported; done for; bound and gagged like an animal; sunk from sight in a pit which was Hell and Sodom and Bedlam combined.

And still hurtled towards it at such speed! It seemed, during the few moments I stood in dumb horror, as though my cellmates were pressing themselves against the walls in order to escape the maelstrom in which I was caught. I shall not dwell now on its humiliations. But at the same time I cannot forget the brute who shaved off my hair and moustaches; he cut me so deep on my scalp in one place, I still had not healed by the time our transport reached Simons Town. Nor how my clothes were given up and replaced with a suit of coarse grey which chafed me. It had a number 10 stitched on the back, large as a house address. How I grieved for them, my clothes, gathered in our gaoler's fist and offered for sale to my companions. The beautiful blue surcoat which I had thought would temper judgment. [2] The waistcoat and cravat. The soft calf boots (which I admit were not worth much in the auction, being worn through in the soles. But my surcoat was sold for 2/-, which was a bargain.).

When this was all done, my hurry subsided. Then next morning early it began again exactly as before. The cell door whisked open, the moans and complaints of my fellows were fanned into life, and I was propelled out into the bare stone corridor, upstairs, and brought to a halt in the lodge-room I remembered from the day I was admitted. Although I was weak with dread, and baffled by the injustice done to me, I was nevertheless relieved to be above ground—and even more so to be away from the stench below.

There was a turnkey, whom I also recognized, and this encouraged me to speak to him. "Sir," I began, or something very like, "I am the friend of Coleridge, of Flax—" but I got no further. The turnkey interrupted by lifting one paw and striking me across the mouth, repeating "Sir" in a little mincing voice, then adding in his own growl, "You are the friend of no one." [3]

It was all I could do then not to weep—and perhaps a few tears did escape me, as I saw that my old life was entirely beyond my reach. The fetters hanging on the wall of the lodge like giant ribbons, and the boards inscribed with the prison rules, all seemed to sway for a moment. I am sure that if I had not controlled myself fiercely, I would have fainted from the insult of the blow. The greater offence of what followed required an even stronger discipline. The turnkey told me I was to be taken down to the hulks at Portsmouth by stagecoach, leaving immediately. I would have a fellow travelling with me, he said—*and* (this was added with relish) "a guard to keep an eye." Whereupon he hoisted down one of the fetters from its hook on the wall, fastened its two irons round my ankles, and shouted through the door by which I had entered: "Come up!"

At once the wretch I knew must be my companion was brought forward—a yellow-faced, red-nosed creature, whom then or later I never heard make any sound except a rumbling sigh. The prisoner-companion I must call a man, though really he was no more than a boy—a thin-faced, hollow-chested boy, whose shivering reminded me of a mouse cornered on a threshing floor. Like me, he was shaven-headed, dressed in the same coarse grey, and also like me he had a number on his back: number 11. Sensible of the differences between us, and seeing that I was old enough to be his father, I held out my hand to him as the turnkey knelt to buckle on his fetters. He ignored me. "What is your name?" I continued. He looked at me straight, then put back his narrow head and laughed so that I saw the whole long extent of his throat. "Eugene Aram," he said, which of course it could not have been. "What is yours?" "I have no name," I replied, which was nothing less than the truth. [4]

The turnkey straightened as this exchange ended, and showed that he did not wish it to resume by giving another sullen lift of his arm. Then he ordered us out of the lodge-house, into a dusty yard. Even now I cannot forget how the fresh air, the first I had tasted for several days, fell on my bare head like cold metal, stopping me in my tracks while I looked up into the heavens. There were only a few moments until sunrise, and the last stars were beginning to weaken as I had seen them do a hundred times when driving the deserted road back from London to Chiswick in my former existence. Then, they had always seemed the dear companions of my gaiety; on this dismal morning, they appeared to shine from beyond a colossal pane of glass, and were separated from me by something more than distance.

The turnkey called to me to keep moving, though I almost at once came to a halt again. The lodge-gate was a huge affair, spiked and studded like an instrument of torture, and when it was unlocked, another identical gate was revealed a few yards ahead. Eugene (I may as well call him that), the rumbling guard, and I, stood jammed together while the turnkey locked the inner door before opening the outer one—all with a great pantomime of key-rattling as though our brief journey might have created a devilish talent for vanishing.

By now, however, my fate lay on me so heavily I had no thought of escape. As I stepped out into the empty street, exactly as the earliest sunlight began flooding the sky, I felt as I had done when looking up at the stars. I was no longer a part of life—but a ghost, haunting the city and its sights. The cobbles at my feet were covered with a battered layer of straw, laid when the Courts were sitting, and when I noticed that this straw was shining with a layer of dew, and smelled shockingly of beer spilt by the crowds which had gathered here previously, the information seemed meaningless. In an effort to shake off this mood, I immediately replaced it with another which proved even more painful. I looked beyond the grim barricade of Newgate towards the dome of St. Paul's Cathedral. The same dome which had soared above me when I stood at hand to lower the coffin of my esteemed friend Henry Fuseli into the earth! The contrast between the proud grief I had felt on that day, and the misery of the moment, was sufficient to turn me briefly from the shadow I had become into a suffering man once more. I could scarcely endure it.

Indeed, I think I would have fallen down stunned on the stones, had the turnkey not roughly bundled me forward again. He was impatient for the coach to appear. If I had in any way wondered about this, it had merely been to ask myself whether we were to be carried in a special, dedicated carriage—and as I now put the question to myself again, the thing itself materialized. It was a common-or-garden diligence with a hungry-looking jarvey on top, swaddled in his greatcoat. Yet, with the horses breathing smoke in the morning air, and the straw-scattering, heaven-swaying, lurching magnificence of the carriage appearing to shimmer as it bowled towards us, it seemed more entirely part of a dream than anything I had yet seen that day. It filled the whole width of the road.

"Climb aboard," said our turnkey, already beginning to unlock the prison gate behind us, eager to let himself back into his kingdom. As I did so, with Eugene and our guard clattering up on the roof behind me, I noticed a woman's fingers closing round the curtain which shielded the interior of the carriage. Four fine white fingers, one wearing a wedding ring.

By some trick of nature, the air seemed colder on our perch, but squeezed between Eugene and our guard, and expecting that if anyone looked up from the streets as we passed I should burn with humiliation, I felt warm enough. Eugene was restless, first untying his neckerchief and binding it round his ankle, inside his iron to protect the skin, then fiddling a clay pipe from the vest inside his uniform, filling it, and lighting it with hungry sucks and gasps. As we set off, smoke trailed over his shoulder, reminding me (which I had not in the least anticipated) of the stream train I had seen illustrated in the newspapers, when my uncle William had been in Manchester with Mr. Huskisson. [5]

With every twist of the road, my heart lifted at the thought of Newgate falling behind us. At the same time, I shrank with dread from the realization of what lay in store. This caused such a confusion in my spirits, that what with the rolling of the coach, and the early hour, and the lack of sleep I had suffered during the past several nights, I fell into a sort of trance. I saw the shining roofs of the City of London sliding beneath me like the flagstones of an enormous pavement. I was crossing them but my body had no weight, and I was able to glance down through windows at women preparing breakfast, setting out loaves and fruit, and at men buttoning into waistcoats, pressing on hats, pulling shut doors behind them. Weightless, I say—but not unfeeling. On my left, St. Paul's continued to mock me with its memories, and beyond it, along Cheapside and the Poultry, stretched the banks and offices where I had laid the foundations of my ruin. I almost supposed they were laughing at me, the gentlemen of the City: the living jeering from their niches in Threadneedle Street, the dead rising up in their winding-sheets from the graveyards of St. Ethelburgh and St. Andrew Undershaft.

On my right, the punishment was worse. As though a second Great Fire had swept across London during the night, and then been extinguished as dawn came up, the whole labyrinth of streets lay smoking in the sun. Everything that I knew was dull and grey seemed white and gold. Everything squalid and muddled seemed beautiful and orderly. I saw the faces of those I had loved, floating like spectres in the mist—no, like faces in the crowd on the Strand, as though they and I might be heading off together once more for George's, or the Coalhole: Lamb and Clare, Hazlitt and John Scott, Fuseli and Blake, Barry Cornwall and John Foster. As I looked at them, they bowed away from me like leaves in a gust of autumn wind, their faces puckering in disgust or sorrow. "Come back," I wanted to call out, my eyes filling with tears. However, I knew that any account I might give of myself would be useless.

We reached Blackfriars and turned left along Upper Thames Street, where the delightful spire of St. James Garlickhythe passed so close to us, I could have reached out and pricked my palm upon its point. But by now I was not in a mind to reach out for anything. Besides, the stench rising from the river alongside us compelled me to press my hands over my nose. The mudbanks, sloping deep into the channel—the tide being out—were littered with waste. From inside the coach beneath me, there came a groaning laugh.

Then we were over Southwark Bridge, and properly on our way. At this point I stopped paying attention to my surroundings. The feeling that had been swelling within me ever since leaving Newgate, the feeling that each turn of the wheels was severing me from the past, was now so strong I truly believed I had become a stranger to myself. In a final, appalling conflagration, the faces of my friends spun through the mist behind me, whizzing up into the heavens and vanishing. Whirling round them, in a million particles of dust and ashes, ascended everything that had been my pride and joy. Shards of my beautiful china. Scraps of prints I had almost blinded myself by gazing upon. Paint flecks and graphite fragments of my treasures by Fuseli and Blake. Canvas threads from Holst, who took me in when the rest of the world spurned me. All gone into oblivion. All blasted out of my life. My love for them, which I had trusted would prove a right to possession, had turned out to be worth nothing. I myself was nothing. A nothing manacled and shamed, with no voice left to influence what might become of me.

1. TGW was tried for forgery at the Central Criminal Court of the Old Bailey on the morning of 5 July 1837. The phrase "ruthless perfidy" comes from the ticket-of-leave appeal that he made in Van Diemen's Land on 18 April 1844.

2. Several phrases in this section are taken from the description of Newgate given by Charles Dickens in *Great Expectations*. The references to the coat, however, are taken from TGW's own writing, where he tells us that during the 1820s, when he was living in style, he owned a pale blue "military-looking surcoat." He also admired the green coat belonging to John Clare, which Clare is shown wearing in the portrait by their friend William Hilton which now hangs in the National Portrait Gallery, London.

3. TGW mentions his friendship with John Flaxman and various other artists in his ticket-of-leave appeal.

4. At least a dozen of the convicts transported with TGW were less than twenty years old. One of them, who was eighteen, and had been sentenced for stealing a hat, gave his name falsely as "Eugene Aram." The real Eugene Aram (1704–1759) was a notorious criminal; he had originally worked as a schoolteacher in King's Lynn, Norfolk, and ended up, like TGW, being the subject of a novel by Edward Bulwer-Lytton.

5. William Wainewright, the youngest brother of TGW's father Thomas, was Parliamentary Private Secretary to William Huskisson, the Liverpool MP and one-time President of the Board of Trade. William Wainewright cared for Huskisson when he was fatally injured by Stephenson's locomotive the *Rocket,* at the opening of the Liverpool-Manchester Railway on 15 September 1830, and remained with him when he was carried "in excruciating agony," and with one leg already amputated, to the house of a friend in Eccles to make his will. "It is an extraordinary fact," said the *Manchester Guardian,* "and evinces the uncommon firmness and self-possession of the right honourable gentleman under such awful circumstances, that after he signed the papers he leaned back, as it were, to place a dot over the i, and another between the W and the H." Shortly before Huskisson died, William Wainewright added a codicil to the will in his own hand.

2

ARE WE?

*T*he confusions of my life began the moment I was born. My mother died within minutes of my entry into the world—though whether this fatal event took place in Chiswick, where my grandfather was living, or in Twickenham, as my good friend Egomet Bonmot once said in rhyme, or at Richmond, I cannot be sure. Had my father lived beyond my ninth year, when I had not yet had the wit to ask him a sensible question concerning my nativity, I might have settled matters. I might also have agreed with him upon a precise date. As it is, I have been compelled to discover the pleasures of being a little imprecise. [1]

The *Gentleman's Magazine,* reporting my mother's death "at the early age of twenty-one," gave the day of our instantaneous joining-and-parting as 4 October 1794. The few melancholy sentences of her obituary—carried, I fear, more as a mark of respect for her celebrated father than for her extinct self—provided one other detail. She was, the elegist said, greatly regretted on account of her amicable disposition and uncommon accomplishments, and was "supposed to have understood the writings of Mr. Locke as well as, perhaps, any person, of either sex, now living." [2]

I have often pondered this judgement, feeling a powerful admiration for the talents my mother did not live to share with me. It is well known among men of a reasonable intelligence (though none of them are hereabouts) that Locke denied the once universal belief which held: there are in the *understanding* certain *innate principles* stamped upon the mind of man. It is also well known that he demanded the replacement of this belief with another, which stated: our *experience* alone should guide us towards our *speculative opinions.*

To speak for myself, this substitute notion has usefully made me imagine my infant mind as a flat and empty place until the winds of the world blew into it, carrying whatever impressions I was capable of receiving, and forming them into valleys and mountains, plains and gentle slopes. I have had enough time since then, God knows, to wander among their shapes, reflecting on how much or how little shelter they give, and how in any case they exist to prove that I am nothing but the sum of everything I know. Which is a curious consolation, in the circumstances.

During my prime, in London, I asked myself these same questions, putting them to my companions and being rewarded with the smiles which seemed a sufficient answer at that leisurely time. My friend Theodore von Holst (who enjoyed his full name, but whom I shall hereafter call merely "Holst," for the sake of convenience)—Holst was more particular. Encouraged by a succession of coincidences I cannot now recall, he had been employed by a certain bookseller to engrave a Frontispiece for that shocking and profound story of *Frankenstein,* by Mary Shelley, the wife of Percy, whom almost alone of his great poetic contemporaries I never met. I knew of this book—all my circle knew of it—but I had never examined a single page until I received a copy from Holst's own hand. Then I fell upon it eagerly, realizing at once that the efforts of the Creature to attain his knowing personhood held up a mirror to my own story. It is all just as Locke indicated. "I ought to be thy Adam," the poor Creature says to the doctor, or something very like, "but I am rather thy fallen Angel, whom thou drivest from joy for no misdeed. Everywhere I see bliss, from which I alone am irrecoverably excluded. I was benevolent and good; misery made me a fiend. Make me happy and I shall again be virtuous." [3]

Make me happy. When I was old enough to consider my situation in life with due gravity, I understood that, in my orphan state, the task of providing for such a thing as happiness must fall to my grandfather, since my actual father was not often at home, and when he was, lived entirely in the old man's shadow. [4]

I have already suggested that my grandfather Griffiths found losing his daughter and gaining me to be less than a fair trade. When I close my eyes and summon him up now, I see a hard and compact bomb-ball shooting towards me to knock me flat, or preferably do away with me altogether. A round body squeezed into a tight black coat; round calves bulging below black knee-breeches; a round red face beneath a white wig; and an angry fizz emanating from the mouth as though the whole construction might go sky high at any moment. Short as he was, I nevertheless see him looming *above* me (this is not to be wondered at, since I was still a child when he died, and small for my age).

At other times, when I am less alarmed, I see him in a dark room where only the white of his wig is visible, so that it seems to have acquired a life of its own, and flown off his head. In the gloom behind this strange and disembodied object—although I can never quite catch her attention—is my grandmother (my mother's mother), who I think is thinner and less kind than our cook, quieter and less comforting than the chambermaid, cleaner and less open-hearted than the groom. [5] Lurking yet deeper in the darkness is my uncle George. I shall come to him in a while.

My grandfather was seventy-four years old when I arrived to destroy his peace, and although I never knew it while he still breathed, he had lived valuably. His own childhood, which I now suppose to have been a dry affair, his family being Presbyterians, was spent at Stone in Staffordshire, where he trained first as a watchmaker, before scraping the county-clods from his shoes, as his acquaintance Samuel Johnson also did, and travelling to London. There he fell in with Jacob Robinson, a bookseller in Ludgate Circus, and through him met another gentleman who dealt in books, named Thomas Davies. This Davies and my grandfather liked each other so much, they soon combined in the publication of an evening newspaper. My grandfather must have enjoyed his work, being a stickler for accurate information, but he also dreamed of a different career. Therefore, when he had made an adequate profit, he sheared off from Davies, and set up a bookshop at the sign of The Dunciad (mocking his own presumption) in St. Paul's Churchyard.

By now my grandfather had reached a point of sufficient confidence to concentrate all his different energies into one, and propel himself towards the great endeavour of his life. This was a magazine, the *Monthly Review,* which was unlike any other then existing, and which would attend to literary matters, and dignify them with the reward of a proper account. So many other minds agreed with his ambition, and supported his labours, that the *Review* remained his whole interest and employment for the remainder of his days. (Which used to strike me as astonishing, since when I first looked over certain old numbers, they seemed like sepulchres full of ashes. Column upon column, all stuffed with dead histories, forgotten travels, exploded theories and obscure theologies. When I eventually learned to peruse them more carefully, and could understand their arguments, I knew better.) [6]

My grandfather and his wife Isabella—with whom he shared much, to the annoyance of his detractors—took almost the entire business of publication upon their own four shoulders, and conducted it with the utmost care and attention. He was a man of definite hatreds: hatred of the established Church, hatred of Tories, hatred of literary name-calling, and hatred of any form of flaunted personality. And also a man of settled sympathies. Everything was to be liberal (with Whig principles sternly applied); and everything must be learned (but fiercely defended). Whether giving his own judgements, or printing the opinions of others, he acted with a spirit at once definite and open, intent to register all new things in general, without exception to any, on account of their lowness of rank.

The contributors to my grandfather's magazine were his mainstays and his guiding lights combined—though none put their own name to their work, merely a pseudonym, or a gaggle of letters thus: XYZ, or ABC. In my uncle George's time, when he had inherited the business, I was interested to unravel some of their identities. William Taylor of Norwich I remember first, for broadening the foundations of everything in his attention to Continental literature, and for creating "the style of philosophical criticism" (as Hazlitt termed it) which has since become the staple of the *Edinburgh Review*. And others I could name. My grandfather's brother-in-law and ally, Dr. William Rose, who on occasion would even fulfil the office of Editor (with Dr. Kippis the Dissenter). William Bewley, the friend of Priestley. John Seddon, the rector of the Academy at Warrington. Cartwright the reformer. Samuel Clarke, the tutor for Dodderidge in Northampton. Samuel Goodenough, later of the Linnaean Society. Owen Ruffhead the radical. How could I have once thought these men capable of dead history? In peace-time and at war, they wrote to defend the elegance of the English tongue. Ruffhead, I remember my uncle saying with an approving nod, berated Johnson himself for cluttering his *Rasselas* with "excogitation," "exaggeratory," and so on. And when the incomparable Sterne, whose writings I have preferred to almost any other—when Sterne produced his "Sermons by Mr. Yorick," my grandfather condemned it as a kind of slander against the Holy Ghost.

Such biliousness, which for my own part I blame on Presbyterian blood, spoils a page in the *Review* now and again. Yet I must not exaggerate its extent. The principal effort of my grandfather's life was to discover a means of becoming freely himself—indeed, to find how *all* men might become freely themselves—and for that I honour him. First and last he loved to scorn ancient authority, whether it was of the Church, or of the dead languages in our systems of schooling. He and his associates—among whom, I should add, he counted that great mind Josiah Wedgwood—looked down from a superior height on the mere taste-mongers of the town and the coffee-houses, reckoning the arts they esteemed were neither moral nor instructive. [7]

It is for these reasons (and not only, I think, because of the attacks on his style), that Johnson criticized my grandfather for "pulling down all establishments." Nor is it surprising that our knobbly-faced Tory chronicler

Tobias Smollett should have set up his *Critical Review* to confound him, ridiculing his politics but, much more grossly, the licence he gave to his wife Isabella in running his affairs. I say it again: I honour my grandfather for all this, which makes the columns of his dead pages live again, and breathe a fine spirit of generosity. [8]

But as I am determined to be plain, I will say there was little love bound up with these feelings of honour. I would hesitate to admit this, even after so many years, were I not encouraged by a certain notorious episode in my grandfather's life. Before I come to my own case, therefore, let me call to the witness stand the author Oliver Goldsmith, whom my grandfather met in the Academy of Mr. Milner of Peckham, when the young author was working there as an usher.

Within a short time of their first meeting, Mr. G. was my grandfather's creature—employed by the *Review,* and housed and fed at his own home—which was soon the ground of difficulties between them. Which is to say: my grandfather was often fierce in his pursuit of justice, and capable of immense feats of diligence; and Mr. G. was feckless, as even his fondest admirers will admit. Therefore, if the young hack took paper from the shop for his own writing, my grandfather accused him of stealing it. If he laid down his knife and fork for a moment at the supper table—the plate was removed from his place. After a little while, these annoyances grew so intense, the two men parted in anger—though in later years they swerved close together once more, and clattered their heads together most painfully, which I cannot now bear to remember. [9]

Mr. G. retired from this final encounter with an ache and a resentment, and my grandfather with an injury to his liberal reputation. No one on earth could be more in sympathy than myself with the notion that a man may not deserve the words spoken about him. But even when I remind myself of the maddening habits of underlings, I still cannot deny that my grandfather's behaviour towards Mr. G. smacks of parsimony. And, admitting this, I draw closer to my own case with a stronger resolve. I mean: the manner in which he was also parsimonious towards me, his grandson. [10]

Yet for the second time I must delay my account of this, if I am to give a clear picture of myself and my earliest circumstances. (My enemies will protest at this point, and say my hesitations show deceit. But surely a man may be cautious and not have something to hide?) I shall, however, make my digression swiftly, because I would blush to give it slowly. At the heart of my grandfather's tangled money interests, there lies a question. How did a person of humble origins establish his *Review* in the first place, and make it prosper? By chance, is the answer; by chance—and in the following manner. There was a fellow known to my grandfather in his bookselling days, whose poverty was such that he had been incarcerated in the Fleet prison. While under guard in that dismal place, this gentleman had passed many dreary hours composing a story. My grandfather, who kept up with this tale while visiting his friend, liked it exceedingly, and eventually made an offer to publish it, paying 20 guineas—which was enough to gain the young man his freedom. When I tell you this author's name was John Cleland, and his story was the Memoir of that notorious Woman of Pleasure, Fanny Hill, the mystery of my grandfather's money is resolved. [11]

My digression is now almost at an end—yet before I am done with it altogether, I must touch briefly on other matters. The first concerns the tedious matter of family history. I say tedious, since while some consider their families beyond price, my own has contributed immeasurably to my unhappiness, as will soon be clear. When my grandfather's first wife Isabella had laid down her Editor's pen for the last time, her widower decided he must live alone for all eternity, since his dear departed had no peer. Yet in due course his solitude proved oppressive, as solitude will—and he married for a second time, his new wife's name being Eliza. Now this Eliza had a sister named Sarah, who married the William Rose I have already mentioned. [12] This William and Sarah, my great-uncle and great-aunt, had three children, and the youngest of them, Ann, married a name I shall struggle to write. Yet I shall write it. Edward Smith Foss. Though it is not *his* name but the name of his son, also called Edward, which makes me actually come to a dead stop. I swear that if he were beside me now, I would revenge myself on him with all the crimes of which I have been accused. I would strike him to the heart. [13]

Nevertheless, in order to continue serving faithfully at the altar of truth, I must say that this cousin Edward Foss showed me charity in my childhood—the charity of calling on me sometimes—for which, when I had means of my own, I thanked him. I also welcomed his son Edward to my rooms, and paid this Edward the compliment of inviting him to sit for a portrait by me. Likewise his sister Frances. Frances, indeed, I might say that I loved, though she has now been lost to me for so many years, I cannot exactly recollect what sensation I felt for her. Only that she was a lovely creature, and an admirer of all I admired, which led me on occasion to send her familiar advice, in the character (as I put it in my letters) of her most obedient oil and colourman. [14]

Furthermore, and as continuing proof of my kindness to those who did me nothing but harm, I should add that when the head of this family—my uncle Edward—passed into the company of his ancestors, I honoured him in a letter I sent to his son. It was written when my own life was at its lowest ebb (the lowest I then knew), yet I felt grievously for his loss, almost as if it were my own. I offered the earnest wish that he and his father might look for another meeting in eternity, of which *I have no such hope* myself. Yet just God (I most sincerely continued) had given me a full reliance on His generous but inscrutable dispensation towards better souls than mine—before I immediately fell to thinking of Locke again, and demanding of my cousin: do we individually exist? Are we? Or is matter nothing but an idea? Is this life a swoon of the spirit and the grave a waking? I had no answer to these questions, nor did I pretend to have one, but I implored my cousin to believe that the Lord of the sun and stars is good, and would comfort them all.

How could my cousin betray such tender questionings? Yet as everyone will see, he did betray me. In the brutal courtroom, he conspired to take from me what was mine.

But let me end my digression at last, and return to my grandfather, and the difficulties he laid up in store for me. I have already mentioned how his journey through the dust-heaps of London began from a shop close to St. Paul's. Yet I have also said that I recollect him in the darkness of a shuttered building, with his wife, etc., around him. Let me now turn my attention to these shutters, and fold them apart. What do they disclose? Why, a window, of course, and not a window letting on to the racket of the churchyard. No. A window opening on to the bright air of Chiswick, where my grandfather has moved in his middle age. Seizing whatever time and profits were allowed him by his *Review,* he has begun turning his house into his castle. [15]

But such a castle! A monument to taste and privilege, where the sturdy centre of an old home has sprouted new wings and glorious offshoots, such as: a conservatory, a glass-house, a stable block. The house itself was an achievement of rare quality, but this was not its sole distinction. It was girdled with a garden of such magnificence, no other place in all Chiswick or Turnham Green rivalled it, save only Chiswick House, formerly the property of Lord Burlington.

What a feeble-hearted muck-worm must he be, who does not feel delicious nature tingle along his nerves, like sparkling champagne, when faced with such a prospect! Often, as a child, I considered the best response I might give to the beauty of my grandfather's estate; it would be to depart from its gravel paths altogether and *take a roll!* For the more decorous reader I had better add that I also admired this garden with a complete and steady calm.

There was a cedar which I especially loved, broadening its green steps towards Heaven year by year. There was a copper beech tree which, when I crouched inside it, spread over me like the night sky, full of star holes. There was the linden tree itself, or lime as it is more prosaically known, which shed its peculiar pale light with such evenness, and such a restful breathing noise, that anyone seated in its shade might almost believe they were lying in clear water on the bed of an ocean, safe from all harm, and beyond the call of human voices.

With these soft lawns and rustling bowers as my playmates, I wanted for nothing. I lived in a trance of summer, dazzled between tree leaves and tree trunks, and dreamed that in years to come I would possess it all as my own.

Aye, there is the rub, at last. There is an end to the digressions I have made, and the hard fact of my disappointment. *I dreamed that in years to come I would possess it all as my own*—and my dream was taken from me. The dream that I would walk where my grandfather had walked with Wedgwood, with Goldsmith and with Johnson. That I would have my kingdom, and my subjects within it. That I would lie in the soft lap of the earth and watch clouds sail freely across, or the swallows come and go and then return once more, remembering their homes from thousands of miles off, and screaming for pure joy when they found them again, after an absence that must surely have been painful, for them to celebrate as wildly as they did.

1. In most of the previous literature about TGW, it is assumed that he was born in Chiswick on or within a few days of 4 October 1794. However, his semi-autobiographical work *Egomet Bonmot* (1825) suggests that he was born at "Twick'nam." Elsewhere he refers to an unnamed place "many miles from the metropolis," and when he arrived in Van Diemen's Land in 1837 he told the authorities that he came from Richmond. Elsewhere again, in his ticket-of-leave petition (1844), he said that his mother's family came from Wales ("A *Descent*, deduced, thro' Family Tradition & Edmonstone's Heraldry, from a Stock not the least honoured in Cambria").

2. The phrase comes from the brief obituary of Ann Wainewright which appeared in the *Gentleman's Magazine* on 7 October 1794.

3. Theodore von Holst (1810–1844), who was a prodigiously gifted painter, and an important friend of Fuseli and TGW during the 1820s and early 1830s, designed the frontispiece for the 1831 edition of *Frankenstein*. See pp. 69–70.

4. TGW's father Thomas seems to have handed him over to Ralph Griffiths as soon as Ann Wainewright died. Little is known about Thomas. He was the second son of Robert Wainewright—a London solicitor who worked in Gray's Inn and lived in Hatton Garden—and Ann Arnold, the daughter of Latham Arnold, a snuffmaker and tobacconist who lived at 6 Newgate Street. His parents were comfortably but not well off: it was said that he was the only person living in Hatton Garden who could not afford to keep a carriage (*Essays*, p. xiv). When he married Ann Griffiths in Chiswick on 13 December 1792 (she was only nineteen years old) he was living in Sloane Street, in central London, but set up house with Ralph Griffiths in Chiswick soon afterwards. If the old man's will is anything to go by, Wainewright and Griffiths got on badly, and their animosity is reflected in the treatment Griffiths later handed out to TGW. It is not known exactly when Thomas Wainewright died, but it must have been before 7 June 1803, since on that date Griffiths made his will, which refers to "the late Thomas Wainewright, Esq."

5. Ralph Griffiths's first wife, Isabella, was eight years older than her husband and died aged fifty-two on 25 March 1764, when he was forty-four. His second wife, whom he married in 1776, was Eliza Clarke, the daughter of a dissenting minister in St. Albans, Hertfordshire. They had two daughters—

TGW's mother, Ann, and another, who died in infancy—and a son, George.

6. See Paston, p. 151. ~~Griffiths edited the~~ *Monthly Review* ~~for fifty-four~~ years, after which control passed to his son George; one admiring contemporary called it "a sole example in the history of the republic of letters of a publication conducted for so long a period under one title and editorship" (Phillimore, p. 466). Announcing itself as "A Periodical Work giving An Account with Proper Abstracts of, and Extracts from, the *New Books, Pamphlets,* etc, as they come out," it helped transform literary journals from anthologies of extracts (as most had been during the mid-seventeenth century to the late eighteenth century) into reviews proper, and opened the way for more combative successors such as the *Quarterly Review, Blackwood's Magazine,* and the *London Magazine,* to which TGW contributed. Contemporary journals such as the *Censura Temporum,* for instance (founded in 1708), or the *Bibliotheca Curiosa,* "only gave notices of a few remarkable publications, and detailed selections from foreign journals" (Anderson, p. 55). Although Griffiths eventually made a decent living from the *Review,* he had considerable financial difficulties at various times during his editorship. In 1761, for instance, he was forced to sell a quarter share of the business to a Benjamin Collins of Salisbury for £755 12s 6d. In 1772 he sold the remaining three-quarter share to Collins (who never interfered with the editorship), but eight years later was able to buy the whole thing back again. For further details, see Sullivan, p. 233.

7. Griffiths's friendship with Josiah Wedgwood is a further clear proof of his liberal sympathies. Wedgwood (1730–1795) opened his pottery at Burslem in 1759, and the more celebrated works at Etruria in 1769. Highly successful in business, he was the friend of radicals such as Priestley, as well as artists such as Flaxman. Wedgwood records meeting Griffiths in February 1765, and then again in October and November of the same year, when he urged Griffiths to review Priestley in the *Review.* Griffiths was also on friendly terms with Wedgwood's partner Bentley, who lived nearby in Chiswick, and visited Burslem at least once. Wedgwood called Griffiths "impatient," but "our dear friend"; he said he "hath one of the warmest places in my heart." Thomas Griffiths—Ralph's brother—was also involved with the Wedgwood family. In 1768 he went to South Carolina to look for new sources of clay for Wedgwood, and sent back some samples which proved useless. Later, in the early 1770s, Wedgwood found that if these samples were mixed with barium sulphate, that did the trick. By this

time, Thomas Griffiths was working full-time for Wedgwood in Stafford-shire.

8. The *Critical Review* was founded in London in February 1756 by an Edinburgh-born printer named Archibald Hamilton, who gave Tobias Smollett *carte blanche* as editor. It was a magazine "established under Tory and Church patronage to maintain principles in opposition to those of the *Monthly Review*" (Walter Graham, p. 213). As far as the *Monthly Review* was concerned, the *Critical Review* was a place for "physicians without practice, authors without learning, men without decency, and writers without judgement"; as far as Smollett was concerned, Griffiths was reprehensibly liberal, and his wife Isabella "an antiquated Sappho, or rather a Pope Joan in taste and in literature, pregnant with abuse, begot by rancour, under the canopy of ignorance."

9. Actually Goldsmith worked hard during his five months with Griffiths, producing sixteen long reviews on subjects ranging from Scandinavian poetry, to Gray's *Odes* (which he admired), to Wilkie's *Epigoniad*. Their last meeting took place in 1759, when Goldsmith was hard up and living at 12 Green Arbour Court, off Floral Street in Covent Garden. He decided to become a hospital orderly, and applied to Griffiths for advice about the interview. Griffiths invited him to review four books, in return for which he would pay Goldsmith enough money to buy a suit. Goldsmith promptly borrowed his suit money from a friend, with whom he left the books as security. When Griffiths heard of this, he demanded either the clothes or the books or payment. Goldsmith replied: "Sir—I know of no misery but a goal to which my own imprudences and your letter seem to point." Griffiths then offered him £20 for a review of a lengthy *Life of Voltaire*, and from this amount the cost of a suit was deducted.

10. Goldsmith and TGW were not the only ones to think Griffiths stingy. John Forster, the biographer of Dickens and an acquaintance of TGW's, described Griffiths as a "mean-spirited tyrant, wielding his whip-lash over a miserable group of hack writers."

11. John Cleland (1710–1789) became a founding contributor to the *Monthly Review* after his release from prison. When *Fanny Hill* was first published in 1750, all 750 copies of the first edition were quickly sold, and a second edition, somewhat cleaned up, did even better—a great deal better than Cleland's subsequent books, which were less explicit, and sank without trace among the mass of erotic novels published during the 1750s. Griffiths was

repeatedly threatened with arrest for publishing the book, but always got away with it. He is said to have made at least £10,000 profit, and not surprisingly defended Cleland in the *Review*, praising his style for its "peculiar neatness" and adding, "As to the steps taken . . . to suppress the book, we really are at a loss to account for it."

12. William Rose (1719–1786) was born into a tolerant Presbyterian family in Birse, Aberdeenshire, and educated at Dodderidge's famous dissenting Academy in Northampton. He began his long and distinguished teaching career in Kew and eventually settled in Chiswick. Rose was well known as a liberal critic of the government, as the editor of Dodsley's *Preceptor* (1748), as the translator of Sallust (1750), and as one who "enjoyed the proud distinction of being almost the only Scotchman [apart from James Boswell] whom Samuel Johnson really loved."

13. When he was in Van Diemen's Land, TGW is supposed to have threatened to return to England and murder his cousin Edward Foss. Foss (1787–1870) was the seventh of fifteen children. He went to the same school as TGW in Greenwich, but overlapped with him only briefly, being seven years older, and when he left in 1804 began studying law. He was a pernickety, conservative and tradition-loving man, became a member of the Inner Temple in 1822, Chairman of the Incorporated Law Society, and Magistrate for the County of Surrey. He also wrote prolifically, contributing to the *London Magazine*, the *Athenaeum*, the *Gentleman's Magazine* and the *Monthly Review*. He shared TGW's interest in the Elizabethans (he edited *The Beauties of Massinger* in 1822), and in 1870 completed an enormous *Biographia Juridicia* (1,600 short lives of judges who had worked in England since 1066). He married his first wife, Catherine Martineau, in 1814; she died in 1841. His second wife, Mary Hutchins, bore him six sons and four daughters.

14. Frances (Fanny) Foss, the third child of Edward, was the recipient of one of TGW's few surviving letters. Although apparently written in the early 1820s, it gives an insight into the relationship he had always had with Fanny: generous, good-humoured and avuncular. At one point, TGW apologizes for the "mighty dull" books he is sending as a present, and adds:

> Faustus is miserably translated; all the character gone, spiritless, vapid. Wordsworths are many of them very simple and majestic; some mild and beautiful. I wish you would read them not skim. Of the German tales some of them are admirably rendered by the Opium Eater [de Quincey]; others wretchedly by mere hacks. The Spectre Barber is very

clever and lively. The Fatal Marksman is very popular in Germany. They have made an opera out of it which ends happily "selon la charte" as we say at Dunkirk. I am afraid you have read most of my friend Allan [Cunningham]'s stories in the [London] magazine but never mind! *read them again*. The *Haunted Ships* is the grandest thing I know in that *line of writing,* as the news-critics phrase it. *"Ezra Peden"* never appeared in the mag.

For many years, Fanny Foss worked as companion-housekeeper to her brother Henry at 42 Devonshire Street, London, when Henry was working in partnership with Thomas Payne, the bookseller. (Payne's nephew or possibly illegitimate son John, also a bookseller, married his cousin Sarah Burney in 1821, and Charles Lamb, an old friend of the Burney family, gave away the bride because her father's gout "confined him at home." TGW was almost certainly a guest at the wedding. See p. 100.) Over the years of their friendship, TGW painted Fanny's portrait in watercolour at least once— and also her sister Emma's god-daughter. Her brothers Edward and Henry were painted in oils.

15. Griffiths had moved into Linden House by 1765, eleven years before he married for the second time. The house stood in the Grove, beside what is now Chiswick High Street, and was described by a contemporary as "a capital mansion" (Phillimore, p. 466). During the eighteenth century, several large villas were built in the area, which was considered handy and salubrious (it is five miles from Hyde Park Corner). Linden House started life as a typical example, but soon became unusually grand, thanks to Ralph Griffiths's additions, and to the even more ambitious schemes of his son George. By the time TGW arrived in Linden House as a child, it was a splendid, white-painted, expensively embellished property with a large formal garden and four acres of "plantations." Linden House was demolished in 1878, and the houses now known as Linden Gardens built in its place. Only a fragment of the old stable-block wall survives.

3

HABITS OF REGULARITY

J cannot remember my grandfather's death, only that it introduced a new regime into Linden House. [1] My grandmother grew more withdrawn; my uncle, the new owner of the property and of the *Review,* welcomed the latter but shrank under the burden of the former. Which is to say: he had known that he would one day edit the magazine, and although he performed his office duties well, his heart was not engaged in them entirely. No, his heart lay at home, which I well understand: in the library and in the billiards room, upon the gravel walks and sweetly rolling lawns, and in the plantations which sprang up as he increased our estate. Truly, I believe my uncle knew the usefulness of his work, but understood better the value of his rest. He would rather have been a gardener than a bookman. [2]

There is no reason for me to complain of the treatment I received from either my uncle or my grandmother when I was a child—except, perhaps, that they left me too much to myself. But—as I have shown in my last chapter—I must speak differently of my grandfather. He had taken me in when I was an infant; he had passed me faithfully into the protection of those who survived him; and he had even planned for my schooling, which I shall come to in a while. For all this I am grateful, and easily forgive him his impatience. What I cannot forgive (because I cannot comprehend his reasoning in this matter) is why he dealt with me as he did after his death. The money that was mine—the money that had been my parents', and which after *their* deaths should have passed to *me* when I came of age—this money he put into a Trust for me. The guardians of this Trust were my father's brother Robert (a solicitor), and my cousins Foss, whom I have already touched upon. It is, apparently, a simple document, yet for as long as I have known its terms, they have filled me with questions. Why should my grandfather have curtailed so severely the amount I might have expected from him? Why, in particular, were *the monies that were my own* barred from me, so that I must be thankful for the little interest which oozed from them, like a poor creature which lives on the spray of a waterfall, but will never bathe in the torrent itself? [3]

I shall say no more now—only this: I pity my poor mother, who married a man for whom my grandfather felt such great dislike he even vented his enmity on that man's son. Myself. And I shall add: the worst of a grievance, as all those who suffer grievance know, is the eagerness with which it escapes its proper channels, and floods into every cranny and corner, every crack and crevice of existence.

I cannot now remember whether I was settled on my seat of learning before or after my grandfather's demise. However, I am able to describe accurately the route which led me to my particular school. My aunt Sarah, the second child of William Rose, had married a young man who taught for a while at her father's academy in Chiswick—a young man from a celebrated family, who bore the same name as his father the musician: viz., the well-known philologer and bibliomaniac Charles Burney, D.D., brother to Madame D'Arblay and companion of Cook the explorer. Doctor Burney's earliest employment had given him an appetite for schoolmastering, so that he eventually opened a place of his own in Hammersmith which, after a few years, he moved to Greenwich, south of the river Thames. I suppose this was for the benefit of its open air, and fresh cargo of pupils from the dockyards, etc., thereabouts. It was certainly the case that many of my colleagues had fathers on the Seven Seas. [4]

This school, having already supplied my cousin Edward with most of what he knew, was in due course considered suitable for me. In those days, the village of Greenwich was overrun by sailors, except that its most splendid buildings contrived to hold their heads above the fracas. Often my legs would carry me busily up Croom's Hill towards Blackheath, where I would gaze upon the fine houses, or down towards the Queen's House of Inigo Jones, or around the Royal College. My favourite of all was the Observatory, which can be said to have given time to the world. Studying its instruments, by which ships make their way many thousands of miles across the ocean, steering through darkness, round rocks and shallows, following a sure route over the trackless waters, I little thought that I would one day curse their existence, which allowed me to be carried so far from everything I love.

Greenwich, therefore, may be described as a place at once bustling and retired: the one time I recall the whole community in a complete uproar was during the lying-in-state of Lord Nelson. [5] Yet, in the ordinary way of things, my fellows and I found scant opportunity for wandering on the heaths or parks, dallying under the elms around Wilderness Pond, or ascending One-Tree Hill, to peer across the misty vales which divided us from our modern Babylon five or six miles off. Not at all. In the ordinary way of things, we were kept at our tasks, our heads low and our minds in a clamp, which is what each of us expected and none of us relished.

Our schoolmaster had purchased his academy when it already existed as a place of education: a tall building set discreetly within a wall at the foot of Croom's Hill, opposite the Spread Eagle. He then proceeded to cram into it one hundred or so pupils, each of whom paid £100 every year for the privilege of their confinement. To speak fairly, however, I must confess at once that we were not entirely confined. Behind the house lay a large stepped garden which ran as far as Royal Hill. This was our playing ground, where I now picture myself as a child who began solemn, soon learned to skip and tumble, and eventually grew tall enough to look down on others who had arrived after me, and were as solemn as I had once been.

The truth of the matter is this. In any place where a tyrant holds sway, those who suffer together will be joined by strong ties of mutual sympathy. For Burney had up-ended my mother's beloved Locke and shaken from his *Thoughts Concerning Education* all those ideas which make children sad. In the spreading gardens, our play was always educational. We were pressed into human orreries when we wanted to run zigzag, and learned the operations of sunlight when all we wanted was its heat. In the schoolroom, tales and other fruits of the imagination were forbidden: all was use. This may appear strange to anyone familiar with the good Doctor's reputation as a scholar (and that must be everyone), but I insist that he was more concerned with order than with education. His object was to establish habits of regularity, and principles of integrity. Learning was his last consideration, since that would easily be added to the other requisites. Even our religious instruction was accommodated within the grand design of usefulness. Burney had made and published a selection of abridgements, which was placed before us on Saturday evenings, and from which young scholars—ourselves—were required to translate a portion, adding, in their proper places, passages from their origin in the New Testament. I cannot say how many Sunday mornings I woke with my head still tingling from these labours.

It would have been easy, for one crushed by such oppression, to have taken refuge in dullness. Yet among the many heads that did sink into sullen stupidity, my own refused to drop. Impelled by what need I cannot say— perhaps by no more than the memory of my grandfather—I chose to make learning the foundation of my happiness. When Burney saw this (and remembering his duties to my family) he took an interest in me, and pointed out to me the many beauties of Greek and Latin, which I later used to decorate my own writings. [6] The Doctor's library, in particular, was a treasure house, with its volumes arranged to admit all the existing editions of the various authors. Few men since the Medicis can have assembled such a wealth of learning, and none with such limited means, and when I remember our teacher now, I most often see him with his "Cherry Nose" (as Garrick called that notorious proboscis) glowing above an open page, and his mouth sunk open as if to swallow knowledge the more easily. He was indeed a philosopher and an antiquarian, and as for his sternness: I can even take some amusement in that, recalling how he would shout "Shut the door" after any of us who did not, since he had a horror of currents of air. (On one occasion, he even made the same remark after two footpads who robbed his coach, and left him open to the night as they departed.)

Yet I cannot enjoy the gentleness which creeps into my tone as I bring this to mind, for the following reason. I have often seen it written that the Doctor was an accomplished man, which nobody would deny. But I have also heard it said that he was remarkable for his kindness to inferiors, and from this I must dissent. To those of us who endured his methods of regulation—even such as myself, who shared certain of his interests—he was not kind. His tone, which was melting with his paymasters, was cruel with his charges. Moreover, he was excessively fond of the cane, which he called his Tickler, and wielded with abandon. It was not uncommon, if we should come across a boy who had recently been punished, to find deep cuts in his skin. Nor was it rare to see a fellow arraigned for the merest trifle in our schoolroom, and his outstretched hand given such attention as made it impossible for him not to cry out. In recent years, as I shall tell, I have seen cruelties I could not believe true, and endured others which have made me long for oblivion. But the memory of my little companions' sufferings is worse than all of them. With each blow of his Tickler, the Doctor drove out of us something that was human, and let in something that was not. [7]

Given the generality of such punishments in the distant-seeming days of my youth, it will surprise no one to hear that it was perfectly common for schools to be shaken by revolution. [8] I cannot now recollect the immediate occasion for our own Greenwich mutiny; nevertheless, I still feel its excitement, which began as follows. On a certain late night, or rather, on a certain early morning, a gang of pupils darted from their beds with rapidly beating hearts. (We slept in large rooms at the top of the school, close together as I have later been accustomed to do in my exile.) After collecting provisions from the kitchen, we then returned to our dormitories, where we barred ourselves in, nailed up the door, and wielded the weapons we had made for ourselves of knives and clubs (which were broom handles).

To our astonishment, the noise of these preparations did not rouse our masters, and our actions were discovered only when the getting-up bell was rung, and we did not appear for our Muster. Very soon after the bell ceased its tolling, however, we were besieged. When we would not yield to any entreaty by our tormentors, Burney fetched a ladder which he climbed to look down at us through a space above the door. If he supposed the mere sight of him would crush our rebellion, he soon found that he was mistaken, for some of the boys gestured at him with their clubs, and flourished their knives, whereupon his cherry face grew as bright as a new sun, and he disappeared. I cannot forget him there, braving the air currents in that window, gazing at the monsters he had created. Never in my life before had I been given proof of the way deeds may alter a case; in my grandfather's house, the only power lay in words. But this new intelligence impressed me, and I remembered it.

When Burney reappeared to us, looking for all the world like Mr. Punch, he too had decided to prefer the power of words. He promised that if we laid down our weapons, we would have the choice of being expelled or forgiven—"generously," he said, and I am sure some of us believed him. Only two boys elected to be expelled. The rest of us stayed for our forgiveness, but I cannot say it was ever granted. Burney circled us cautiously for a short while, then by degrees returned to his old ways with his Tickler and his harsh tongue. I do not think it is imagination which tells me that those mutineers he most disliked were often punished for their other misdemeanours with extreme severity. This was a lesson for me as well: how we suffer for sins besides those for which we are arraigned, whether we are guilty of them, or not. [9]

Thus do our days continue, when we are in our childhood, with no knowledge of how our lives must change. The tide of time sweeps us along and we do not stretch out to grasp at the bank; I mean, we do not delay our progress by clinging to moments we cherish, or situations we envy. We think we shall find them again, later in our journey downstream, and are impatient to hurry forward to our next pleasure, or remove ourselves from our most recent disappointment. When I look back across the enormous width of earth and water which separates me from my young self, I see my days rushing me forwards rapidly, until everything seems composed of flickering sunlight. A streak of light and then a patch of shade. Dust motes floating in a schoolroom, then a ridge upon my finger, dyed black where the ink has stained me. Myself in a looking-glass, experimenting whether to part my hair on the right or the left, then deciding to be content with the centre. The scent of newly mown grass, then the taste of pennies upon the tongue where a snowflake has melted.

All of which makes me consider: what is it that makes a life? I cast a line over the river of my past, reel in a memory of Burney and broomsticks, and believe it has a meaning I can calculate. Another time I throw out my line and catch only a sunny silence. Yet who is to know which has the greater importance? Who is to say that a thing I recollect has shaped me more profoundly than another thing I have forgotten—a thing which might be so trifling no accidental witness would have troubled to remember it either? Truly, we are as much a mystery to ourselves as to others. The wind blows, the dust of the world filters into our heads, and settles into valleys and mountains, and we walk among them marvelling at their strangeness, as though they are nothing to do with ourselves, rather than being our exact definitions.

I have already said: my young head was innocent of such thoughts. I saw Burney's sarcasm and severity. I felt (more lightly than some) his blows upon my body. But these things seemed to me like scars which healed, not like openings where an idea might lodge and grow. I considered them meaningless as soon as I no longer thought of them—which for the most part was immediately, since almost the whole of my attention was fixed on the day when my labours would cease, and I would return to Linden House, which was the destination I most desired.

Although this day of my translation could never arrive quickly enough, it did eventually heave into view, whereupon my guardians began to increase their concern for how I might get my living in the world. I told them I did not intend to follow the example of many of my young friends, and set off across the Seven Seas; I had no stomach for that. I added that I supposed I should aim myself towards a University; and, after that, set my head between the mashing wheels of the law, as my father's family had done. In the event, I was delivered a more surprising solution—one that half pleased me, half perplexed me.

In spite of the severities I have described at Greenwich, Burney had also encouraged artistic ambitions wherever they showed in his charges, allowing them to shoot like weeds among the heavy slabs of his regularities. It had been discovered, in this way, that I possessed a talent for sketching, which I was licensed to do at any time I could escape our lessons. I quickly learned to take trouble with my drawings, seeing that they won the admiration of those about me, and also absolved me from other pastimes I found less agreeable. I would portray the faces of my friends for their love, my enemies for a shilling, and my masters for twice that. No feature was too difficult, and the art of flattery came easily to me. Fetch a dandy lock across a forehead, smarten a cravat, stretch a neck here or five fingers there, and my subjects paid me the more willingly.

It began as a form of game, but soon grew serious, as things will in our lives. Burney directed me to prints in his collection so that I might learn the sublime lessons of the Old Masters; I found in my grandfather's collection certain examples of Claude and Poussin (their gentler subjects). Whether or not I believed in my own genius was always a question with me, as though I had already looked to the depths of myself in secret, and had seen what could be done, and what was impossible. Yet at the same time I was not daunted. It seemed that Burney, after many years of shaving at my edges, preparing to fit me into a box of a size and shape which did not fit me comfortably, was abruptly convinced I should be at liberty. I should apprentice myself, he said, and make my name.

Make my name! He did not know what he was saying, the good Doctor. All the drawings I have done since I left his Academy, the paintings and the portraits and the inventions, are the quintessence of my Self—and through my own choice not one of them bears my name. In this respect, therefore, I look upon my schooldays as a brief time of success, which was the preparation for a life of obscurity. Yet in the same breath, I must add that my name follows me in this obscurity like the wind itself, searching me out wherever I am hidden. It can never be forgotten, although the world and I both insist that I am no one.

1. Ralph Griffiths died at Chiswick on 28 September 1803, aged eighty-three, and was buried in the north aisle of Chiswick Parish Church on 5 October. The *Annual Register* wrote, rather stiffly: "[He was] the original instituter of the *Monthly Review,* which, with unremitting perseverance, he conducted for 54 years, assisted only by his son in the latter period of his life. Dr. Griffiths was a steady advocate of literature, a firm friend, a cordial lover of the enjoyments of domestic happiness, and a zealous and successful promoter of the charms of social intercourse" (28 September 1803). The *European Magazine* was more effusive, hoping that Griffiths had left behind a volume of memoirs which would be published posthumously, since "he must have become acquainted with more characters, anecdotes and circumstances . . . than perhaps any other critic from Dionysus of Helicarnassus" (4 January 1804, p. 3). No such memoir existed.

2. Although George Griffiths continued to add distinguished names to the roster of contributors to the Monthly Review—Byron among them—the impetus of the magazine faltered when he took over. What had seemed original in the 1750s looked dusty when compared to the combative style of the *Edinburgh Review.*

3. Ralph Griffiths made his will, which was witnessed by Samuel Rose, the lawyer son of his friend William, on 7 June 1803. It said:

> Whereas on the marriage of my late daughter Ann Griffiths with the late Thomas Wainewright Esq I advanced a certain sum of money and covenanted that after my death a further sum should be paid by my personal representatives as a marriage portion for my said daughter and whereas my grandson Thomas Wainewright is become entitled to such property as advanced by me to his mother my will is that neither he the said Thomas Wainewright nor my trustees for him shall demand any further sum out of my estate as I hereby declare that the sum already paid with that which is covenanted to be paid is all that I intend for my said grandson.

What this meant in practice was: Ralph Griffiths left TGW £5,000 in trust, and this produced an annual interest of around £250 a year.

4. The Burneys were a remarkable family. Dr. Johnson said of them: "I love all of that breed whom I can be said to know, and one or two whom I hardly know, I love upon credit"; Hazlitt wrote that the family "produces wits,

scholars, novelists, musicians, artists in numbers numberless. The name alone is a passport to the Temple of Fame."

Charles Burney (senior; 1726–1814), author of a four-volume *History of Music,* was the son of a dancing master from Chester. When he moved to London as a young man he was articled to the composer Thomas Arne, and later held various prestigious musical posts before becoming the Organist at Chelsea Hospital in 1783. He was a vigorous social climber, knew everyone, and was duly showered with honours, including membership of the Royal Society. Macaulay described him as "an amiable man of good abilities, a man who had seen much of the world. But he seems to have thought that going to court was like going to heaven; that to see Princes and Princesses was a kind of beatific vision" (Lonsdale, p. 324).

His daughter Fanny (Madame D'Arblay; 1752–1840), was the author of *Evelina* (1778), which Burke "sat up all night reading," *Cecilia* (1782) and *Camilla* (1784). Thanks to her father's influence she was also Mistress of the Wardrobes to George III.

James Burney (1750–1821) fought with Wolfe at Quebec, travelled with Captain Cook on his second and third voyages (he took charge of the *Discovery* after Cook had been killed), and wrote books on his adventures and on whist.

Charles Burney (junior), TGW's schoolteacher, was born in Norfolk on 4 December 1757 and educated at Charterhouse and Cambridge, from which he was expelled for stealing books in October 1777. The effect on his personality was immense. After considering whether he should commit suicide, he became—by way of atonement—strenuously ambitious for himself, and severely demanding of others. After finishing his university education at Aberdeen, he edited the *London Magazine* for a few years, while also beginning to teach in schools—first in Highgate, then Chiswick, then Greenwich. Here he took Holy Orders and, after running the school for twenty years, left in 1813 to become Chaplain to the King. Burney was a formidable scholar, producing countless articles (mainly for the *Monthly Review*), and editing many major Classical authors, including Aeschylus. When he died on 28 December 1817 his vast library was bought by the nation for £13,500 and housed in the British Museum. It contained some fourteen thousand printed books, a manuscript collection which included the Townley Homer, and four-hundred-odd books on the history of the stage. His school in Greenwich was eventually demolished in 1839, and Burney Street laid out over the site of the house and gardens. Some of the outbuildings remain, at the side of 6 Croom's Hill.

5. Nelson's body lay in state in the Painted Hall of the Naval College, from 23 December 1805 to 8 January 1806, after it had been brought back from Trafalgar. On the first day alone, seventy thousand people came to pay their respects, and this number increased steadily until the coffin was eventually ferried up the river with great ceremony to be buried in St. Paul's Cathedral.

6. The attention given to TGW's Classical education was by no means routine. John Stirling (1806–1844), for instance, who went to Burney's school shortly after TGW, was taught (according to his biographer Thomas Carlyle) no more than "competent skill in construing Latin, I also think an elementary knowledge of Greek, cyphering to a small extent, Euclid perhaps in a rather imaginary condition, a swift but not very legible or handsome penmanship, and the copious prompt habit of employing it in all manner of unconscious English prose composition, or even occasionally in verse itself" (Carlyle, p. 238). On the other hand, John Rennie, son of the engineer Rennie who built Southwark Bridge, and who attended the school in 1807, said in his *Autobiography* (1875):

> Dr. Charles Burney was considered one of the best Greek and Latin scholars of the day, and was the intimate friend of Porson and numerous other literary celebrities. His school was therefore very highly esteemed for classics, but for little or nothing else; for although a certain quantity of arithmetic and the elements of algebra and geometry were taught, yet these were quite secondary to the classics. I therefore made little further progress in anything but classics, in which I became a tolerable proficient (p. 3).

7. The Master of Salem House, in Dickens's *David Copperfield*, also refers to his cane as a "Tickler," as does Mrs. Gargery in *Great Expectations*. One old boy of Burney's school remembered (in a letter dated 17 April 1818): "We had heard from an Officer of the Guards, who not infrequently smarted under [Burney's] castigations, that . . . he was a grand assertor of the ancient discipline" (Scholes, p. 237)—and in his own writings on education, Burney said threateningly:

> During the latter part of [my career] the difficulties, the toils and the solicitude of a School Master's occupation have been gradually and greatly increased: not nearly so much, let me add, by the *evil days,* in which *we have fallen;* as by those extraordinary indulgences, with which children are most gratified, during the seasons at which they are under the roof of their parents.

8. There were mass risings against unpopular teaching methods at Eton in 1810 and 1832, Winchester in 1818, and Rugby in 1822. The eighteenth century had seen an even greater number of these mutinies.

9. John Graham, a pupil of Burney's, described a revolt in the Greenwich school in a letter written on Monday, 24 February 1808. A transcript is preserved in the Greenwich Local History Library.

4

SIMPLICITY AND FINISH

*I*n childhood, when we feel our disappointments with extreme pain, we do not enjoy our pleasures with a comparable intensity. Our pleasures simply occur and are accepted as of right. The day I quit Burney's school is an exception to this general rule. When my carriage groaned up Croom's Hill towards Chiswick for the final time, I could scarcely contain my happiness. I was passionate for Linden House, and the future which awaited me there. [1]

If I say this made me excitable, I should add that in this respect I was no different from other young men. There was nothing vicious in me except perhaps a love of ease, which could have become a love of luxury, only had I possessed the means to express it. As it was, I could do no more than dream of what I might accomplish in this respect, which proved a harmless enough way of passing idle hours.

How often are our plans interrupted, and our hopes! I had barely taken up residence again, when my grandmother thought better of continuing under the same roof as me, and quit this world. [2] In my grandfather's lifetime, when I was a child, I had been kept from death as though it were a contagion. During the afternoon on which his widow went to join him, I was led to her bedside by my uncle, and required to make my farewell in person. I shall not give any detail of what happened as I inclined my lips to her forehead, except to say that her skin was like paper to my touch. Although I examined her face closely, I felt nothing with any force.

Following this loss, it fell to my uncle to direct me into whatever career I chose—which, according to the encouragement given by Doctor Burney, I announced as: Painter. As soon as this was said, my uncle (relieved to be spared the difficulties of making a decision himself), lost no time in sounding out that skilled artist John Linnell as my instructor. Trading on the good name of my grandfather, and on the poverty and youthful eagerness of Linnell himself, an arrangement was soon made. Whereupon it became my routine, once or twice a week, to leave the shade of my beloved linden trees and

arrive in London to stare for a morning at a dead branch laid upon a table—
or sometimes at the shivering form of a man brought in for the purpose. I
was not disinclined to shiver myself. Linnell had been reckoned good for me
since he was then coming into fashion, and might teach me how to earn
money. This did not seem likely, just by the look of him: a small, narrow-
faced man with a pinched nose, very enthusiastic for drawing, and with an
equal reverence for the Scriptures. (He was a Baptist, and used a poetic tone
in everything.) The best I can say about his conversation is that he spoke to
me often of Professor Henry Fuseli, at whose feet he had once sat. I soon
found myself in a complete fascination with this Professor, who had lec-
tured Linnell in several languages, and terrified him into excellence by cor-
recting errors with a thumbnail he kept purposely long and sharp. [3]

Linnell was a good and gentle man, but lived too much in the eye and not
enough in the imagination. I had been with him only a matter of weeks
before I grew impatient to leave, and find another teacher that excited
me more—though my uncle, who was anxious about my gaining useful
employment, would not let me stray off where I wanted. Accordingly, I was
plucked from one kind of boredom and set down in another. I mean, in the
studio of Thomas Phillips, where I was bound apprentice for a year in his
house at number 8 George Street, close to Hanover Square. [4]

The sufferings of my schooldays, the hours I spent in solitude as a child,
the absence of a mother and father—all these were as nothing compared to
the tedium I endured during the next part of my existence. To do him credit,
Mr. P. was another kind teacher, and my capabilities were equal to the tasks
he set me. Yet the life I expected for myself was nowhere to be found. I was
shut off from the pleasure of thinking my own thoughts, and insulted by the
confusion my teacher made between his art and money. I had money, or I
supposed I had; it was not at this stage a concern of mine. It was mystery I
wanted, and Mr. P. had nothing to tell me on this score. Some men set themselves to understand what they see in front of their eyes. Others, on the contrary, aspire to examine inwardly, and to report on what can only be
imagined. Under the disapproving eye of Mr. P., I became one of the latter,
and realized that I had chosen the harder task.

If I had known what trials lay ahead, at such a distance from everything
familiar, I should perhaps not have complained as I did. Yet because we cannot see into the future, I filled many sad hours, lamenting what a miserable
wretch is he who has the practice of painting. Often I would wander about
the city in great distress of mind, seeking everywhere for I knew not what.
No sooner was my pencil in my hand, and my eye fixed on some object

before me, than my brains went round like a whirligig, and started away in every direction they should not.

The recollection of my unhappiness makes me breathless. So let me, in the long aftermath of my life, steady the scene as I could not at the time, and describe what it contained. I should guess that, when he took me in, Mr. P. was in his early forties, a little over twice my age. (For some years he had been grey-haired, which gave him the appearance of being old and young at once, since his face was still handsome and unlined, with a delicate nose and mouth.) [5] He was in every respect an intellectual man, who would often talk of science, as well as poetry and novels. But he was a shy man too, and for this reason lacking in that subtle method of relieving his sitters of all consciousness of observation, which his rival Sir Thomas Lawrence had in abundance. His interests made him progressive, urging his pupils *each day* to acquire some literary or factual knowledge in order to relieve their minds and strengthen their understanding, and to study wherever possible the works of Turner, which he believed gave evidence of such application. [6]

The tastes of Mr. P. were reflected around him. I shall show them in his house first. Because he had lived in St. George's Street for many years, his Painting Rooms were extraordinarily cluttered—a kind of cave, which seemed more probably the abode of a bear than a man. Portraits were leant against the walls in a profusion of different states: some complete and shining, others with an eye missing, or a cheek, as though their skeletons were beginning to appear. If this were not mortal enough, white busts (mainly of plaster) looked down from an assortment of plinths and stands, their unseeing faces all waiting to become my subject, and the structure of their anatomies my daily task. However I progressed with my studies—and I do sincerely believe that my skills increased during this time—I could not shake off the sensation that far from equipping myself to celebrate the living, I was in fact learning to associate with the dead.

Our Painting Rooms were two lofty affairs at the back of the house, lit by skylights as well as two windows overlooking a yard which ended in a high wall. On the same floor, but in the main body of the house, was a large sitting room where Mr. P. would sometimes entertain me, with his wife, to a glass of wine. (Of the floors above this I saw little, only the room where I sometimes slept, if my other lodgings failed. This was a narrow cell which also looked upon the blank wall whose foundations I knew so intimately from my hours in the Painting Rooms. There were hours when I felt the weight of every individual brick pressing on me.)

Mr. P. had a low voice, yet a forceful way of speaking which made his eyebrows, which had remained dark, perform with a life of their own. He would often speak of Lawrence, who not unnaturally interested him as a competitor, but from whom he never tried to poach. (Nor from Hoppner either.) Such was his courtesy, indeed, that his definite opinions were often veiled. In the rare times I was able to draw him out, I discovered that he agreed with Reynolds in his belief that the whole beauty and grandeur of art consists in being able to get above all singular forms, local customs, peculiarities and details of every kind. It is certainly true that his own works, like those of Lawrence himself, endeavoured to do this. At the same time, he also felt the authority of Reynolds had produced in certain painters a desire to tamper with nature, and give what is called a flattering likeness. He would not have spared Lawrence this criticism, nor Romney, nor Hoppner, nor himself. Yet he was powerless to reverse the effect, out of concern for others' opinion, and from a desire to keep his pockets full.

In later years, I learned the patience to enquire: did I misjudge my teacher? My answer came to me clearly when Mr. P. published his *Lectures.* Perusing these, I found again the honourable aim to preserve the practice and application of painting *pure and unadulterated,* the admiration for intellect over senses, and the roll of magnificent names he had once told me in person: Raphaello and Michel Angelo, the Flemish Masters, Rembrandt—whom I remember him calling "astonishing." And these were all fine sentiments! Yet if ever the dazzle of an imagination showed too brightly, it was spurned—and therefore Giotto was spurned, and others of divine genius. Truly, I was never capable of enjoying the world, unless its poetic mysteries were explored, and this my teacher could never understand.

Honourable, respectable Mr. P. Tedious Mr. P. My time with you passed in a simmering anger, which had really begun to bewilder me before our ways parted. I do not know now whether you are alive or dead. If dead, I ask forgiveness of your spirit for my disgrace, and in return for this I forgive you the crime of your dullness. If you are still alive, then as a mark of respect for your patience with me, I will do you the honour of recollecting the day in your company which I prize above all others. I mean, the day Lord Byron visited our Painting Rooms for his portrait. [7]

I do not recall the route which brought him to your door. Had Mr. Murray admired your portrait of William Blake, and made a recommendation? In any case, the hour came that he appeared (I would do better to say *paraded*) before us. There was a great performance of scowling, and not a

37

little discussion of how he should show his face—fully, or in profile. Eventually this was settled in a compromise, and when you went to work, you took pains to barber him ten times o'er, to plumpen his face a little, and to cast everything into a chiaroscuro, so that the subject seemed to be meditating on his certain and imminent death.

I confess that I found the entire proceedings ridiculous. Notwithstanding my admiration for His Lordship's writings, and my humble curiosity in meeting his person, I could not happily reconcile the agonies of his imagination with the fussing of his manner. Myself, he ignored, saving that he was envious of a pair of yellow gloves I had recently acquired, and demanded to know where he might buy the same. [8] This was a brief conversation, but I suppose it must have allowed him to look at me more closely, in which case he would have noticed a sort of imitation of himself, that I had constructed from existing pictures. There was nothing excessive—a curl upon my forehead and an open-necked, turned-down shirt when I was at my easel—but it may have disturbed him where it was meant to flatter.

When I made my own portrait of Byron, standing close beside Mr. P. as he worked, the Lordly gaze more often seemed to sink through me than fall upon me. This made my amusement turn into something like scorn, which I dare say crept through my brush into my canvas, where the face of my sitter, turned a little further off from the viewer than in Mr. P.'s account, shows a sign of pride, and a lasciviousness, that I never saw in other portraits. Yet in spite of my impatience with him, I insist that I painted what I saw, and not my own faults.

I was at that time not familiar with the humiliations which often accompany truth. Indeed, to be spurned by Lord Byron (even in a glancing kind of way) made me suppose that I might quicken my progress through the world by following *in*directions, rather than by taking the main path.

This idea increased my giddiness, and before my year with Mr. P. was out, I had moved back to Linden House again, where I was determined to recover myself. This was not so easy as I had imagined. It was during the spring of 1814, the year when I reached twenty years of age, and even though I was so young, I already felt a presentiment that my life would fail. I had been a scholar whose learning was no more than a heap of untried opinions and jumbled phrases. I was a portraitist who did not sufficiently love the sight of real faces, preferring instead the visions which rose into my head in solitude. I was the member of a family which could not exactly call me their own, and would not expel me into the world either. And yet even as I made preparations to settle back into the comforts of my old ways, trusting that I could live well enough on clean air and a love of fine things, my uncle was enquiring again: what would become of me? I cannot say who was the more astonished, he or I, when on a sort of whim I told him that I had decided to postpone my pencil to the sword, and the next time he laid eyes on me I would be in uniform. [9]

1. We do not know exactly when TGW left Burney's school. It was probably in the summer of 1812, when he was seventeen.

2. Elizabeth Griffiths died on 24 August 1812, and was buried beside her husband in Chiswick Parish Church.

3. TGW began his apprenticeship with John Linnell (1792–1882) in 1812, though details of the arrangement are obscure. The only reference to it appears in Linnell's autobiography (see Kerr, p. 837). Linnell was a precocious child who became a pupil of John Varley's when he was twelve, and a student at the Royal Academy in 1805, the year after Fuseli had been elected Keeper. (Fuseli called Linnell his "little giant.") He was a well-connected young man, knew George Griffiths as the editor of the Review, and made his more famous friendship with William Blake through George Cumberland. Linnell lived on a similar plane of spiritual thought to Blake, and later became an important biographical source for Gilchrist in his life of Blake, saying, "I never saw anything the least like madness." At the end of Blake's life, Linnell was one of the few people to give him financial support.

4. Thomas Phillips (1770–1845) was almost as widely admired by his contemporaries as the leading portrait painter of the day, Sir Thomas Lawrence. He was born in Dudley, Warwickshire, and when he left school at thirteen, his guardians (his uncles) decided that "my future station in life was that of a japanner." After serving an apprenticeship near Birmingham, he moved to London, where he studied at the Royal Academy. His career as a portraitist took off when he was commissioned by the Third Earl of Egremont (of Petworth House, also Turner's patron) in 1796. Thirty-six of his portraits still hang in Petworth. In 1814, he was commissioned by John Murray to paint a series of portraits of writers—including Byron (twice, in 1814), Crabbe, Scott, Southey, Coleridge and Campbell. (He had already painted Blake in 1807; in the course of the sittings, Blake told him that "the arch-angel Gabriel" had described to him "the paintings of Michel Angelo"; Phillips called this "a good authority, surely.") Phillips was appointed Professor of Painting at the Royal Academy in succession to Fuseli in 1825 and resigned owing to ill health in 1832. Some of his fellow artists criticized the social-climbing element in his work, but much of it shows an impressive grasp of personality, as well as a gorgeous polish.

5. Phillips was forty-three in the spring of 1813; TGW was nineteen. Phillips was already grey-haired by 1802, according to a self-portrait done

that year. In 1816 his wife said, "If Mr. P. [sic] were a little stouter than he is, his face would be very handsome but that perhaps would rather lessen than improve the expression of intellectual refinement which was always very valuable in my eyes."

6. TGW said that Phillips, a "great man of colour," was inferior to Lawrence in the "subtle method of rescuing his sitters from all consciousness of observation."

7. Phillips's Sitters' Book, preserved in the National Portrait Gallery, London, records that he produced 854 portraits between 1800 and 1829. During 1813 he painted Lady Russell, the Prince Regent, the Earl of Egremont and several others before turning to "Ld Bryon for Mrs. Leigh" on 23 September. This portrait, the so-called "cloak portrait," is not to be confused with the more spectacular portrait, also by Phillips, of Byron sporting Arnaut dress, which was finished on 4 April 1814. (Four copies of the "cloak portrait" were made by Phillips, the first for Murray in December 1814.) TGW also painted his portrait of Byron in September 1813. Initially, it was owned by Robert Francis Cooke, a partner in Murray's publishing business, and was sold in the name of Cooke at Christie's on 29 February 1892. It was bought by Colnaghi, then disappeared from view until it was sold by Baroness d'Erlanger to Newstead Abbey (where it remains) in 1935. (See plate 8.) There is a second portrait of Byron, "As a Dandy in a Stand-Up Collar" (present whereabouts unknown) which may also be by TGW, since it was once the property of a W. W. Wainewright, who was possibly a descendant of TGW's son Griffiths.

8. Byron once told Lady Blessington, in Genoa, that " ——— was the first man I saw wear pale yellow-coloured gloves, and devilish well they looked." The erased name is almost certainly "Wainewright" (see Norman, p. 11).

9. TGW's résumé of the first twenty-odd years of his life reads as follows:

> As a boy, I was placed frequently in literary society—a giddy, flighty disposition prevented me from receiving thence any advantage. The little attention I gave to anything was directed to painting, or rather to an admiration of it, but, ever to be wiled away by new and flashy gauds, I postponed the pencil to the sword; and the noisy audacity of military conversation, united to the fragrant fumes of whiskey-punch (ten tumblers every evening without acid), obscured my recollections of Michel Agnolo as in a dun fog.

5

I BECOME A RENEGADE

*I*t is a curious thing, but when I look back through my life, some parts of it are strange, and others familiar, regardless of their actual distance from me. My childhood under the linden trees (I could not get further from myself than this) might be yesterday: I still see the shine on the leaves, and the gossamer threads linking them one to another. My apprenticeship with Mr. P., which is some fifteen years nearer, is strange and shadowed. I look towards his face, towards Byron—who glances back with a haughty tilt of his head—as though I am peering into a gloomy vault. (Once, diverting into the country around Oxford, I happened upon a gang of men digging a canal tunnel into a hill. I remember it now, abruptly, as I recall Byron. I stared into the darkness, my nostrils full of the scent of the wet earth, and perceived the labourers in the cavern of their own making, travelling away from me on a wooden cart, one of them holding a lantern so their faces were flaming as they disappeared.)

The next part of my life has become the most obscure of all. I will not say that I decided to quit my apprenticeship on a whim, rather that my unhappiness accumulated gradually until I could suddenly tolerate it no longer. Mr. P.'s flattery of his sitters—I scorned it. His faith in everything polished and perfect—it did not interest me. It was easily within my capacity to execute works as precise as his, but this seemed child's play. I had decided that faces in the phenomenal world were not the subjects I cared for most. Rather, I desired knowledge of what I could not see, which lay darkened in my brain. Mr. P. could not be my guide to this other realm.

Nevertheless, I cannot recall what made me suppose that I might live without my blessed Art entirely, and become her renegade. By which I mean: I do recall, but hesitate to describe. I must first point out, to earn myself some indulgence, that this time of my volte-face was unique in my life. It was a time of peace and, in order to remember it now, I must once again picture Bonaparte on his island of Elba, from which no one expected him to remove himself. In the same way, I must also see again the pipe smoke

42

which hung thickly above the parks of London, like morning mist which could not be burned away. By day we would watch sea battles on the Serpentine, and always come away victorious. By night, fireworks would scatter their harmless blazes upon the booths and towers, the drinking stalls and hawkers, the upturned faces and the empty patches (empty save for a few dawdlers here and there), which had been turned by the crowds from green oases into sandy deserts.

Among these crowds—and bemused, I admit, by the mist of smoke, etc.—I was far removed from the society in which I had been raised. I met military men, in particular, swaggering in the flush of their freedom, men with gay stories to tell, and grateful hearts to win. Encouraged by their example, my natural giddiness increased to such a degree I persuaded myself that I preferred the noisy audacity of their conversation to any other form of talk on earth. Wherever I was led by their chat—across the bloody plains where Bonaparte had been challenged, hunting the enemy through forests and ruins—I felt the ghost of my grandfather melting, and likewise the figures of the Revd. Burney D.D., my uncle, and Mr. P. All of them were put to flight. I did not live once in the reality of a battle, but always in a dream of glory, with a plume above my head, and my spurs jangling as I dismounted from some adventure.

Not to beat about the bush, and yet to the surprise of all who knew me, I became an ensign in His Majesty's 16th Foot, though I believe I may subsequently have become a party to some uncertainty on that score. Be that as it may, I will now say plainly that the 16th was indeed my regiment, thanks to the money I offered, and its acceptance. [1]

I should have anticipated that my new world would not afford me the liberty I desired. I looked upon my uniform as a magician might look upon his robe: as a means of transformation, which would deliver extraordinary power into my hands. Yet, to my eyes, the yellow of that costume soon came to resemble nothing so much as a kind of jaundice, and the facings a mere tinsel. Perhaps this was my punishment for not showing a greater willingness to get myself killed. But in truth, who is eager for death, when the choice of life is easy? I had selected the 16th carefully, knowing I would spend more time enjoying the companionship of barracks than the din of battle—since I had been informed that the regiment was not often preferred for active duty. No sooner had I settled into my new routines, however, than I discovered that even a soldier will grow sick with waiting, and lose sight of the day when he might go back into the world and pretend his time has been glorious. In the fog of a mess-room, whether it was in London (where I began my new career); or in Ireland (where the fog was heavier, the drink poorer, the society as dull as peat-water); or in Portsmouth (where I last repaired), I can say that my disillusionment increased steadily. I can say, in fact, that eventually I came to a state of complete misery.

I do not know what dark star shone at my birth, that I should have been so humiliated by this unhappiness. I had done nothing to deserve it, except lose patience with my birthright. Nothing. As I search my memory now for some good which might have come of that time, the one comfort I can find is this: the 16th restored my natural affections to the place they most obviously belonged. When I put myself back in Fermoy, and call to mind the sweating faces of Captain John Gallway, Lieutenants Hasleham, O'Brien and Mahoney, and my fellow ensign John O'Donnell, I see again that they are men who would have preferred to butcher a pig than learn the name of Michel Angelo. Wherever they are now, I cannot feel sorrow for them. They are a part of the waste of my existence, that is all.

I would prefer to forget them immediately, but there is one thing I must add. Fermoy to me is no more than a miniature, in which I see myself at a window, suffering a dreadful vacancy of spirit. I could almost say the same about Portsmouth, as far as excitement was concerned. But there my view was across the harbour, where my future—had I known it—lay at anchor. As I looked across the glistening waters, I saw those dungeons full of terror and dismay, those sinks of devilment, those horrors: the prison hulks. There were eight or ten in those days, mighty vessels of war stripped of their masts, and girdled about with enormous rusted chains. I would stand in the sun and watch the new arrivals (the convicts) taken up from their ferry boats and swallowed in darkness. I would watch others brought stumbling into the light and then conveyed to more limber vessels bound for Australia. I would shake my head over this, then forget it all as I turned back to my dullness.

Describing my entry into the 16th, I noticed that however gradually thoughts might build in a man's mind, a moment will come when their accumulation requires a sudden change. So it was at the end of my life in the military. Although my brain became addled by infinitely slow degrees, the news that Bonaparte had escaped his confinement, and was again pursuing his warlike ways, immediately stirred me from my slumber. In the space of a few seconds, I chose to seek an alternative way of killing time and humans. In the space of a few days, I sold my ensigny whence I had purchased it, and returned to Linden House, whereupon my feelings, parched, hot, and tarnished, were at once renovated with cool, fresh blooms—beautiful to the simple-hearted. [2]

I wish that I might say: this renovation did me a lasting good. Yet the comfort I so urgently desired, and briefly found, was a satisfaction I could not possess for long. In my childhood and early youth, I had sometimes succumbed to strange fits of melancholy, as I have already confessed. These had always raced overhead like sudden showers, dropping their drenching load in a hurry before the sunlight returned and my spirits lifted. This new mood, however, was misery of a different kind, rolling towards me like a fog off the sea, dense and clinging, and leaving me perplexed on the shore of my own life. I had dreamed of bettering myself and winning the honour of those for whom I felt respect—I mean my parents and my grandparents. But I had achieved nothing. I had imagined myself a figure, but had become a failure.

Let me call my condition the *passio hypochondriaca,* which has ever been the curse of the poet and the wit, and the great tax upon intellect, the bar to posterity and renown. Let me call it this, and keep some dignity in my despair. If only I could have laid hold of it, like a dog, and shaken it loose! But everything that was real to me was not real in the world, and vice versa. The phantom of fear was always about me. I felt it in the day at every turn, and at night I saw it, illuminated and made horrible in a million fantastic shapes. Like my friend Coleridge, but not thinking of him at all, or of anything sensible, while my passion was upon me, I marvelled at how much of the inexplicable and astonishing this world includes, and how inexplorable the labyrinth, to which our experience leads us. [3]

In plain English, I might say that I was almost insane—and should certainly have become insane, were it not for the ministrations of assorted angels. My uncle, under whose roof I lay, was a very present help. I shall not forget the noise of his footsteps on the gravel path below my room, as he went to and fro in his garden. It was to my ears the sound of goodness, of the rhythms by which leaves disappear and shoot again, by which rivers swell and diminish, by which flowers bloom and die. These soundings of him were more healthy to me than any words he might have spoken.

Then there were the ministrations of ———. Having not mentioned her until now (and meaning hardly to mention her hereafter), I do not know how to introduce her. Let me call her my most delicately affectionate and unwearied (though young and fragile) nurse, and give her full names immediately: Eliza Frances Ward. Now I have said as much as that, I see that I may as well continue and say more—but I find I cannot. I shall therefore let matters rest there.

Yet I cannot prevent myself from adding that I should not have survived my difficulties without the help of my Eliza. I am certain of that. Even today I see her angel's face at the door of the library, where I am reclining before the fire. I feel her touch on my arm as she guides me beneath the trees and into the sunlight. I have been without her now, I calculate, for almost as many years as I had lived when she first became my nurse. These two times of absence are the periods of emptiness enclosing my life; she is its bright centre. [4]

My other saviour lives more easily in my mind—in *all* our minds, since the person I speak of is the poet Wordsworth. His writings did much, very much, towards calming the confusing whirl of necessity which followed my departure from the military; I wept copious tears of happiness and gratitude over them. [5] The shorter lyrics would have been enough for me. But reading the *Excursion,* especially, I found my spirits reviving rapidly. In the solitude incident to the rambling life it describes, its lines release in the poet a power that keeps alive a devotedness to nature (one he had known in his childhood), together with the opportunity of gaining such notices of persons or things from his intercourse with society, which has qualified him to become a teacher of moral wisdom. This is the boldness and originality of Wordsworth's genius, and it was the foundation of my recovery. I am brave to say this, but I know that I speak for a fit audience. Lamb often told me the same.

When we are guided to nature, then we discover what exists within us. Nature becomes the source of ourselves. That is what Wordsworth taught me, which I took into my heart. The sublime language of his rocks and stones and trees brought me back to steadiness. I believed once more, through my love for the world around me and its creatures, in the power of my own spirit.

I could not have said, as I recovered my happiness and pleasure, that I was equipping myself for a new existence, full of new faces and arrangements. Our lives are not created with such clarity, however we dream of the future. We might aim ourselves like an arrow at a target. We might march like a soldier towards a particular battery. But while we are passing from moment to moment, we are tossed in the torrent of a thousand accidents and chances. We are buffeted hither and thither, unable to see ourselves clearly, or our way ahead. I had known this from my studies of Locke, when I was a boy. But I had forgotten it—or perhaps I should say I had not allowed myself to remember it. My mind had become overlaid by other men's traditions, so that my identity had first sunk and then shattered under their weight. When I re-collected myself, I knew that I was whole. Only then could I begin my journey at last, to become my true Self.

1. TGW was deliberately misleading about his year in the army, implying in one essay that he had been a Dragoon, and stating in another that he had been a cornet in a yeomanry regiment. Barry Cornwall (whose real name was Bryan Procter, but who wrote under the pseudonym Barry Cornwall, and is referred to as such throughout this book) believed that "he had originally been in some regiment of the line." Others supposed that "he had held a commission in the Guards" (see Curling, p. 46). In fact TGW bought an ensigncy in the 16th Foot, otherwise known as the Bedfordshire Regiment of Foot, on 14 April 1814—for which he paid £400 to a Mr. Brett, the agent acting on behalf of the regiment at 16 Gerrard Street, Soho, London—who left out the middle "e" in his name when signing him on.

The regiment had been founded in 1688 to fight supporters of the Prince of Orange when they threatened James II, and had since seen active service at Blenheim and Ramillies, and in North and South America. Immediately before TGW joined, it had suffered heavy losses to disease, first in Surinam, then in Barbados. Early in 1814, most of the regiment was shipped off to Monkstown in Canada. It went from Quebec to Chambley to Montreal, then back to Quebec in July 1815. Subsequently, it travelled via Portsmouth to France, where it arrived two months late for Waterloo. TGW missed every one of these journeys. Since the regiment was awarded no battle honours for its part in eighteenth- and early-nineteenth-century campaigns, its soldiers were often and ignominiously referred to as "The Peacemakers."

They did, however, have a glamorous uniform, which no doubt strongly attracted TGW. In 1751, the facings of their "regimentals" were changed from white to yellow; they were also equipped with three-cornered hats bound with white lace and ornamented with a white loop and a black cockade, red waistcoats, red breeches, white gaiters reaching to the knee, white cravats, and buff cross-belts.

2. The 16th Foot was in Canada from March 1814 until August 1815, but it is clear from the Regimental Monthly Returns that TGW stayed in the Depot in Fermoy, Co. Cork, in the south-west of Ireland, from 25 June 1814 until Christmas Day, then moved to Portsmouth, where he remained until 25 May 1815. He had sold his ensigncy on 23 May, and returned to London soon afterwards.

3. Ladbroke Black suggested that TGW's illness was "sleepy sickness" (*encephalitis lethargica*), which he claimed "to be responsible for a cerebral

derangement that may result in an honest man becoming an habitual criminal" (p. 55). Other commentators have been less specific. Havelock Ellis, for instance, said that TGW was "on the verge of insanity, if not, as is more likely, actually insane" (p. 54), and Curling added: "There is no reason to presuppose madness in accounting for the incongruities of his nature, although his youthful melancholia may certainly have impaired his moral judgement" (p. 83). The only clear facts of the matter are that TGW had a breakdown after what he called the "sudden mutations" of his early manhood, and was better by 1816. His illness, however, may be taken as a sign of instability which later returned in other forms.

4. Eliza Frances Ward was the eldest daughter of a Mrs. Abercromby (née Weller) of Mortlake; she was born in 1796 (the exact date is unknown) and baptized on 29 September that same year. (I am grateful to Paul Hopkins for this information, which he conveyed to me in a letter dated 19 June 1999. Dr. Hopkins intends to publish his research on TGW, which is referred to elsewhere in my notes, in "Thomas Griffiths Wainewright, his in-laws and Wimbledon Manor.") Eliza had probably once lived in Turnham Green, in which case she may have known TGW as a child (see Hammond, p. 6). TGW very rarely mentions her in his few surviving papers, she plays no part in his *Essays,* and only one or two of his friends make any reference to her. Those who do show an unhelpful prejudice—Barry Cornwall, for instance, calls her "a sharp-eyed, self-possessed woman, dressing in showy, flimsy finery," adding, "She seemed to obey [TGW's] humours and to assist his needs; but much affection did not apparently exist between them" (Procter, p. 190). If, as I suggest on pp. 108–09, Eliza was the model for Bertalda in TGW's Royal Academy picture of 1823, she was a stockier figure than Cornwall implies, with long curling auburn hair, large brown eyes, and a full-lipped mouth.

Like Eliza and her other children, Mrs. Abercromby is a shadowy figure. Her first husband was a Mr. Ward, with whom she had one daughter (Eliza) and a son; with her second husband, a lieutenant in the army, she had two daughters, Helen Frances Phoebe (born 1809) and Madeleine (born 1810). Following the death of Lieutenant Abercromby in 1812, she was left with a legacy of approximately £100 per annum. To supplement this, she started taking in lodgers, and also applied to the Board of Ordnance, which gave the children an annual allowance of £10 each. This has led TGW's critics to assume that she was always and irredeemably hard up during her widowhood. In fact the Ward family "had been prosperous illegitimate gentry offspring, and even after a catastrophe about the time of Eliza's birth retained the wreck of their fortune" (letter from Paul Hopkins to author, 18 April 1999).

5. In his *Autobiography* (1873), John Stuart Mill said much the same thing as TGW about the healing properties of Wordsworth's poetry. But by the time Mill came across Wordsworth's work, it was safely established in the canon—even though Mill felt that he had made a personal discovery. When TGW read him, Wordsworth's reputation was much less secure. In 1814 he had published a two-volume edition of his works (probably the one TGW read), which for the first time adopted the classification that has since troubled and fascinated his readers—"Poems of the Fancy," "Poems of the Imagination," "Poems founded on the Affections," and so on. Admirers like Keats, Hazlitt, de Quincey and Hunt (who called Wordsworth "the greatest poet of the time") received it warmly. Wordsworth's detractors were sufficiently vocal to restrict sales severely. This is important, since it shows TGW acting independently in his reading. He would later find himself in strong agreement with Lamb, whose remarks about the *Excursion* are incorporated here (see *Selected Prose*, p. 78). Lamb told his friend the Quaker poet Bernard Barton on 15 May 1824 that "A line of Wordsworth's is a lever to lift the immortal spirit! Byron can only move the spleen."

6

THE BOLD LOVER

J clapped my hands, and set out upon the golden road to town. One of my ministering angels, my uncle, flew into my pocket, placed some money there, and flew out again. Another, Wordsworth, flew into a second pocket and made it his perpetual home. The third, the angel of my affections, flew back to Mortlake, where she prepared to make darting journeys into my life and heart.

My new lodgings allowed me room for my work—that is the best I can say of them. And I must immediately add, this was a trouble to me. Since I had ended my days in the 16th, the memory of boredom had inflamed my desire for pleasure, which of course my circumstances had prevented. Now that I was well again, this desire became an insatiable longing, and I do not exaggerate if I say that the best part of my income, and of my energy, was spent trying to get satisfaction. [1]

I told myself: you are a London man, an Artist, you are coming into your prime—you should conduct yourself accordingly. Looking round at my new world for encouragement in my ambitions, I thought I could do no better than settle on the figure of Beau Brummell for inspiration. I do not presume to suggest that I considered myself a rival to this alternative Majesty; but I shall happily admit that I envied his fine eye to discriminate, which allowed him to move freely amongst those who otherwise would have considered him an inferior. His looks and manner were like a ticket-of-leave, enabling him to visit most places and say most things. His art was the cultivation of the Self: an eye to see beauty, and a pulse to feel.

It is often said by gossips that this art was entirely composed of gaudy colours and effeminate ways; but gossips know nothing of the dandy's skill. Brummell's appearance was in its own terms severe, and always serene. I have heard that his collar, which was worn *fixed* to the shirt, was so large that, before being folded down, it completely hid his head and face; the white neckerchief was at least a foot in height. To be so sheathed gave him a proper disdain for lowly things, since it prevented him from looking down on them altogether. It also, I believe, meant the head could not be turned sideways—and I did hear of one case when a man starched his own collar so frostily, he cut off one of his ears, attempting to converse with a neighbour. [2]

My affection for my own ears being considerable, I relaxed the demands I made upon myself as far as collars were concerned. (But I did love a long neck, as anyone who has even glanced over my paintings will confirm. I loved especially the long neck of a beautiful woman—my Eliza!—stretching in eagerness, perhaps with a black band drawn across, and the veins charged with blood, as I have often shown.) Neither did I aspire to wide hats and thin-waisted coats, nor to that system of buttons and straps which, when they are passed beneath the foot, allow a man's inexpressibles to hang without a wrinkle.

That said, I had no choice but to design an appearance for myself, since fate had thrust me into the world without any close guide to help me—and I soon built myself into a very superior sort of edifice: a family, an estate, and its noble effects, all rolled into one. My blue, military-looking surcoat—that was a well-fitting thing which I flourished as though it had been my coat of arms. My spurs—I jangled those dangerous items at George's and elsewhere, when my only charger was a bowl of punch. My white top hat—that was the banner flying from the flagpole of my tower. And the diamond rings on my fingers, the antique cameos on my breast-pins, my cambric pocket-handkerchief breathing forth *Attargul,* my pale lemon-coloured kid gloves? These were the treasures in my castle boudoir. These were the flashes of fire which illuminated the corresponding glow of a rare binding, or the milky eyes of my porcelain, winking from the surrounding gloom. Even now, at such a cruel distance, I see them rise again. My tables groan with the weight of volumes of Raphaello, Michel Angelo, Rubens, Poussin, Parmigiano, Giulio, etc., etc., and the massive portfolio cases open wide their doors, disclosing yet fresh treasures within. Then do I riot in immeasurable delight—I am great as Sardanapalus—I hold Sir Epicure Mammon in contempt—I am a concentration of all the Sultans in the Arabian Nights. Everything and everybody seems *couleur de rose!* The coffee is exquisitely fragrant; the salver and spoons become gilt, the Worcester china the rarest oriental.

I confess (where else might one confess, except in a *Confession?*) some have thought these things made me into a fop—a weakling, a sentimentalist, a languid drowser. I say in my defence: I have done no more than live in ways I considered indispensable to gentility. This is why dress became a favourite interest, and, next to dress, horsemanship. (I mean the exercise I took upon my noble steed Contributor, who, like his master, would not stand the whip, being apt to kick.) No one should suppose that when I call myself giddy, I mean fainting. Or imagine that when I say flighty I mean careless. I was, rather, someone who had the fondness of a savage for finery, and whose passion for beauty was barbaric.

I shall prove what I mean immediately, and take a look at myself as I embark on this latest stage of my career. I shall adopt, as I have done before, a precise form of annotation. Let me suppose the *date* to be 1816 or 1817— never mind which; my *age:* the age anyone would be, who had been born when I came into the world—i.e., twenty-two or twenty-three; my *height:* 5'5" (and a half-inch); my *complexion:* pale, but coloured sometimes with rouge, for health; my *head:* oval (yet seeming a little elongated by the device of fine curling moustaches); my *hair:* ah! a question to juggle with. Dark, on occasion. Light, on occasion. Generally—BROWN (I would do better to call it "my own") and worn to my shoulders, with a central parting; my *forehead:* high (also: crammed, ingenious, lofty, aspiring, clear); my *eyebrows:* I refer to hair; my *eyes:* grey—but weak, and therefore often behind a quizzing-glass; my *nose:* still breathing (I mean long); my *mouth: I* would say average, my enemies large, voluptuous, sensual, gloating, sneering; my *chin:* firm, or rather—a sprouting-point for my beard.

Other remarks? I am unable to make any, since the vision is fading. No! My remark is this: the portrait that I have given here is the portrait of someone who does not exist.

I was ambitious to live upon the town, yet the size of my uncle's allowance did not permit me to do so without working. Neither, at this stage, did I myself wish to be idle. The recovery of my health, and the recent long practice I had given to the fine art of yawning, made me impatient to seek my fortune.

Impatient, yet when I look back upon this time of life, I detect in myself a hesitancy to undertake anything which might easily win the applause of a public, or tarnish the good name of a gentleman. I was content to execute a likeness for those who sought me out—my cousins Foss, among others— and to line my pockets with whatever they cared to pay me. In the same way, I was pleased to admit one or two pupils into my Painting Room, and to pass on to them such skills as I had learned in earlier days. This, however, was never a profitable exercise for me, and I am certain that my own disaffection with prolonged study created confusion and alarm in my pupils. [3]

I admit, there was a tincture of self-criticism dropped into my pride.

During my infancy, when men such as Flaxman and Stothard and Westall had often passed through my grandfather's house, I had presumed that a great talent was an easy thing to acquire—and once acquired, equally easy to develop. In my apprenticeship, I had learned otherwise, which had bred in me a perpetual disappointment with myself. Such polite work as I completed, I would not sign with my own name. Such attention that I received, I merely reflected back in the flash of bright buttons and a blue surcoat. I felt myself a species of crustacean: my shell a gorgeous carapace, my interior a mystery even to my own eyes.

Nevertheless, my new life began to occupy me more and more. I have already said, in speaking about Mr. P., that I had little sympathy with the tendency in British art to honour mean, bald matters of fact, and undiscriminative imitations, which did not take due care for the satisfaction of the mind. Accordingly, since I now had the liberty to do so, I gave almost the whole of my admiration to works I would later call *poetic*—examining them in the print shops, and all manner of private collections. By *poetic* I mean especially the works of Henry Fuseli, and (though these were a far rarer sighting) of William Blake.

Now, no man should willingly admit to being an imitator—since forgery is such a grave offence—but the artist who will not learn from his betters is a foolish one. Looking over these works by Fuseli, and admiring his ingenuity in giving solid expression to the inventions of his own mind, or in putting solid flesh on the insubstantial forms of men and women from the Drama, I felt a light creeping across the dim surfaces of my brain, which showed me the shapes of those ideas I had long wanted to express. I took encouragement from this, and began reading what I believed Fuseli must have read. Furthermore, I made a habit of copying his works, and making them my own by devotion. I might mention as an example my scene of lovers embracing, or my rendering of *Zephyr with Aurora Playing,* which I took from Fuseli's imagining of that scene in his *Euphrosyne.* Also, *The Bold Lover.* [4]

These images leapt into my brain as though they had been freshly snatched from the stream of my own existence. Yet they never were! I had manufactured something from nothing. No sooner have I said that, however, than I must continue by wondering how a man might make something from nothing if he does not exhibit his creation. How may a thing exist, if it exists in secret?

The answer in my case is a delicate one. These little drawings of mine celebrated the amity which may exist between human bodies, as did others I would execute in due course: melting love pictures, for which I received particular praise and encouragement from Fuseli and Holst. They are not pictures for the general, and if they had been, their power would have been diminished. I cannot easily say more than that; but in withdrawing from the subject, I will turn towards another which presents me with equal difficulties, since it involves my Eliza. I mean the subject of Love itself.

It is a marvellous thing, how the occasional companions of childhood (as Eliza was the companion of mine), whom we look upon in our salad days with no special admiration, may change gradually in our eyes, and become the goal of all our tenderness. My own convergence with Eliza was all the more remarkable for the differences between us. When I felt my heart begin its journey towards her, which was during my illness, I noticed our discrepancies and thought nothing of them. She had no wealth: I did not care. Her days were encumbered by her mother, and by her two half-sisters Helen and Madeleine: I did not care. She had a fragility in her appearance: I did not care (indeed, I thought her exceedingly beautiful). She was not expert with the names of those artists and writers whom I expected my friends to have by heart: I did not care. She had a habit of smoking a cigar sometimes, after dinner, which seemed a curious thing in a woman: I did not care. Everything that was strange or not suitable became, as my affections gathered into a passion, a reason for loving her all the more dearly.

Such forms of fascination are dangerous. The years pass, the heart cools, desire fails, and blemishes which had once seemed delightful are exposed as their simple selves: blemishes indeed. Yet to speak for myself (I cannot speak for Eliza; I shall not) I may say freely that our fate was not so simple. I first loved Eliza when she was my nurse and I her charge. Her sympathy never diminished through all the long while we lived as man and wife, and neither did my demand for her comfort. It was not our differences which finally thrust us apart—as I shall prove. It was the ways in which we resembled each other.

Now let me be as good as my word, and leave Eliza, unsullied at the pinnacle of her beauty and kindness. The nurse who had lifted me from the black waters of my unhappiness with so sore a struggle had become the whole object of my wish to please. Our marriage plans were the crown and glory of all my ambition in this world.

Would that my uncle had felt the same. His heart, which itself had never known the heat of adoration (except perhaps for an orchid coming into bloom), beat out of rhythm with ours. I will not do him the injustice of saying that he turned against us. But I will say that he did not turn towards us.

Did he consider Eliza's mother and half-sisters a burden? He was not so bold. Did he suppose Eliza's mother had designs on his own affections—for he was a quiet man, and had a hermit's readiness to believe the world was full of plots and stratagems? I cannot tell. All I am sure of is this: in the grandeur of youth, which achieves its shape by mingling pride with fear, Eliza and I decided to marry in secret, abetted by two friends of the time who have both since sunk into oblivion. When it was done, we were so in thrall to one another, the opinion of the entire world might have tipped against us and we would not have felt it. She had redeemed me, and now stood at my shoulder as my life began in earnest. I felt that the ropes which had tethered me to the shore were suddenly cast off, the current was strengthening to catch me, and my attention was swinging round towards a bright horizon. There was the lift of a sea breeze in my face, and overhead the big topsails were snapping open and filling. [5]

1. We do not know where TGW lived when he moved to London, nor exactly when he left Linden House. It was probably early in 1816, and his rooms were likely to have been central—perhaps near the church of St. Martin-in-the-Fields, since he was living in that parish when he got married.

2. The Regency world of Brummell and the world of the Romantics were contemporaneous but mutually exclusive. However, Hazlitt—as well as Byron and TGW—was interested in Brummell, and realized that his priorities were subversive as well as entertaining. Brummell, said Hazlitt, has "arrived at the very minimum of wit, and reduced it 'by happiness or pain,' to an almost invisible point. All his bon-mots turn upon a single circumstance, the exaggerating of the merest trifles into matters of importance, or treating everything else with the utmost nonchalance and indifference, as if whatever pretended to pass beyond these limits was a bore, and disturbed the serene art of high life."

Several of TGW's other contemporaries regarded such flamboyance as merely suspicious, and made their feelings plain in their remarks about his own appearance. Barry Cornwall, for instance, called him "absolutely a fop, finikin in dress, with mincing steps, and tremulous words, with his hair curled and full of unguents and his cheeks painted like those of a frivolous demi-rep." Hazlitt referred to him in his "Dandy School" essay as a "dandy scribbler." Talfourd spoke of him, shudderingly, as having "a sort of undress military air, and the conversation of a smart, lively, clever, heartless, voluptuous coxcomb." De Quincey commented on "the dandyism which overspread the surface of his manner."

George Bryan Brummell (1778–1840) was the son of Lord North's private secretary, educated at Eton, and as a teenager became friendly with the Prince of Wales, who gave him a cornetcy in the Coldstream Guards in 1794, at the tender age of sixteen. Thereafter, he became the epitome of irresponsibility, making absurd wagers (running a five-minute mile in the Edgware Road), dressing with great elegance (Tom Moore once said the Prince of Wales "began to blubber when told that Brummell did not like . . . the cut of his coat"), and in all respects redefining social orthodoxies. He lived far beyond his means, fled to France in his early thirties, was imprisoned for debt in 1835, and declined into misery and insanity during his pathetic final years. His achievement was significant but inevitably febrile: he was the wittiest and most original of those men who, led by a pleasure-loving Prince, created the *Zeitgeist* of the Regency, and whose tone influenced later figures such as Wilde and Baudelaire. (Baudelaire called dandyism "the last gesture of the heroic in an age of decadence.") It is the concentration on matters of identity (or lack of it) that links Brummell with TGW most strongly. A later dandy, Barbey d'Aurevilly, said, "Brummell left nothing but a name mysteriously sparkling in the memoirs of his time," and Catherine Cecil, in *Adventures of a Coxcomb* (1841), said tellingly, "A dandy is a nobody, who has made himself somebody, and given the law to everybody."

3. Only three portraits by TGW survive from 1815 to 1816, and only "six portraits of friends and relations dating from about 1820 to 1825 are . . . known, one of which (a study of John Payne, now in the New York Historical Society Collection) shows both the conservatism of Phillips and the stylized patterning and linearity of Blake" (Kerr, p. 837). Curling also claims to have seen some "immature sketches in charcoal on brown paper, dated 1814 . . . [of] little ability . . . [showing] a woman's feet, hands, wrists and ankles" (p. 24).

4. TGW's *An Amorous Scene* (?1821) is described in the British Museum catalogue as:

> A park of undulating ground with thickets; a tall lady with a sunshade is moving away from the foreground, looking with scandalized or envious eyes at a couple seated on a bank (left) and ardently embracing; in the background, among the thickets, three other pairs of lovers are similarly engaged.

This conveys the generally lubricious atmosphere of the picture, but does not recognize the debt that TGW owes to Fuseli for his subject and techniques. The same applies to the contorted embrace of *Zephyr with Aurora Playing* (which has its source in Milton's *L'Allegro*) and *The Bold Lover*—which according to TGW's inscription on the reverse shows how Lothaire of Bourgoine "discovers the *amour* of his wife with the High Constable and thereby procures his own death." In fact, as David Weinglass points out in his *catalogue raisonné* of Fuseli's work, the scene illustrates Margaret of Navarre's *Heptameron*, XVI, which Fuseli had studied in Berlin in 1763. TGW's claim that his source was Baraut's *Histoire des Ducs de Bourgogne*—which was not published until 1824—is false.

5. TGW and Eliza were married in the church of St. Martin-in-the-Fields; their marriage certificate reads: "Thomas Griffiths Wainewright of this

Parish a Bachelor and Eliza Frances Ward of the Parish of Mortlake in the County of Surrey a Spinster were married in this Church by Licence this thirteenth Day of November in the Year One thousand eight hundred and seventeen by me John Tillotson, Curate. (In the presence of Edw Foss and Jn Taylor.)"

7

GODS OF MY WORSHIP

As I entered the next chamber of my existence, I thought my eyes were open for the first time. I saw what was beautiful in my daily life; in my work I discovered the means to make something out of nothing. For this, I must thank Eliza, who steadied me when she was at my side, and, when she was not, became my Muse, my argument, and the object of my fervent study. (Sometimes her half-sisters Helen and Madeleine—who would often shelter under our roof, to make us a complete family in an instant—also sat for me.) The greater debt, I owed to Professor Henry Fuseli. [1]

In my present wilderness, I look at his name where I have written it, and am astonished at my impudence in calling such a man my friend. Yet such he was. Friend of my heart and intellect. Friend of my fears and hopes. When our friendship began in earnest, the Professor had already enjoyed his high office as Keeper of the Academy for several years. This made him a king in my eyes—something almost divine. Yet because he looked so kindly on my more modest talents, and encouraged qualities in me which should more properly be called his own, I soon realized that this genius was a man, with a man's ordinary needs and habits. Whether this was because he habitually lifted me up to his own exalted plane, or descended to my lowly one, I cannot tell. All I know is this: after some cautious circlings we drew more nearly together, until scarcely a week would pass without our being in each other's company. I do not shrink from saying that this time became, accordingly, the most blessed of my life.

Let me summon him up again, notwithstanding the pity of seeing him waste his sweetness here, on the desert air. He was of small stature, yet on his minute and slender body was the head of a Jupiter, his blue eyes (a very light blue) set far apart and shooting piercing glances from beneath overhanging brows. These brows were white, the same as his hair, which he wore unpowdered in thick tumbling masses. This would have given him the appearance of untidiness (considering his habitual old flannel dressing-gown, tied round with a length of rope), were it not for the quickness of his movements.

The look of Fuseli made him extraordinary; his talk made him wonderful. In the Academy when he was teaching, he showed a fearless audacity of expression. Sometimes he spoke in a slow solemn utterance, which gave to the simplest phrase the pomp of a Roman oration. At others he spoke with such irascible wit that not a few of the younger members of his profession would provoke his ire deliberately, merely for the pleasure of hearing him storm. I myself have heard him produce all manner of oaths, roarings, boastings, deprecations, rushes between languages (I believe he knew eight), and have often seen him hurl himself out of the room altogether to show his disgust at a thing done badly.

Yet his disciples, of which I counted myself among the most ardent, easily forgave him this strangeness, knowing that they would catch something worth treasuring in memory, to increase their understanding. This something was akin to the qualities I had formerly admired in Byron at a distance, and which I now saw close up, in a whirlwind. The pell-mell of his conversation showed a knowledge of the Classics which would have silenced the Reverend Burney D.D., and a fluent memory of all that he had seen which made him a veritable encyclopaedia. It engendered in me a sense of largeness, and excitement, as though I was leaping through a vast landscape of boulders, not treading a gravel path.

What I call largeness here I also consider the mark of greatness in his work. During his time in Italy as a young man, he had shaken hands with the ghost of Michel Angelo, and in all that he subsequently produced, he doted upon this Master's example. There are enemies who claim his admiration issued in a kind of superhuman ponderousness—pointing to the engravings he made to accompany Cowper's poems, and saying that in each of them a peaceable scene has been transformed into a conspiracy of giants, whose dresses are as fantastical as their minds. To this I say: you may hate Fuseli but you cannot forget him, which is the prerogative of true and high genius. Furthermore, we should be careful how we condemn; the fault may be in us, who have not the same power of delivering our minds, at will, from the restraints which the rules of polished society and tight breeches have placed on the expression of the passions.

I have broadcast my estimation for the Professor in numerous places, before now. In my teaching, I have fixed the minds of my pupils on the principles of his *Six Lectures*. In my conversation, I have used his many and excellent aphorisms concerning beauty and dignity of tone, questioning in the same breath the wisdom of encouraging mere historical painting to glorify Old England. In my articles, I have echoed his own views in most things—emphasizing the great ingenuity of Dürer (but also repeating the opinion that he did not *invent* a style); describing Raphaello as the father of dramatic painting; saying that Leonardo was more fit to scatter hints than to teach by example; expressing the fear that Reynolds, by courting the applause of his own time, must reckon on the neglect of posterity; praising Rembrandt, and Masaccio, and Giorgione, and Caravaggio; enjoying the coalition of light and darkness achieved by an imperceptible transition in Correggio; relishing especially (I shall write it again) the sublimity of conception, the grandeur of form, the breadth of manner, the united magnificence of plan, and the endless variety of subordinate parts in MICHEL ANGELO. [2]

Yes, I have shared Fuseli's opinions and won his gratitude, I believe, for my pains. A greater proof of our affection—greater, even, than my purchase of numerous of his works—is the knowledge that when we examined our imaginations in secret, we discovered resemblances which proved the consanguinity of our spirits. To put this more simply: my Professor was a left-handed man—left-handed in his daily practice, and somewhat sinister in his delights. The visionary power of his work created a dimness, a bloodless pallor, a mental blight which was visible to the corporeal senses, whether it be in his depiction of Prometheus tethered upon his rock, or Macbeth confronted by his wife, or his infamous *Nightmare*. Recollect how the damsel slumps upon her bed, while the vile incubus gloats over her. Poor unprotected girl! Recollect then how the demon is the product of her own brain, and no one will be amazed that my Professor was called the Painter in Ordinary to the Devil.

This aspect of Fuseli's genius has become a common property, and does not need my comment. But as I walk again through the anguished landscape of his imagination, seeing once more those fissured rocks upon which mighty heroes lie shattered, I am bound to remember there are critics who still cling to the safety of a conventional opinion, and so condemn him. Is it to be supposed that the storm-tossing, white arms of his Chriemhild, the future wife of Attila the Hun, were tied down by the shoulder straps of Mrs. Bell's corsets? Is the first appearance of Undine in the cottage of Ulrich a matter for teacups and mild greetings? What other world is possible for the delivery of Prometheus, except an abyss which yawns between him and his saviour, who rises on the opposite peak, while the moon shines out broadly without a cloud on the ghastly scenery, and where blank desolation is unbroken by a shrub, a stump, a weed, or even a pebble?

These are mighty pictures—the workings of a mind roaring at itself; they would have struck at me fiercely wherever I encountered them. By reason of the fact that I generally saw their creator at work in his studio, they entered my soul. As Keeper of the Academy, the Professor was given accommodation in Somerset House, below which was a set of dungeon-like rooms that would have excited the admiration of Horace Walpole himself. They formed a long suite of narrow and irregular apartments, very dark, being lit only from little round windows close to the ceiling. The awful picture of the Lazar House was at the very furthest end of this dim gallery, entirely covering the wall. The pale and ghostly forms, in every variety of human pain and woe, seemed actually real. The wide walls of this cavern were also completely covered with paintings, legendary, historic, scriptural; all ages and countries seemed to have furnished their most tragic scenes and most renowned characters, invested with somewhat of the superhuman, from the genius of Fuseli; while confusedly piled in corners all sorts of artistic lumber were visible.

I would often be summoned here to drink his wisdom, in the company of Eliza and her two half-sisters, Helen and Madeleine, so that he might perceive my female companions as a kind of coven, and conceive of them as a suitable subject. In the strange light of a few candles, I watched him working at his easel in a frenzy, his white hair seeming to glow in the dimness; or I sat in a trance while he explained to me things I already half understood but needed his guidance to see whole.

I recollect him, in particular, imagining in that suspicious place that he must plead the cause of a murdered man—a speech which put my own hair on end, and made my eyes jolt in their sockets. "Why should not every supposable circumstance of the act float before my eyes?" he said. "Shall I not see the murderer, unawares, and rush in upon him? In vain he tries to escape—see how pale he turns—hear you not his shrieks—his entreaties?—do you not see him flying, struck, falling? Will not his blood, his ashy semblance, his groans, his last expiring gasp, seize on every mind?"

It is common for artists of all kinds to enter the souls of their creations, be they cheerful or criminal. I will not hear it said the Professor did more than any other man in this respect. Yet he had a special sympathy with the moment at which our human controls dissolve, and we are exposed to the same wild furies, the same ungovernable passions, that hold sway in beasts. It is marvellous that a man who (in spite of his storms) was yet so well regulated and reasonable in his behaviour was so fully equipped to comprehend everything terrible in his imagination. Some will think it is also marvellous that I allowed my wife and her sisters to accompany me on my visits to him. To them I say: the division between the Professor's sociable self, and his creating self, was well defended. My wife, in any case, was firm-minded enough to know good from evil. Her sisters were sillier—though Helen in particular was of a sweet nature—and yet I am sure they came to no harm. When I remember them across this great distance which now divides us, I see their pretty faces like gleams of moonlight in those dark and alarming apartments, conjured up by the Magician (I mean Fuseli himself) where no moonlight came in fact. They were valuable to him in their innocence— valuable and secure. [3]

I must leave my Professor there, in the near-darkness, lest the story of my own life be consumed in the account of my love and respect for him. Yet as I turn to his (I might almost say to *our*) protégé Holst, I must mention one link among several which united the two painters. Even when Fuseli drew women engaged upon their usual tasks, he contrived to create the strange mood of a dream. In his private drawings, where he relied upon "the animal of Beauty," as Dante calls it—and which I must immediately say my Eliza etc. never saw—this dream was of a more delicious kind. (I am speaking here of his love paintings.) I have known women who started from his brain enter my imagination with the power of a thunderbolt. I cannot describe them. I have felt myself a pygmy in comparison to the muscular strong haunches, the immense neck cords, and the towering head-dresses of those creatures. [4]

As I say, I cannot describe them. But I will mention that Holst shared our liking for these curiosities, and even—which was somewhat surprising, since he was so much our junior in years—led us on to them a little.

My first meeting with Holst was in the region of Fitzroy Square, where he always remained, and where I see him still. [5] His studio was a most quaint room, full of artistic appliances of various descriptions, old swords "by rust embrowned," that would have made an antiquarian's teeth water to look upon; ponderous volumes, "iron clasped and iron bound"; beaverless helmets and broken gauntlets, inlaid guitars, foils, masks and fencing gloves, damask draperies, German drinking glasses, and earthenware from Holland. Upon a table in a dark corner of the room lay a crucifix and skull, the forehead of which was decked with a wreath of faded flowers; there was also a long row of pipes of various patterns, for even at that early age he was a confirmed smoker, of opium as well as tobacco.

Holst himself seemed to belong to a bygone age, being dressed in a kirtle of grey cloth reaching to the knees, confined at the waist by a leather girdle, his dark waving hair falling low on his shoulders, and his lip slightly shaded by a moustache. His features were regular and well developed; his brow high and marked; his eyes large, dark and bright as a gazelle's; his form slight but graceful.

Making all due allowances, I might say that we resembled one another, as far as our looks were concerned, and our tastes. That pleasure in the vague and the terrible, which our Professor had kindled in me (but which had always been eager to burn), flamed passionately in Holst. His love groups were as delicate and beautiful as can be conceived, and among his other subjects were such glimpses of sublimity as I would have felt proud to call my own. I am thinking especially of his *Wild Huntsman Careering in the Storm Blast,* of his *Demon Lover and His Mistress,* and above all of his *Fiendish Dance round the Gallowstree.*

We had dreaming days in our friendship, yet we were diligent, for all that. As I have said already, we had chosen the harder task, by endeavouring to show what was contained in ourselves, not merely what lay around us— since only by dwelling on that which lies within can the finite mind respect the eternal act of creation in the infinite I AM. (I have seen a similar thing written by Schlegel: "Wie kann das Unendliche auf die Oberfläche zur Erscheinung gebralt werden? Nur symbolisch, in Bildern und Zeichen.") [6] Therefore, we were scornful of the reality which lay so clearly and intelligibly on the foreheads of gentlemen in their fine portraits. Therefore, we also demanded to know where, in Wilkie or Haydon, was the light of genius, the crystal which lives within the light it transmits, and which is transparent like the light itself? Therefore, we answered these questions: it does not exist. It cannot exist in their unremarkable histories and heroics.

Let me give instances. There lives more wisdom in one dream by Goethe than in the whole waking intelligence of my instructor Mr. P. There is nothing in the whole of West which shakes the heart like a page by Motte Fouqué. In his *Undine,* all the principles of the imagination are set out so that we may comprehend them while suffering the harsh lessons of the world: the perishability of earthly things; the fading of beauty; grief which comes whether we deserve it or not, and which alone among our memories will not fade. [7]

I have come close to discussing my own case here, which in this part of my Confession I did not propose to do. Let me therefore instantly forget myself again and say there was a third, besides the two I have already introduced, who understood what I mean. I am speaking of William Blake, who unreasonably mocked himself when he said that another of Motte Fouqué's works, *Sintram and His Companions*—that sublime and deeply pondered effusion of genius—was better than his own things. [8]

It was not until close to the end of his breathing existence that I knew this man, though his name had often been in my ears when I was a child. I had not then understood what I soon came to know: namely, that there are some on this earth who have no conception of Heaven, and others who never lose sight of it. Blake was eternally one of the blessed, and indeed when he and his wife Catherine moved to Fountain Court, soon after I became their frequent visitor, he seemed already to have half completed his journey to the Eternal Father. I would make my way from the Strand towards the river, and on entering the dark tunnel into that Court, begin my ascent to his rooms in the certainty that I was learning a lesson of the spirit even before I knocked upon his door. Here was nothing of the dungeon gloom of the Professor, or the antiquarian confusion of Holst. Here was pure simplicity which gave a glimpse of the life beyond.

It was not within my capacity to endure many such visits, but I kept Blake in my thoughts, and praised him. I mentioned his "Jerusalem" in the *London*, calling it a tremendous piece of ordnance and other such things, and all at a time when I felt like a voice crying in the wilderness unheard. [9] I also purchased examples of his work, hoping thereby to comfort his mortal body even as I celebrated his immortal soul. I cannot easily do justice to the pleasure they gave me, since they brought me into the presence of beauty which lay far in advance of our general comprehension. I have studied Blake's figures and not known whether their faces are turned towards Heaven or earth, whether their strong limbs are equipped for above or below. I have clambered among the lines of his writing and understood them partially, as if I were reading by lightning (as my friend Coleridge said elsewhere). I have been drenched with his gorgeous umbers, spattered by the gold leaf which he put on at my bidding, rejoiced in the density of his sunsets—and all the while I have felt that I was breathing the purest ether. Where did such a man originate, who was able to combine so many diverse thoughts in one moment? What immortal fire consumed him when he passed from us at last? Truly, he was a saint among infidels, who although he sometimes outraged common sense and rationality by the opinions he advanced, nevertheless drew from me all admiration possible. [10]

. . .

I have attempted here to give the portraits of three courageous spirits who made my existence happy—and who are now further off from me than the most deep-dwelling creature in the profound ocean. It is impossible for me to pay adequate honour to the mental journeys they undertook. Each stood alone and spoke for all: we can ask no more of our great Artists. What man will have folly enough to study the principles of the blazing luminaries of Florence, Rome and Parma, if it is only to be insulted by the preference given in certain quarters to such trifles as *Crossing a Brook, The Dog Stealer, The Cock Fight,* and *The Approach to Mr. Plummock's Grot?* Who will not prefer to compliment these poetical Masters I have counted among my friends? [11]

I can ask no more (which is more than I deserve) than this: that my part in their lives be remembered. My enemies say that I robbed them of their accomplishments and adopted their wisdom as my own, and many will not even say that, since my words and my work have evaporated from the earth like dew. If there is any fair commentator left, he will more reasonably show that I shared my faith with them. The fact that the attention of such a fickle and capricious thing as the public has now swung elsewhere is a matter of no moment. Honour will return to their names, and they will inherit in posterity what they were often denied in life.

This is a comfort to me, as it should be to us all. But it is not a complete redemption of myself. The days of glory are gone and cannot be restored. The link is broken. With the Professor to guide me, I held a candle in the labyrinth of a working brain, and saw the fantastic shapes of all our hopes and terrors. With Holst I woke into a dream, and saw visions of beauty I would call true. With Blake I walked in the fields of Heaven itself. Now I am left alone on the sordid earth. The meanest wind that blows, carries a dust from the scrubland hereabouts, which settles on my page and might be the ashes of all that I have lost.

1. Henry Fuseli was born Johann Heinrich Füssli in Zurich on 6 February 1741—he changed his name to Fuseli in 1779. He was the son of a minor painter with impressive friends: Gessner, Klopstock, Wieland, Mengs and Winckelmann. He studied at the Zurich Collegium under Bodmer, met Lavater, and was ordained into the Zwinglian Church in 1761. The following year he and Lavater published an attack on a local magistrate and left Switzerland for Germany; in 1764, Fuseli moved to London, working as a translator and critic. In 1770, encouraged by Sir Joshua Reynolds, and backed by Sir Thomas Coutts, he left for Italy to study painting. (According to Allan Cunningham he "ate and drank and slept and waked upon Michelangelo.") On his return to London in 1778, he fell in with radicals clustered round the publisher Joseph Johnson, who published his translation of Winckelmann's *Reflections on the Paintings and Sculptures of the Greeks*, and his own *Remarks on Rousseau*. He met Mary Wollstonecraft (who fell in love with him) and William Blake. The paintings he exhibited at the Royal Academy in the 1780s—especially *The Nightmare*—made him famous. He became an Associate of the Royal Academy in 1788, a full Academician in 1790, Professor of Painting from 1799 to 1805 (and again from 1810), and Keeper from 1804. In 1786 he contributed to John Boydell's famous "Shakespeare Gallery," and in 1799 inaugurated his own "Milton Gallery." This was a financial disaster, but it did not stop him becoming, for the last two decades of his life, the centre of a distinguished circle. As Professor at the Royal Academy he taught (among others) Benjamin Robert Haydon, David Wilkie, Edwin Landseer, William Etty, William Mulready and Charles Leslie. After Fuseli's death in 1825, Sir Thomas Lawrence said, "In poetic invention it is not too much to say [Fuseli] has had no equal since the fifteenth or sixteenth centuries."

We do not know precisely when or how Fuseli met TGW. It may have been during TGW's childhood, when Fuseli was visiting Ralph Griffiths; it may have been through John Linnell, who had been a pupil of Fuseli. The surviving work produced by TGW during the late 1810s suggests that they were on good terms by 1818 at the latest. (On 21 October 1818, for instance, a note from Fuseli's apartments in Somerset House says, "Mr. Fuseli will be happy to be favoured by Mr. Wainwright [*sic*] and the Ladies [i.e. Eliza, Helen and Madeleine] tomorrow Evening at Tea.") The evidence of other letters suggests they were in close and friendly contact throughout the first half of the 1820s, and since TGW attended Fuseli's funeral in 1825, we can

be confident that their friendship lasted until Fuseli's death. In the years following, Fuseli's reputation took a "gannet-like plunge" (Todd, p. 81), and in
1868 his most famous picture, *The Nightmare,* was sold for £1. During the
twentieth century his fortunes revived, and he is now celebrated as an exceptional draughtsman, and as a founding father of the psychological and
"poetic" school of Romantic painters (see p. 113).

2. Fuseli trusted TGW, but obviously had some mixed feelings about his
artistic judgement. In a letter from Fuseli to an unknown addressee written
on 2 September 1820, for instance, he writes, "Permit me to observe, that, if
the Drawings which Mr. Hn [William Hilton] exhibited, are the standard of
his Method they certainly show more what to shun than what to imitate as to
'the mechanical part' which Mr. Wainewright commended [in the *London
Magazine*]."

  TGW, on the other hand, came close to idolizing Fuseli, praising him in
print at every opportunity. He also owned at least one item/painting by his
"Master"—and possibly several. In a catalogue of drawings by Fuseli sold
at Christie's on 14 April 1992 (drawings from an album once owned by Harriet Jane Moore, the granddaughter of Fuseli's friend Dr. John Moore),
"Mrs. Wainwright" (*sic*) is given as the previous owner of nine. Martin Butlin, in his introductory essay to the catalogue, suggests this "could well be"
TGW's wife, who disposed of her collection some time after TGW had
been transported to Van Diemen's Land. Most of these nine drawings show
young girls; one is a sketch of Prometheus and Io, and two are salacious
sketches of "lovers embracing by a keyboard instrument." (Seventeenth-
century Dutch paintings of women playing the spinet had made this last
scene a standard symbol of sexual availability.)

3. Fuseli had a number of regular female models: his wife, pre-eminently;
the daughters of his patron, Thomas Coutts; and Eliza Wainewright's two
half-sisters, the Abercromby girls. After his death, his friend Mrs. Balmanno
remembered the studio cellars beneath Somerset House: "Amidst this chaos,
the white head of Mr. Fuseli might be seen afar off, his figure robed in a large
flowing robe, looking like some old magician. He had a picture before
him . . . As Mrs. Fuseli advanced . . . two very pretty young girls sprang forward and saluted her; they were the sisters Helen and Madeleine Abercromby, one of whom had been sitting for the portrait of Undine."

4. Prominent artists of the Regency period produced a good deal of erotic
work—almost all of it anonymously—sometimes as an expression of sym-

pathy with the "counter-culture," more often as a profitable sideline. Reynolds, for example, did a set of drawings of a "notoriously free tendency as regards subject" for the Prince of Wales, and so did Holst.

Many examples of Fuseli's erotic work were destroyed by his widow after his death. Those that survive sometimes show straightforward scenes of sexual intercourse, and occasionally depict more complex arrangements. (After studying in Rome, Fuseli admitted to enjoying "the pleasant gratifications of a luxurious city," and Haydon rather heatedly said, "The engines of [Fuseli's] mind are . . . Blasphemy, Lechery and Blood.") Ruthven Todd (p. 82) describes these erotic drawings as "among the finest of Fuseli's works . . . [T]hey possess an extraordinary atmosphere, where the faces of the actors are quite unmoved by the strange actions they perform; Fuseli's hair-fixation appears in the elaborate head-dresses of the women, where hair, poured and moulded into fantastic shapes, suffers no disturbance from the static violence of which they partake."

Similar pictures held by the Victoria & Albert Museum are interesting cases in point: they show a powerful mixture of fantasy longing and neurotic misanthropy. But are they all in fact by Fuseli? Museum authorities are inclined to think so, but none of the drawings is signed, and they show marked differences of style and technique. Max Browne (p. 76) argues convincingly that *Ithyphallic Man and Two Women with Elaborate Hairstyles* (Plate 14, present location of original unknown) is by Holst. TGW seems not to have been responsible for any drawings in this series, but he clearly produced similar work. Talfourd, for instance, said that he "exhibited a portfolio of his own drawings of female beauty, in which the voluptuous trembled on the borders of the indelicate," and W. C. Hazlitt said, "He devoted a great deal of time and attention to the treatment of subjects intended for his own private portfolio." The only example mentioned by Hazlitt is "the well-known leg-comparing episode related in Gramont's Memoirs, in which one of the Court Beauties, Miss Price, is made to figure" (*Essays*). In this context, it is interesting to wonder how much time TGW spent looking through his grandfather's most profitable publication, *Fanny Hill*.

5. Theodore von Holst (1810–1844), although now almost entirely forgotten, was one of the most extraordinary figures of his day. He was born in London of Livonian/Russian parents who had recently arrived in England, and was introduced to Fuseli in 1820, when he was only ten years old. Fuseli was immediately impressed by his facility (and also by the sympathetic odd-

ity of his imagination), and arranged for him to have tuition. When, the following year, Thomas Lawrence, the President of the Royal Academy, gave him three guineas for a pencil sketch, his career was launched. By 1824 Holst was a probationer at the RA, and his erotic drawings were much in demand by the Prince of Wales (see Max Browne, pp. 13–14). Holst was only fifteen when Fuseli died, but the older man's influence dominated him for the rest of his own short life. His "private" work often includes copies of figures taken from works by Fuseli; his "public" works generally show scenes from his own imagination or from literature (Goethe, especially), which have a similar mood. Less monumental than Fuseli's, but often as violent, they describe extreme states of horror, disillusionment, or rapture—as their titles suggest: *Satan and the Virgin Mary Dancing at the Edge of the World*, *The Water Witch*, *The Treasure Seeker*. Towards the end of his life, Holst began producing calmer works which show him loosening his ties with middle-European Romanticism, and anticipating the more serene qualities of the Pre-Raphaelites. (Rossetti called him "a great painter.") He was a key figure in the "poetic school" of which TGW formed a part, and the great-uncle of the composer Gustav Holst.

6. "How then can the infinite be made to show up on the surface of things? Only symbolically, in pictures and signs."

7. Benjamin West's *Death on a Pale Horse* was shown in London in 1817 and, although generally popular, was derided by various discerning judges. Keats, for instance, complained, "There is nothing to be intense upon. No woman one feels mad to kiss; no face swelling into Reality." *Undine: A Romance*, by Baron Frederick de la Motte Fouqué, was translated from German by George Soane and published in London in 1818. Today its sentimental saga of love and loss seems glutinous and often unintentionally comic; for TGW and his set it told an impressive story of spiritual endeavour. Moreover, its heavily symbolic style suited ideas about the imagination that TGW developed with Fuseli and Holst, and which were common among the Romantics generally.

These ideas were strongly influenced by the work of the German Romantics, and TGW, like Fuseli, Holst and Blake, owed considerable debts to writers like de la Motte Fouqué and Goethe, as well as to painters like Friedrich and Runge. TGW was one of the first critics to praise Goethe's *Faust* in England before its first successful translation in 1833 (he devoted the first of his *Sentimentalities* in the *London Magazine* to twenty-six illustrations of the poem), and to develop its themes of human folly, seduced innocence and spiritual fantasy. Significantly, Barry Cornwall (Procter, p. 78) recalled that TGW "spoke especially of German art, which he admired, and of German literature, which had then . . . scarcely begun to make way in England. Mr. Westall [Richard Westall, the painter] and I found that [in the mid-1820s] he had . . . contracted intimacies with some German art-students, and that he had been buying and dealing with scarce old prints and etchings to a great extent."

8. William Blake moved from South Moulton Street to Fountain Court, off the Strand, in 1821; TGW's friend Allan Cunningham described the set of rooms as "a garret." TGW possibly met Blake in childhood, since Blake's friendship with the sculptor John Flaxman (1755–1826) brought him to the edge of the Wedgwood circle, of which Ralph Griffiths was a part. (Blake called Flaxman "a sublime archangel, my friend and my companion for eternity.") TGW more certainly met Blake through Fuseli (who, incidentally, also admired Flaxman's work very much, but was less polite about his personality, and referred to him as "the Reverend John"). Although Fuseli's nonpolitical stance, his intellectualism and his (comparative) Classicism set him apart from Blake, Blake learned a great deal from him. He put Fuseli's draughtsmanship in the same league as Michelangelo's, realized that his imaginative work was "a hundred years beyond the present generation," and once dittied:

> *The only man that e'er I knew*
> *Who did not make me nearly spew*
> *Was Fuseli: he was both Turk & Jew,*
> *And so, dear Xtian friends, how do you do?*

Fuseli, in return, said Blake was "damned good to steal from," and sympathized with his embattled integrity: "It is the lot of genius to be opposed, and to be invigorated by opposition." In 1805 he recommended Blake's illustrations to Robert Blair's blank-verse poem *The Grave*, and at other times bought several of his works. In many important respects, their visionary art served different purposes, aspired to different ideals, and sprang from different impulses. Yet they are linked by a similar early Romantic faith in the power of the symbolic imagination—and it is this which drew TGW to them so strongly. It seems possible that TGW "introduced Holst to Blake's designs, although several other artists and connoisseur acquaintances of Holst were also friends or patrons of Blake during his last years including John Varley, William Young Ottley and Sir Thomas Lawrence." (See Max

Browne, "A Blake Source for von Holst," *Blake: An Illustrated Quarterly,* vol. 29, no. 3 (winter 1995/6), p. 81.)

9. This phrase comes from an article TGW published in September 1820—an appreciation of Blake (as Viscomi points out, p. 353) which includes a brilliantly punning elucidation of the themes of "Jerusalem," and a subtle analysis of its explosive power:

> Dr. Tobias Ruddicombe, M.D. [i.e. Blake—who had reddish hair] is, at my entreaty, casting a tremendous piece of ordnance,—an eighty-eight pounder! which he proposeth to fire off in your next [number of the *London Magazine*]. It is an account of one ancient, newly discovered, illuminated manuscript, which has to name Jerusalem the Emanation of the Giant Albion!!! It contains a good deal anent one "Los" who, it appears, is now, and hath been from the creation, the *sole* and fourfold dominant of the celebrated city of Golgonooza! The doctor assures me that the redemption of mankind hangs on the universal diffusion of the doctrines broached in the MS.

TGW's devotion to Blake is one of the most important (and neglected) aspects of his life as a collector. He seems to have owned, among other things, copy "X" of the *Songs of Innocence and Experience* (Viscomi, p. 154), copy "C" of *Milton* (Viscomi, p. 352), copy "I" of *The Marriage of Heaven and Hell* (which was finished in gold; Viscomi, p. 352), and also copies of *Job, Chaucer's Canterbury Pilgrims* and *Jerusalem.* These purchases made a vital contribution to Blake's finances, and were a valuable proof of trust in his genius.

10. The final phrases here are John Linnell's, who used them when writing of Blake in 1855, twenty-eight years after Blake's death on 12 August 1827. When Linnell arranged his friend's funeral, he contacted TGW among others, asking for help to keep Mrs. Blake in funds. Eliza Wainewright replied on 15 August, two days after the funeral in Bunhill Fields:

> Mr. Wainewright is out, but I beg in his name that you will accomplish your intention of favouring us tomorrow. We shall indeed *deeply* sympathize with you on the loss of so great an Artist, and I fear Mr. W.'s regrets will be most poignant that he did not enjoy once again the pleasure of an hour with him.

This is one of very few surviving letters by Eliza.

11. Thanks to the preferences of the Victorians, Fuseli's "poetical" school was marginalized, suppressed or dispersed during the nineteenth century. Holst died in obscurity, and acolytes such as Alexander Runciman, John Brown and James Jeffreys all died young. The Pre-Raphaelites made some of their ideas fashionable again, but it is really only in the last part of the twentieth century that these minor figures have been given the credit, and the major ones the high praise, that they deserve.

8

THE FAIREST RELICS OF THE PUREST TIMES

I have sometimes sat upon the banks of our inland streams here, which run very fiercely, and seen a fish rise towards me through the dashing waters. Whatever my mood—even when I was wearing the foul uniform of the canary, which I must soon describe—I found this charming. To feel I could discern something clearly in the bother of the current! To make something from nothing!

Until the dawn of my first happiness, which I have just described, the course of my life had been confused and obscure. Now at last I felt that I was coming towards the light. I shall prove what I mean by supposing that I am once again living in the year 1820—the summer, and a torrid one as I recollect, following a bitter winter.

Eliza and I had lately abandoned our lodgings near to St. Martin's and taken up residence with her mother, Mrs. Abercromby, in Mortlake, for our mutual convenience. (Besides which, I was concerned about the effects of the London air upon our health. Some afternoons the filth and soot were such I was required to change my shirt two or three times in as few hours.) For our convenience, I say, but also for my inconvenience, since it was often imperative for me to be somewhere else.

Good morning! let me therefore say, in imitation of my old self, and let me call it a Saturday morning. I am almost too late: engaged to meet some prime coves of the fancy at twelve; then to the Fives Court; must be at the Royal Institution by half past two; take my twentieth peep at Haydon's picture on my way back; letters to Belzoni till five; dinner *chez moi* with a little philosopher and the doctor at six; don our azure hose for the Lady Cerula Lazuli's Conversazione at half past nine; then opera—applaud Milani—and sup with the Corinthians in St. James's Square at two on Sunday morning: and so for a moment goodbye—hope to see you at church tomorrow, if up in time—or meet you at St. Joseph's tonight. [1]

Anyone may wonder: how, in such a helter-skelter slide, was a body able to undertake any useful work? Not easily, I would reply, without much caring how I answered. A drawing lesson here. A sketch executed briskly there. Once I was known to assist Leigh Hunt with his *Pocket Book*. Another time, I gave *Blackwood's* and the *Quarterly* the benefit of an opinion. Yet another, and I set a new studio in order, where I discussed with myself the magnificent works I would soon begin. Such activities were all I wanted (and they were more than enough) of everything that could not be called pleasure—or more precisely: life on the town. [2]

When they say that a man is *on the town,* they mean he is buried within it. This was my experience, at any rate; I turned aside from the orderly streets, where we feel counted upon, and keep regular hours, and entered instead those dark and winding ways where the catalogue of delights is more surprising. There I encountered the benefits of losing time and travelling incognito, like a man in a forest who is lured out of his way, and instead of succumbing to hopelessness, finds himself rewarded with the sight of rarer flowers, and stranger creatures, than any he could otherwise have imagined.

It was a dazzling time; yet through it all I did not waver from my devotion to my blessed Art, or my favourite style of worship. I am coming now to my addiction to that most ingenious of marvels, that most fabulous orchestration of varied skills, that most marvellous expression of genius: the PRINT. (Truly, I may call myself not picture-, but print-learned.) The print: which allowed the glories of a thousand Exhibition Rooms to shower their riches into the parlours of even such a humble enthusiast as myself. Which permitted me to feel that Michel Angelo, Raphaello, Rembrandt and the whole godly company were the companions of my days, and the fellow spirits of my nights. If I had the gift of poetry (and not merely the talent of rhyming) I would say with that quick-witted money-man Sam Rogers:

> *What tho' no marble breathes, no canvas glows,*
> *From every point a ray of genius flows!*
> *Be mine to bless the more mechanic skill*
> *That stamps, renews and multiplies at will;*
> *And cheaply circulates, through distant climes.*
> *The fairest relics of the purest times.* [3]

I have often rehearsed these lines to myself (marking that *cheaply* with a smile) on my travels through the treasure-troves of London. At Mr. Colnaghi's shop, in particular, I delighted to find ways of proving how "my low roof the Vatican might recall"—as later I sometimes had occasion to tell in an article, when I advised the inexperienced to use *my name* as they pursued a portfolio of Alberti or Polidori, or romped in a wilderness of Leonardos. Seeing my pen travel across the page now, I imagine my hand lifting once more to grasp the handle of Colnaghi's shop (shining with use!) in Cockspur Street. Once more I hear the sweet voices of caged birds greeting me. Once more I see Mr. Paul Colnaghi bow his shining head. (The elegant large ring on his little finger throws a dull light; his eye-glass flashes on the black ribbon around his neck). There again are his boys, Mr. Dominic and Mr. Martin, tall and hook-nosed like their father, telling me how they have just heard from Constable, how they have some lithographs of Bonington, how John Keats pressed his face briefly against their window this morning, admiring their portrait of Sands, the destroyer of Kotzebue. [4]

The entire room ahead of me is one large press of people, but Mr. Paul's terrier senses my approach, and picks his way between ankles of beauty and fashion, giving a gracious wriggle of recognition. I pet him affectionately, and make my advance. Here are English marchionesses and foreign princesses—knights, dames, squires of high degree (at Cambridge) and damozels. I pass edgeways between a rich cluster of living flowers, treading as gingerly as a cat among china, and thankfully do no damage in my passage until—alas!—the rowel of a long brace spur (one of the pair I have worn as decoration) catches and so draws away, unperceived, a dangling Brussels lace shawl from the shoulders of a young lady . . .

It can be seen from this: I possessed an active mind, and could not subsist for long without sustenance of some kind. Therefore, notwithstanding the high price of many desirable images, I went after them with gusto. The Argument of my Collection, as I termed it to myself, was created by my good angel (I should more properly say my *bad* angel since she involved me in such expense), who propelled me willy-nilly against portfolios of Bonasoni, Ghisi, Aeneas Vici, etc., until I was battered into acquiescence, and unable to resist them.

In my noviciate, I would submit to this pummelling almost daily, weakened by the force of my desire; in my prime I was the victim of an even greater appetite, and knew there was no help for me. My enjoyment was too immense. Modestly and coyly would I begin my adventures, inquiring for a *single* subject from Correggio or Giulio, only to find the panting shopman hurl on the table a whole elephantine portfolio teeming with Volpatos, Mullers, Longhis, etc. Had I resisted, I should have been more than mortal. Alas, I did *not* resist. I bought prints one, two, three. I threw down the payment with desperation, refusing all offers of porterage, and dashed home by the shortest ways, to view my acquisitions with unmixed delight for a matter of minutes, before regretting the absence of those other two volumes, which were indeed their companions.

I have said too much. I have said enough. My walls at Mortlake were soon more lavishly decorated than the Academy itself. My wife's mother—Mrs. Abercromby—rolled her eyes over them with a marvelling anxiety, expecting that at any moment I should complain of want of room (which indeed I felt). Eliza was more plainly quizzical, wondering how all this luxury might be paid for. I myself was in a sort of delirium, knowing that her fears were well founded, and that if I was determined to pursue my mad career, I should do more than labour with little reward in my Painting Room, or torture a pupil on occasion.

She was always charitable to me, my Eliza, fearing that the black moods she had once nursed with such attention, were now kept out only by the ferocity of my self-pleasing. Yet I knew that I should heed her advice. I should put myself about in the world with more purpose, and win benefits.

I therefore took it into my head to become an author, even though I had not yet developed a proper confidence in my qualifications. To be precise: I cherished an ambition that I might be employed to some effect by that estimable man John Scott, who was then proposing to launch his *London Magazine*.

Having respect for my grandfather's life in his *Review*, it may be considered a heresy for me to admit that I loved the *London* the instant I clapped my eyes on Scott, and his grand design. So be it. I believe that a periodical was never begun with happier auspices, or numbering a list of contributors more original in thought, more fresh in spirit, more sportive in fancy, or better qualified by nature and study. [5]

It was Scott's special genius to have a respect for personality which allowed those who wrote for him to feel themselves part of an affable band of comrades. He knew that much of what he encouraged struck a blow at convention, yet no man was conscious of appearing before the public as a desperado. (Though Scott himself was a swarthy man, not tall, and with a fierce expression.) Furthermore, no one he took up was spared his enthusiasm—however it might make him seem unsettled, one day distracted, and the next calm. On a certain occasion, for instance, I have seen him giving audience to some young aspirant at his breakfast, quite unconscious of the newspapers, reviews and uncut novels lying about in a fascinating confusion. On another, I have watched him in his office preparing an edition—his passion manifested in a judicious and steady superintendence of the whole.

"National character" was a term ever at the end of his pen and the tip of his tongue, which was the reason he indulged my interest in Goethe and suchlike, and why he deplored the notion that the metropolis should for so long have languished unrepresented in the strenuous competitions between periodicals that raged in those days. In every one of his issues as editor, he proved the unique endowments of Britain, and therefore showed why she was bound to oppose the false philosophy of France, and to sound the true note of Liberty. To sound it in the ears of Parliament, and in the Courts of Chancery, whose ears are plugged with the fat of their own corruption. I have already indicated that I am a man with no more than a slight interest in politics, and yet I have an equal and opposite enthusiasm for Liberty, and I cherish its principles.

But I am digressing again. As I have said, I first made the acquaintance of Scott when his *London* was in the process of turning from a chrysalis into a butterfly. Which is to say: I was in at the beginning. Taking notice of my enthusiasm for Art, and pitying my low estate, Scott immediately requested me to put down on paper *for his first number* some of the feeling I was moved to express in my conversation from time to time, concerning the mighty works of Michel Angelo, Correggio, Rembrandt, etc. With some modifications as to plan, I cheerfully obeyed him—not that I entertained any hope of carrying my attempt beyond two pages of MSS. [6]

Why not? For the simple reason that it struck me as something ridiculous, that I, who had never before *authorized* a line, save in Orderly and Guard Reports (and letters for money, of course), should be considered competent to appear in a new, double-good Magazine! I actually laughed outright, to the consternation of my cat and dog, who wondered, I believe, what a plague ailed me. Yet in due course a reaction commenced, and I put so much gaiety and spirit into my first contribution that Scott was obliged to cut sheer away every alternate sentence (that at least was the agreeable turn he gave to the cursed excision). After such an auspicious beginning, I was amazed—that's weak—I was astonished—astounded, confounded.

On the other hand (I told myself), although Scott cut me, he did not cut me altogether. Indeed, within an instant of my first appearance, he said of me, with Bottom, "Let him roar again, let him roar again!"—though truly on this second occasion I aggravated my pen as gently as a sucking dove. But once more with only partial success. This time, above *one third* of my work was abolished—*Deo gratias*—and that third was the *best part;* I looked at it in my rough copy on some later day—quite a curry, credit me! though not exactly conformable to Pegge's *Forme of Curie.*

I wondered, as any young penman in my situation might have done, whether one day I should be reduced by my editor to nothing at all. Yet for all these doubts and lacerations, my progress in this new role of critic delighted me, not least because it brought me to the attention of that most charming of companions Charles Lamb, of whom I shall say more in a moment. [7] And also, I must admit, because I was able to undertake my labours, perform my word-tricks, and suffer my disappointments, without surrendering my good name among the traders and jobbers of the common marketplace. Indeed, at the *London* we were all expert at the fine art of self-concealment, Lamb being "Elia"—who never spoke a falsehood—Hazlitt being "Mr. Drama," etc. My own pleasure in this game was so much the greatest, I took not a single name but three. One moment I was "Janus Weathercock," a fickle bird but able to look every way, and tell the direction of fashionable weather (which caused my editor to pronounce me "licentiously singular in plurals"). Another moment I was "Egomet Bonmot"—twice the wit I was in my own person, yet my own person absolutely. Then again I might be "Cornelius Van Vinkbooms" (or "Stinkinghorne" in the opinion of certain friends)—a very learned gentleman, who could be trusted to tell all ye need to know pertaining to prints, and the news from Europe—and who in truth was a little out of patience with the swivelling Mr. Weathercock, and the indulgent Mr. Bonmot (though he shared their tastes) for all their gauds and fripperies.

How delicious, to dissolve and lose ourselves and yet to keep our heads on our shoulders! What a divine freedom! How superior to be no one and everywhere, rather than someone and fixed in a single place! I may have learned from that gallant soul Mr. Yorick in gaining the liberty I am describing here, but the figure I most resembled to myself (which self is that, pray?) was the sublime Puck. Look once, and you might find me flying through the heavens, squeezing the potent drops of my thoughts into the wide eyes of readers. Look again and you might see me as a trusty companion of the earth, decanting a bottle of sweet muscatel with an all-too-solid hand. Here and there. Now and then. Present and gone. That was the thing (which was no thing at all). To live behind disguises which told more than a face. To practise until I was perfect as a puppet master, hidden aloft in the darkness while my creatures did my bidding—quaint, whimsical, ridiculous, yet always with a purpose. [8]

"And what purpose might that be, my dear Vinkbooms?" "One too learned for your tastes, Mr. Weathercock, with your words falling over one another in their eagerness to please!" "Now, my dear Dutch master, think better of yourself than to criticize Janus so meanly. I . . ." "Mr. Bonmot, we would expect 'I' from you, who can think of no one but yourself . . ." Etc., etc. With a snap of my fingers, I could people all the chambers of my brain and become someone, though no one in particular. I could pun myself into such humour I laid hold upon a Lamb's tail. I could dazzle and be droll, or lower and be learned. I could be a painter in words and deliver the delicacies of the fine arts, or a crusty critic, determined to correct taste. I could spin a sentence like gossamer, or explode like Yorick himself into a warfare of asterisks and leave off my work unfin- . . .

Ah, but I could also be diligent and sober-suited, if the occasion demanded. I should explain, in an aside, that I am referring here, in particular, to my edition of that most slippery, lingering, under-water-caressing, heart-beating and heart-bathing poem *Hero and Leander*. This work was a culmination of my interests. Everything I wrote for the *London* showed my affection for that most glorious time, the Elizabethan. Did I not always babble of green fields and run to them? Did I not fly hurry-skurry over park, over pale, thorough bush, thorough briar? Did I not meet an obtuse apprehension in some dull fellow by recommending that the unfeeling muckworm be whipped? Did I not (enough of "Did I not!") arouse all England, and advance the boundaries of taste, calling forth the ruddy wood-loving Genius of English mirth from slumbers. The Golden Age was to return, and that honoured tree of high Romance, which, blasted by the scathing from Cromwell and the Puritans, was once again to shake its green head in the wind, and shower plenteously its refreshing dewy blossom over all the thirsty fields of Albion, the white Isle!

But I forget myself once more. I was with Marlowe. Marlowe (see how sober I can become in an instant) seemed always to me to have had a considerable leaning to voluptuous, reposing fantasies, and to have dallied with love like an accomplished amorist. For my own part, with a wife at my ("shoulder" I almost said, "side" would serve better)—with a wife at my side, I confess that even when I wrote my article upon him, perusing his tale of true love for the twentieth time, my throat swelled, and my eyes filled with tears. (Perhaps, however, there was something congenial in the season—the grey and watery sky above, the dark grass below, and flagging Auster blowing heavily against the trees, shattering the tawny leaves.)

I suppose if any man look now at what I wrote, knowing what all the world knows of my history, he will remark on my insistence that Marlowe had a devil in him, and ponder how this inward-dwelling creature might have spoken to me directly. To that charge—if charge it be—I can but say: "Sir, I am a bad hand at swimming. *Pah!*" Besides which, how much more truly present in this poem (devil or no) is the genuine nature of woman, and therefore how much more lovely is it to a healthy mind than the outrageous personifications of ill-timed chastity, so common in romances thirty or some years ago. I shall say it once more, as plainly as I may: a wonderful exuberance and display of mental riches exists in all the Elizabethan writers: they give full measure, heaped, and running over. It is to me "no more difficile,/Than for a blackbird 'tis to whistle," to discourse upon their virtues. [9]

There is, I believe, a deep knowledge of the human heart displayed in Hero's longing shamefacedness. It wears a semblance of hypocrisy, yet it is not hypocrisy. May I admit something of the same to be true of myself? In all my articles, I wore the face of laughter, knowing it might appear merely false. I intended, however, that it might be both true and false *together*. True in its high spirits, which were my own, and born from love of my blessed Art. False in seeming the one mood that I possessed.

A time came when laughter seemed a more uncertain thing—a time, indeed, when it seemed a sin. And now I must sorrowfully arrive at that time again. Our esteemed friend Scott was murdered. There! I have no other way to recollect it, except bluntly, and I doubt it will soften the blow to say that this happened when editors were at one another's throats in general, and violence had become a modern ecstasy. [10]

Before I arrive at the scene itself, I shall give the pre-amble. During the year of his greatest triumph with the *London*, I mean the year 1820, Scott had enraged his enemies at *Blackwood's* to such an extent, he felt that he was defending no less a thing than the honour of literature itself. The villain Lockhart (editor of *Blackwood's*), nevertheless continued to bandy words, which rapidly drove things from bad to worse, and in the new year he enlisted the support of his agent in the south, John Christie. Christie immediately took Lockhart's quarrel upon himself, and challenged Scott to a duel. They arranged to meet by moonlight, at Chalk Farm.

I suppose the open country of that area will by now have disappeared beneath the villas and shooting boxes thrown up around London, its grass gone up in smoke, and its wide spaces criss-crossed with the lines of the railway. On the night I mean, with the moon high and almost at the full, the chalk pits glimmered like caves in the surface of that amorous planet, and the men assembled there were like shadows born of shadows: Mr. Trail to oversee; Christie and his second, Mr. Darling; Scott grim-faced with Mr. Patmore at his side.

Christie behaved well, and when all was ready for the first fire called out, "Mr. Scott, you must not stand there: I see your head above the horizon; you give me an advantage." (For it was understood that he meant no actual harm, only to end the business—and indeed both men fired their first shots in the air.) After the pistols were reloaded and everything ready for the second fire, Trail called out, "Now, Mr. Christie, take your aim, and do not throw away your advantage as you did last time." Scott called out immediately, "What! Did not Mr. Christie fire at me?"—to which Patmore answered at Christie's ear, "You must not speak: 'tis now of no use to talk; you have now nothing for it but firing."

Whereupon Trail gave the signal, both guns spoke, and Scott fell. Noble breast, gored and ravaged! Brave spirit, broken and ruined! When I first arrived at his sick room, and saw him upon his bed with his gown soaked through and his face shining, and heard his voice aloud, I imagined that he was speaking to himself in a delirium. But no; he was dictating to his enemy Lockhart, dictating with the tenderness which had always lived in him. "Revere yourself, my dear boy," he said, "and think you were born to do your country better service than this species of warfare!" Then when I moved forward to be near him, and the air (at once hot and cold) wafted from his body on to my face and hands, I saw that I must make my farewell swiftly or not at all. As real as if it were now, I still experience the feeble, kindly clasp of his fever-wasted hand, hear again the faint whisper of his entire trust in my friendship—the voice dropping back again—the look!— one stronger clasp! May the peace which rested over his last moments remain with him for ever! [11]

Poor Scott. Poor Janus Weathercock. Where next might he lay his heart—and his pen with it? In such a vale of sorrow, what appetite is there for plumes and gauds, and all light-hearted mischief? I returned home after that dreadful bedside encounter, supposing the death of my editor to be the death of my own hopes. In a little more than a year I had been licensed as three selves—licensed, tested and proved. Now I was almost a nothing again, and immediately I felt the fire of my pleasures waning, and the energy of my desires failing, until I was travelling the road home with no more sense of my position than a common cur, slinking from doorpost to gateway, wondering where it might find sustenance. Poor brave Scott, as I say: how I envied you in your cold shroud. Poor Weathercock, rusting so immediately on his spike that he was unable to feel the breeze turning in any new direction.

1. This passage, which repeats more or less exactly a passage from TGW's *Essays* (p. 105), more probably refers to the time when he was in Great Marlborough Street, slightly later in the 1820s, and not when he was in Mortlake. In both places, however, he lived almost entirely "on the town." Haydon's picture, *Christ's Entry into Jerusalem,* was on show at the Egyptian Hall, Piccadilly.

2. In Van Diemen's Land TGW claimed to have written for Leigh Hunt's 1819 miscellany, *The Literary Pocket Book.* There is no evidence of his making a substantial contribution, though it is possible that he compiled the list of "Eminent Living Artists," and the inventory of print and plaster-cast shops in London, and the catalogue of that year's Somerset House exhibition. If these things are really by TGW, they "testify," as Curling says, "to little beyond his ability to read, write and reckon." There is no proof that he did any of the work he claimed to have done for *Blackwood's Magazine* or the *Quarterly Review.*

3. The print trade between Britain and Europe had been thriving before the French Revolution—as Hogarth's career indicates. In 1789, however, it virtually petered out, then took off again after Waterloo. Although there were many specialist collectors like TGW, who spent a great deal of money on rare and early prints, these connoisseurs were outnumbered by others who looked on prints as a way of "gilding" their "humble walls" with modestly priced reproductions of Old Masters (as Samuel Rogers does in his "Epistle to a Friend," quoted here). TGW's friends all accepted that prints played an important part in their education—and their cultural life generally. Hazlitt, for instance, in his essay on "Gusto," mentions works known to him in this form by Van Dyck, Titian, Michelangelo, Correggio, Raphael, Rubens and Claude. Hunt decorated his cell in Horsemonger Gaol, when he was incarcerated for libelling the Prince Regent, with "Portfolios of Prints." Keats spoke eagerly of "reading" prints, and "quotes" Titian, Claude and Poussin in his poems. Paul Colnaghi's shop at 23 Cockspur Street, which opened in 1799, was a Mecca for all such enthusiasts. Its place at the centre of TGW's world was reinforced by the fact that Colnaghi's daughter Caroline was married to John Scott, the editor of the *London Magazine,* who first commissioned pieces from TGW. Eventually, "the 'refined taste' associated with the cult of the painter's etching, and the development of photography for repro-

ductive purposes, together spelled doom for the kind of print that had been so popular and valued through the eighteenth century" (Clayton, p. 284).

4. Colnaghi was one of the first people in England to appreciate John Constable, and helped him to organize his reputation-making show in Paris. He also commissioned Richard Parkes Bonington early in his career. Keats was a frequent visitor to his shop, and it is possible that TGW met him here. The reference to the playwright August von Kotzebue is taken from Keats's letter to George and Georgiana Keats, written on 17 September 1819.

5. John Scott was born in Aberdeen in 1783, worked briefly in the War Office, then turned to journalism. As the editor of *Drakard's Stamford News* (for which Lamb wrote "briskets and veiny pieces") he began making his reputation in a series of "vigorous, straightforward attacks on abuses of power" (Bauer, p. 59), then confirmed it as Editor of the liberal *Champion*, which he abandoned to travel for a while (fed up with "the anxieties of literary Gladiatorship") before taking on the *London Magazine*.

The *London* was announced in November 1819 as a liberal journal "to be continued monthly, which is intended to combine the principles of sound philosophy on Questions of Taste, Morals and Politics, with the Entertainment and miscellaneous information expected from a Public journal." About half its 125 pages were reserved for literary matters, and the remainder divided between music, fine art, drama, humour, comment and current affairs; every issue opened with a leader which, after the sixth issue, was known as the "Lion's Head," and for a while was written by Thomas Hood. Scott edited fourteen issues of the magazine, and when the first one was published in January 1820, he had already gathered round him most of the contributors who would make the magazine famous—among them Charles Lamb, William Hazlitt, John Hamilton Reynolds, Horace Smith, Octavius Gilchrist and TGW himself. Later contributors included John Clare, John Keats, Barry Cornwall, Thomas Noon Talfourd, Thomas de Quincey, H. F. Cary and Benjamin Robert Haydon.

6. TGW wrote nine articles for Scott: "A Modest Offer of Service" (January 1820), "Sentimentalities of the Fine Arts" (February), "Mr. Bonmot's Visit . . ." (March), "Sentimentalities II" (March), "Sentimentalities III" (April), "Janus's Jumble" (June), "Janus's Dialogue on the Exhibition at Somerset House" (June), "Much Ado . . ." (June), and "Mr. Weathercock's Private Correspondence" (September). Like his later articles, these generally combine art criticism (of current shows, of print collections, of

favourite artists) with a large amount of autobiographical chit-chat—all of it dotted with specialist knowledge, and written in a gushing, bravura style.

Although Scott was initially keen on TGW's pieces, he soon stopped commissioning him regularly, and often cut his copy. In a note added to one article, the *London* even went so far as to tell readers: "We have made a little free with the following article from one of our most estimable correspondents; but a man who makes so free with others must consider a little liberty with himself allowable—besides, he is too exuberant not to spare something, and too lively not to forgive much." By the time of Scott's death in 1821, TGW could no longer think of himself as a regular contributor.

The reasons for this are obscure—though it seems likely that Alexander Gilchrist was right when he said Scott was "rather discomposed by [TGW's] systematic impertinencies and flippancies" (quoted in Curling, p. 117). It is also possible that Scott was annoyed by an adhesive eagerness in TGW's manner, since TGW himself admits, "I continued to sentimentalize until S[cott], becoming aware that his friendly purpose had taken its full effect on my mind and body, began to rap me on the head, as one sees a cat deal with an elderly kitten which restraineth its lacteal propensities over due season" (*Essays*, p. 307). TGW's return to the magazine when Taylor and Hessey took over as editors was due largely to the friendly influence of Lamb and Hazlitt, and strongly motivated by his deepening financial worries.

7. Charles Lamb (1775–1834) was born in the Inner Temple, educated at Christ's Hospital, and worked as a clerk for most of his life: in the accountant's office of the East India Company from 1792 until 1825. His home life was tragic—he looked after his sister Mary, who in 1796 had killed their mother in a fit of insanity—and his writing life productive. He turned out poems, plays, children's books (*Tales from Shakespeare* [1808] being the best known), but his most durable works are his letters and his pseudonymous writings, *Essays of Elia* (1823) and *Last Essays of Elia* (1833), the earliest of which were published in the *London Magazine*. ("Elia" was the name of someone he had met clerking at the old South Sea House, and is pronounced to rhyme with "desire"—i.e. to suggest that the author is "a liar.")

Lamb was loved and admired by many, especially by Coleridge (who had been at school with him), by Hazlitt (who first persuaded him to write his Elia essays), and by TGW (whose own style he deeply influenced). His circle was also drawn together by other less simple and sunny things. Although Lamb was generally called "honest," "guileless" and so on, he was not the cultural teddy-bear that the Victorians made of him. (He once told

Coleridge, "For God's sake ... don't make me ridiculous any more by terming me gentle-hearted in print.") His "intimados," he said himself, were "in the world's eye a ragged regiment. He found them floating on the surface of society; and the colour, or something else, in the weed pleased him" (*Selected Prose*, p. 227).

Many commentators have found it peculiar that TGW and Lamb got on so well together (for instance, see Lucas, vol. 2, p. 38)—generally because they are embarrassed by Lamb's liking for someone who turned out to be a criminal. Lamb never knew about TGW's fall from grace.

8. In the eighteenth century, it was normal for magazine contributors to publish anonymously: none of the pieces in the *Monthly Review* was signed by a writer using his own name. The pseudonyms of the *London Magazine*, however, existed for pleasure as well as concealment, and were generally as "thin as gauze" (Bauer, p. 168). That said, no one—not Lamb as Elia, Hazlitt as Mr. Drama, de Quincey as The Dwarf, or Clare as The Green Man— took as much pleasure in the concept of an alter ego as TGW. Although his were originally conceived to reflect various aspects of his personality (fun-loving Weathercock, learned Van Vinkbooms, romantic Bonmot), the differences between them soon faded. Written within one false identity, or playing about with several, TGW's essays are at once a typical period game, and a suggestion of something more extremely—even pathologically— volatile.

His dandified prose style expresses a similar sort of ambiguity. Playful and intimate in ways that obviously derive from Laurence Sterne, quaint and affected in others that owe debts to the Elizabethans, it is an exaggerated example of something briefly typical. "A vulgarization," as Ian Jack says, "of the taste of the *London* group, but the vulgarization is more a matter of style and presentation than of critical opinion" (p. 86). Yet at the same time as TGW used "ornamental" phrases as a way of having fun, he also realized that they pointed up his questions about "the verisimilitude of authorship." Over the years, this has attracted a lot of hostile criticism, with most of his readers saying that he "lacked discrimination," or was frankly "ridiculous." Actually his intentions, especially if they can be considered apart from his crimes, seem very focused and well judged. Phrase by jewelled phrase, his writing develops the questions embodied by his various pseudonyms. What is true? What is the foundation of an opinion? How can a stable view be constructed from fragments? What is the connection between a high and a low style?

9. TGW wrote his 51-page, anonymous Introduction to Marlowe's *Hero and Leander* in the autumn of 1820, finishing on 8 November. The edition, published the following year, had been commissioned by his neighbour and friend Samuel Weller Singer, who worked for the Chiswick Press, and whose reprints were often praised by TGW in the *London Magazine:* "Singer's *Chapman*" in April 1820, and later *Spence's Anecdotes* ("a book full of amusement"), *The Legend of Cupid and Psyche,* and so on. (I am grateful to Marc Vaulbert de Chantilly for clarification of these details.)

The Introduction to *Hero and Leander* is as allusive and full of digressions as TGW's pieces for the *London Magazine;* it includes a four-page quotation from Leigh Hunt, and a nine-page selection from C. A. Elton's *Musaeus.* It traces the controversies of authorship, lamenting the lack of reliable editions of Elizabethan works in general, and sincerely (but modestly) appreciating Marlowe's sensuality. The edition is dedicated to Fuseli, the "god" of TGW's "worship."

In the same year, 1820, TGW also did a frontispiece for Singer's Chiswick Press edition of John Chalkhill's poem *Thealma and Clearchus,* which had been first published by Isaac Walton in 1663. The engraving is called *Anaxos in the Cave of the Witch Oranda,* and shows a naked woman on a stone seat being kissed by a handsome Renaissance youth while a third, hooded figure looks on disapprovingly. In the Introduction to the poem, Singer says, "For the elegant and spirited design which embellishes the book, I am indebted to the kindness of my friend T. G. Wainewright, Esq., whose 'mastering hand' should not confine itself to the gratification of a select circle of friends, when it might be hailed an ornament to Art and to his country." It is also possible that TGW contributed the unsigned decoration that ends the book: an ornamental "W" (the first letter of his own name, as well as that of the printer C. Whittingham), surrounded by branches of vine and honeysuckle.

10. The magazine market in the early nineteenth century was highly competitive and political, with reformist journals (the *Examiner,* the *Political Register* and the *London Magazine*) warring with Tory reviews such as *Blackwood's Magazine* and the *Quarterly Review.* The antagonism between the *London* and *Blackwood's,* edited by John Gibson Lockhart, was especially fierce. Scott referred to the arguments as "merry ruffianism," but a good many of them were more serious than this implies, damaging careers as well as self-respect. It was one thing for *Blackwood's* to refer to "pimpled Hazlitt," or to Haydon's greasy hair. It was more seriously hurtful to Keats's

sales, and therefore his career, for "Z" (i.e. Lockhart) to abandon poetry and return to the "plasters pills and ointment boxes" of his life as a doctor.

11. Scott was wounded on 16 February 1821, and died on 27 February. The April number of the *London Magazine* announced his death, as well as the death of Keats in Rome. For further details of the duel, including a discussion of its illegality, see Leonidas Jones, p. 219. No survivors in the case were convicted—though they all stood trial.

9

GENTLE-HEARTED JANUS

*F*ollowing the tragic death of Scott, I briefly forgot my friends. No, I
do not mean I forgot them. I mean my grief hid them from me. Yet
true friendship is adamantine, and many hands reached down to me into my
blackness. Lamb I can see again, and Hazlitt, both advising me to continue
working, and recommending me to John Taylor, the new editor of the *London*. In gratitude for their kindness, I shall devote this next part of my story
to a reminiscence of their good nature, and of dear friends all. Come, then,
ho! A glass here for amiable spirits! And another for silver tongues! And a
third for golden hearts!

Yet wait. Before I drain these bumpers, I have other duties to perform. I
have a family gathering to attend: the wedding of Thomas Payne, a friend of
my cousin Foss, who is to marry Sarah Burney in Westminster in the spring
of 1821. [1] I shall hurry through this swiftly, making certain my spurs catch
on no dragging shawls, and ensuring that any compliments I pay my cousins
do not appear in the least extravagant. There. I am ready to depart already,
having stayed long enough to prove that I am not quite alone in the world,
and also to show that I deserve some respect for the difference of my tastes
and expectations.

Stop there, Janus; what differences do you mean! I shall explain, Bonmot.
Or is that the voice of Van Vinkbooms? The question is immaterial. What I
mean is: after the last several hugger-mugger years in Mortlake, hoarding
our estate as best we could (which was not well), I was able to bring my Eliza
to a far superior abode. Namely: the sweet centre of fashion. A bower where
my library and all other delights could shine as I longed for them to do. A
gilded meeting place for my kindred spirits. Great Marlborough Street! The
name alone quickens my pulse, reminding me how I made my mark where so
much grace already existed. Which is to say, and without blushing: a previous occupant had been that most renowned and glorious tragedienne Mrs.
Siddons, whom Fuseli made immortal in the character of Lady Macbeth, and
her ghost (purged of its horrors) still patrolled the rooms that were now

mine, conversing easily with Mrs. Thrale, with Thomas Lawrence, with Reynolds himself, with the great Sheridan . . . These all became my friends, shaking off the dust of the past to sparkle again in the gay company I made for them in the present. [2]

Made in what manner, Janus? I shall tell you exactly, giving a day in particular and sparing no detail (or only those details which are actually poisonous in their splendour). I have risen late, leaving Eliza still drowsing, and taken a refreshing stroll into town, my blue military surcoat as bright as a cornflower, my cane strict, and my hat ever ready to tip a greeting—good day to ye! I am on the way to the Strand, the first street in Europe, where after the exertions of my journey I entertain myself at number 213, otherwise known as George's, declining the partridge-flavoured gravy of a veal-and-ham pie, a handsome loaf, a fine ripe Stilton, etc., and settling instead for an excellent bowl of soup (ox-tail), amiably harmonized by the running accompaniment of home-brewed ale—pale, amber-coloured, foaming—contained in a capacious brown store-jug, silver-tipped.

Stay, though! Not too much! For I am playing host this evening—the entire *London* set—and even as I speak my man is out in his drab coat, doing the bidding of the house, weighing himself down with delicacies.

Now: I have an hour or so left to myself. Shall it be Colnaghi's? Or a further step down the Strand to Somerset House, where I may nourish myself with a canvas or two? On reflection, neither of these. I shall return home. Come with me, quick march (but not too military). Follow me through my front door from the street, where not a sound of the busy world may penetrate. Pause to enjoy the opulent stairway, sweeping upward to the heaven of my rooms. Tarry to inspect the fluted newels and elaborately twisted balusters. Steady yourself as you ascend, and prepare to feel the luxury of my Collections.

First, however, I shall exchange my surcoat for a chintz gown, then immediately light this lamp to shine your way—a new and elegantly built French affair, having a ground-glass globe painted with gay flowers and gaudy butterflies. Then, summoning my Muse or maid-servant, a good-natured, Venetian-shaped girl (having first placed on the table a genuine flask of as rich a Montepulciano as ever voyaged from fair Italia), I require the door of my chamber to be closed, which (as with my entry at ground level) is achieved gently but firmly, and the whole operation rendered airtight by a gilt-leather binding. Dismissing my Muse, I toast myself in complacent consideration of my own figure, which may be seen in a large glass placed opposite the chimney mirror. Thus are my preparations made. Thus am I soothed into the gentlest sort of self-satisfaction, so necessary to the bodying out of those deliciously voluptuous ideas, perfumed with languor, which occasionally swim and undulate, like gauzy clouds, over the brain of the most cold-blooded men.

Now is the moment at which I judge myself ready. Now are the splendours of the hour irresistible, though I shall prove them in an orderly fashion, giving everything the attention it deserves, thus: *Imprimis*—the very good-sized room in which we find ourselves. And within it—*item:* a gay Brussels carpet, covered with garlands of flowers. *Item:* a fine original cast of the Venus de Medici. *Item:* some choice volumes in still more choice old French maroquin, with water-tabby-silk linings. *Item:* some more volumes covered by the skill of Roger Payne and "our Charles Lewis." *Item:* a piano, by Tomkisson. *Item:* one cat. *Item:* a large Newfoundland dog, friendly to the cat. *Item:* a few hot-house plants upon a white marble slab. *Item:* a delicious, melting love painting, by Fuseli—and last, not least in our dear love, *we,* myself, Janus! Each, and the whole, seen by the Correggio kind of light, breathed, as it were, through the painted glass of the lamp!

All this is wonderful, but it is not everything I possess. It is but the antechamber of my delights, a preparation for the Argument of my Collection. Follow me once more, bowing if you will beneath the laurelled bust of Apollo, who gazes down from his perch above the folding doors as we pass into my library. I call it a library, for who may subsist long without books, yet it is a jewel cabinet of more than volumes—a luxurious recess, which intoxicates absolutely. I may as well call it a boudoir, if that will help body forth the shape of a thing unknown. Imagine an octagon of about thirteen feet diameter and a full sixteen feet in height, into which the light streams through rosy panes in the top—other windows it hath none. There are two doors, concealed with bright blue silk drapery, bordered with crimson velvet and barbaric fringe. The walls are covered with a very rich crimson French paper, formed into panels and compartments with gilt mouldings; and the oak floor is spread with a glowing Persian carpet. A sweeping Ottoman, matching the curtains in hue, offers its elastic cushions to the voluptuary, opposite the fireplace; in either side of which stand marble-slabbed chiffoniers containing my established books.

Here we may come to rest. Here we may enjoy our senses to the full. Here you may survey me at your leisure, the deity of the place, reclining on the well-squabbed Ottoman I have mentioned, beside a blazing fire, my back guarded from the draft by a large folding Indian screen, and my face from the flame by a pale ditto of yellow silk and rosewood. Beside me is placed a small ridged snuff-box, and several antique cameos and intaglios. Other oddities are to hand—a bulb cabinet, a brick from Persia, a genuine bit of terracotta from the hand of Michel Angelo, a suit of sixteenth-century German armour. And the pictures? Fuseli, as I have said, yearning divinely— also, views of the River Dart by Lewis, as well as prints in double ranks of De Wint and Hilton, of Bonasoni and Poussin, of Giorgione and Watteau, of Raphael and Correggio . . .

I must interrupt myself. I perceive from a certain commotion in the air (I *hear* nothing; I *see* a shimmering), that the first carriages have arrived, and our evening is about to begin. Yet before I propel myself forward in a greeting, I must unburden myself of a confession, lest anything that follows should appear like a boast. I mean: for the sake of honesty, I should admit that I was taking a leaf from other books in holding a gathering such as this. Taylor our editor, when he first took over (I had better say *took on*) the *London* from Scott, met with his contributors regularly for an excellent dinner above his premises in Fleet Street. Many a time have I visited him there, and felt the fences and restraints of authorship cast off. Many a time have I seen Lamb uttering his quaint snatches as Bacchus took him into his embrace. Many a time . . . [3]

But it would suit me better if I stayed true to my word and gave a "one" rather than a "many," if I am to recover the force of those pleasant hours. Let me, therefore, before I continue with the little history of my own entertainment, stay longer with Taylor in Fleet Street, and remember my happiness around his table there. On his right hand sat Elia, of the quick smile and the quicker eyes (Cornwall said of them that they "looked as if they could pick up pins and needles"), and a wit to keep pace with both. Next to him, shining out verdantly among the grave-coloured suits of the literati, like a patch of turnips amidst stubble and fallow, behold our Jack i' the Green— John Clare! In his bright, grass-coloured coat and yellow waistcoat (there are greenish stalks, too, under the table), he looks a very cowslip. Elia, much more of a House Lamb than a Grass Lamb—avowedly caring nothing for pastoral—cottons, nevertheless, very kindly to the Northamptonshire Poet, and still more to his ale, pledging him again and again as "Clarissimus" and "Princely Clare," and sometimes so lustily, as to make the latter cast an anxious glance into his tankard.

And where am I in this portrait, this *mise-en-scène*—I who am as warm as I am light-hearted, a very comical sort of fellow? I am listening to their talk, and responding with a graceful instinct that seeks to bend their subjects to my knowledge, so that I may prove my opinion on any thing. It is not a difficult task. I know as much of each man's pursuit as may enable me to make myself agreeable by a reference to it, and as little as makes it natural for me to seek modestly for information when a theme is broached. I may say, also, that I am paid the compliment of attention for these attentions. My writings—which I have offered to Taylor as the earth offers a sprinkling of dew to the morning, delightful but soon gone—have taken an eye here and an idea there. I have called myself critic, fiddler, poet and buffoon, yet my modesties have been disbelieved and I have been translated into "Mr. Fine Arts." I was once perceived as a side-show, a gamester, but my new editor has told me that I have caught the mood of the entire Fair.

The entire Fair!

But I am falling behind myself. Or stumbling over myself. Or running away with myself. One of these or all together; it makes no difference. I must return to the dinner table. Not to the editor's table any longer, no, let that be folded up and put away. I must return to my own table, to Great Marlborough Street. Now; where was I? Let me see. Yes, yes: I was hearing a carriage shake the air—and now immediately I discern the soft tread of pumps on my stairway, the laughter of friends well met and well matched. Come, follow me once more, where I may see it all with my painter's eye. We shall have a group portrait! The entire fair exactly. Everyone together. Daylight is failing at the window and firelight is swelling in the grate, cloaking my Collection in a delicious chiaroscuro. My snowy old Newfoundlander appears—Neptune—thrusting his muzzle into my hand, receiving a stroke on his shaggy head. And then Eliza stands forth, receiving no such unmannerly thing. And now at last I am ready! Everything is ready! [4]

See Taylor enter, with his severe dark face, who never asks a direct question or gives a direct reply, but continually saps your information by a secret passage, coming at it like a lawyer examining a witness. See Hessey, too, dressed in black, with a boyish face which makes him a great favourite with the ladies wherever he goes (they like him for his great cheerfulness, and because he sings a little, plays a little, and dances well). See Woodhouse, their assistant, red-haired, who loved Keats and talks of him with fervour, his eyes blazing at you from beneath the remarkably straight and strong bone of his brow.

See Lamb again, starting across my carpet as if he had already had some conversation with Bacchus. See him, and look closely upon him, who was my bosom friend. His black hair curls crisply about his expanded forehead; his eyes, softly brown, twinkle with a varying expression (though their prevalent feeling is sad); the nose is slightly curved, and delicately curved at the nostril . . . It is a head made for deep thought to strive with humour; where the lines of suffering are wreathed into cordial mirth. No one who ever studied the human features (in such a manner as Lavater had taught Fuseli, as Fuseli had remembered to tell me) could ever pass by Lamb without recollecting his countenance for the whole remainder of their lives. It was full of sensibility, and it came upon you like a new thought, which you could not help dwelling upon afterwards; it gave rise to meditation, and it did you good.

The degree of good, anyone may judge for themselves. It was Scott who first brought me together with Lamb, and by the time I had produced my "Third Sentimentality" I was already bold enough (after an expostulation upon Bonasoni, if I remember correctly) to praise him in public as one who was superior to colloquial oily vulgarisms. This was but the first of many such amiable references I made—and I had the compliments returned on more than one occasion, sometimes even to the extent of his taking the hint of a subject I had dropped for him. Nor did our friendship consist merely of one giving pats upon the other one's bonnet. Our liking for the speech of Old England also made us friends. That venerable sage of Norwich, Sir Thomas Browne, was our "bosom cronie"—so were the masters Burton and Fuller. In our amorous vein we dallied with that peerless Duchess of many-folio odour; and with the hey-day comedies of Beaumont and Fletcher. I understand full well that on occasion our love for these geniuses led us into extravagance—but where is the harm in that, if all that comes of it is gaiety? Yet I insist that it was the peculiar strength of Elia, in spite of all his gaudy shows, to enjoy everything that is familiar and ordinary, and to see that nothing ordinary is simple. Consider his subjects: "The Old Margate Hoy"; "Old China"; a "Chapter on Ears." Verily (I say again) his own words on the acting of Munden could most happily be turned upon himself. The gusto of Munden, he says, antiquates and ennobles what it touches. He stands wondering, amid the commonplace materials of life, like a primeval man with the sun and stars about him.

All this is true, yet it is less than the truth: too nearly a *proper account,* too finicky. The reality of our friendship—of all friendships, indeed—is that it was a haphazard affair, wandering from dinner table to dinner table with no idea in its head, save the certainty that we should be of one mind about books, pictures, theatres, chit-chat, scandal, jokes, ambiguities and a thousand whim-whams. And if I am to speak soberly for a moment—also the idea of knowing what we preferred to avoid. I had met Lamb's sister, that most unhappy matricide, and had paid her a compliment in an article, for which her brother thanked me. (He had endured some temporary frenzy of his own at one time.) I am not saying here that he denied an interest in things offensive, and in everything that might be reckoned criminal. Rather, that he took a personal and sharp interest in such matters, which was *deep enough for him to imagine forgiveness.* I can say no more to comfort myself, and prove the largeness of his spirit. [5]

Therefore let me pay him homage again. Marry! the black bile would sometimes spill over his tongue; then would he spit it out, and look more sweetly for the riddance. How wittily would he mistake my meaning, and put in a conceit most sensibly out of season! How elegantly he would talk, yet without affectation! I say "without affectation," for nothing rubbed him the wrong way so much as pretence: then the sparks flew about. Yet, though he would strip and whip soundly such beggars in velvet rags, the thong never flew in the face of a wise moderation. He had small mercy on spurious fame, and a caustic observation on the fashion for men of genius (vulgarly so termed) was a standing dish . . .

Alas! I have fallen into a sort of hallucination here, making one guest so welcome I have forgot the rest. I shall embrace these others more briskly, and let the festivities begin. As Lamb takes his seat, Hazlitt comes in beside him, seeming to breathe a colder air than the rest of us. He is most complimentary to Lamb upon his taste and idiosyncrasies (which he does not confuse with the common artifices of authorship); yet he is somewhat withdrawn. See his hanging brow and strange twisted way of sitting, as though he had wound himself up to strike. See his shoes splotched with mud spots got between his carriage and my door. I shall be plain and admit that we are wary friends—and for a simple reason. I believe, as I have said, that such work as I did for Taylor was given upon the recommendation of Hazlitt (and of Lamb). Yet my light-hearted manner of thanking him for this drew him into some argument with me upon the very pages he had helped to make my home. In particular: I chid him, in his real, old, original person of "Mr. Drama," *par nobile fratrum,* for visiting the minor theatres and preferring the company there of a certain Miss Valency—who, my hairdresser informed me, was a bouncing Columbine.

I chid him, and he rebuked me in return, humorously, and afterwards continued to speak flatteringly of Janus as not absolutely inefficient, nor the worst of periodical scribblers. Yet at the same time as he watered our friendship, I felt him damp down some of his former warmth, as he also did in his disquisition "Upon Vulgarity." I confess: this seemed not sufficiently pleasant. But did I charge at him with my pen in retaliation? I did not. Did I so much as complain? I did not. I invited him to eat, and he accepted. I swirled round about his dark head in an atmosphere composed of Macassar oil and eau-de-Cologne, hock and Seltzer water, Attar of Roses and Pomade Divine—and delighted in his delight. If this was not amiable in me, then—

But I have insisted already: I do not complain. In any event, I must record a most general sympathy for Hazlitt's stormy, anxious and uncomfortable life, which might have quelled the blithest spirit. In Lamb, the division of his Self into "Elia" and "gentle-hearted Charles" required no surgery, and neither was any severe operation required to unite them again. Hazlitt made no such separation, yet was much more cruelly divided. One part of him was full of indolence; one of energy. One part dreamed of a great artistic intention; one writhed in disgust. I have often supposed that he directed such fierce anger against Fuseli for this reason. He recognized, in the sublime works of the Professor, agonies he knew but could not acknowledge as his own, calling his ideas gnarled, hard and distorted, like his features; his theories stalking and straddle-legged, like his gait; his projects aspiring and gigantic, like his gestures; his performance uncouth and dwarfish, like his person.

Would that our "Mr. Drama" had admitted his own resentments more freely, and thereby purged himself of their poison. For truly, he had reasons enough to feel soured by spleen. Some years previously, the disgrace of Bonaparte at Waterloo had left him staggering under a mighty blow of disillusionment. And it is no secret—since he has broadcast it himself in his *Liber Amoris*—that during the time of which I am speaking, he was caught up in the violence of a more personal passion. This book of his exploded a mine under his own feet, which made it difficult for him ever to regain his balance. Yet I remember him fondly, as I have said. Never will such intellect and such discrimination be united in a single mind. Scowling friend, take your place at my table; you are welcome! [6]

So are *you* welcome, our Jack i' the Green, John Clare—a more comfortable friend altogether in those days, yet soon overwhelmed with a far greater difficulty. But tell me, why do you look heated and out of sorts? I shall broadcast the explanation to the whole company, and make a jest of it. Seeing you creep in from the street, and modestly wait to ascend the stairs, our gentleman's gentleman believed that you were a country messenger, coming with news for one of the guests above, and nodded you to a seat beside the door. I shall make amends now by having him wait on you himself, paying all observances to you as one who is an eccentric notable of the Corinthian order, disguised in rustic. [7]

It is some years now, since you first cast your eyes over our seven days' wonder, this metropolis, and not much less since its romance faded for you into a reality. Yet there remains a freshness in all you say which I marvel at, as I also wonder how easily you abolish the difference between our manners, and discover the sympathies which bind us together in friendship. Never did I speak with such fellow feeling about the abundance of nature and the goodness of her creatures. Never did I meet a man who possessed such little vanity. As you take your place at my table, and the punsters around you begin to crackle, I see a jug of prime ale is borne away from your place— and you follow it with your eyes—then with your outstretched hands—and then insist the tankard is good enough for you, you will dispense with the refinement of a glass. Here is the proof of how when a hubbub threatens to consume you, you sweetly hold your note. It is the living proof of the origi-nality of your genius.

All broken now, both of us gone down in different seas; wrecked and broken. "Princely Clare," Elia would call you. Never again shall you and he be engaged in such high combats, such wit-fights. Never again shall his com-panionable draughts cause you an after-look of anxiety into the tankard!— no more shall he, pleasantly malicious, make your ears tingle and your cheeks glow with the sound of that perplexing constrainment, that conven-tional gagging-bill, that grammar, till in the bitterness of thy heart thou cursedst Lindley Murray by all the stars! Never again shall your sweetly sim-ple Doric phrase and accent beget the odious pun.

And yet take your seat once more at my table, John Clare, and receive from me one more word—and if it be a strange one, as a stranger give it welcome. I have known jovial nights, and felt deeply the virtues of the grape and the barleycorn; I have co-operated in "the sweet wicked catches" 'bout the chimes at twelve, yet I say to thee wherever thou art: shut thy ears in the abounding company of empty scoffers; ever hold it in thy inmost soul that love and perfect trust, not doubt, is the germ of *true* poetry. Thy hand, friend Clare. Others may speak thee fairer, but none wish thee solider welfare than Janus. [8]

I must break off, and rapidly seat these others, who throng upon me apace. Cary first, our modest Reverend, the very model of a country parson. I have heard his mind travel further than any man's into the mysteries of religion, but now it is satisfied with the dish of pheasants my fellow brings in, which he will soon relish and digest as though they were the Birds of Aristophanes. Good Sir, let me gaze upon your features again. This is the gentle visage that stopped the Mariner upon the sands at Littlehampton:

"Yours is a face I should know—I am Coleridge." These are the deep eyes which have scanned the writings of Dante, and the noble Ghibelline now recites his verses in your eloquent and classical English undefiled. Everything you have done is unique for closeness and facility. The poetry of your own heart offers proof of its legitimacy in a sister art, and your taste there is singularly grand, pure and consistent. These are my own words, but they show the feelings of all. [9]

Mild and tactful Barry Cornwall, you are next. Or do I give you your true name of Bryan Procter? Since there is no one present who does not have a false self with which to multiply, let me set aside names altogether, and welcome you as my old brother dilettante. Friend of Elia! Poet of Woman! These are the most grateful titles to your ears, honey-tongued singer of Beauty and its mother, Night! Ghostly you seem at such distance as you stand from me now—your face dapper and delicate. Wherever the world has placed you, let your mind still be its own kingdom; and should the envies blow your tender beauties with their foggy breath, doubt not the advent of true guerdon.

Close on your heels comes Talfourd, that anthery Cicero, glad of your courtesy to him—but more grateful still to be in sight of Elia—and reminding you of your genius. Next, and to speak truthfully, more to my taste, comes Hood, with a clever thing upon his lips if I had but a moment to hear it, and whose gusto will fire us all. I have known him dream articles, think articles, write articles, and perform all the most irksome parts of authorship as though they were a labour of love. Our Lion's Mouth, you are welcome with your pleasant impertinence and ridiculous criticism.

And with your brother-in-law Reynolds, who now enters with Cunningham and completes our party. Cunningham, that stalwart man, very Scotch in aspect, who will later perhaps sing sweetly to us—which I may accompany on my Spanish guitar, or my Tomkisson. Large art thou in body and soul! Thy poetry germinates from the divine seed—love of all things lovely and good. There find I set down, without straining and ambitious fustian, the elements of your own mind: pathos, innocence, hilarity, disdain of petty craft and cant, deep affections, native delicacy, and a deep enthusiasm for spiritual cheer. So it is also with Reynolds, our "Edward Herbert." See him already exercising his smartness, his gamecock-looking head and the hair brushed smooth, fighter fashion, over his brow—with one finger hooked round a glass of champagne, not that he requires it to inspire him, for his wit bubbles up of itself. See him engage with our Jack i' the Green. Hear Jack declaiming him the most good-natured fellow he ever met, and his face the three-in-one of fun, wit, and punning personified.

You are welcome, welcome all. And so are these other humanity-loving and savoury souls also welcome, who do not appear in their earthly forms, but hover round us in the warming air: the Opium Eater; Coleridge and Keats; numbers numberless of the brave hearts who are now the guardians of my spirit and the light of my desolation. Let me not lose you at last! Distant and darkening, you are my close companions still, who stood around me in the time of my glory, and were pleased to call me friend. Elia and Clare, Mr. Drama and Mr. Brunetto; Cornwall and Hood. Your names are the stepping-stones on which I tread across to the isle of my contentment. When your voices rise round me, then I am most myself. Come then, gather close. Here once more we shall have the gaiety of boys with the knowledge of men, and hearts as gentle as ever sent tears to the eyes, and talk like grains of fine gold, which we shall beat out into whole sheets. Have you found your places? Be seated then at last, and I shall shut the door upon us with its well-oiled click. Stay close and companionable, and do not leave me. [10]

1. John Thomas Payne, a bookseller and nephew of the Payne who worked with TGW's cousin Foss, was married to Sarah Burney at St. Margaret's, Westminster, on 14 April 1821.

2. TGW and Eliza moved into 49 Great Marlborough Street in 1821 and lived there for the next seven years—in circumstances that broadly resemble those described by Thackeray in *Vanity Fair*, when he is telling the story of Becky Sharp's married life in Curzon Street at about the same time. They obviously rented their rooms (TGW's name does not appear as a rate- or tax-payer), but how they afforded them is hard to say. Presumably George Griffiths still paid an allowance to top up the interest TGW received on his Trust Fund. TGW also seems to have dealt in prints, taught a little, finished a few commissioned portraits, and borrowed heavily from money-lenders.

In an architectural review of 1734, Great Marlborough Street was described as "one of the finest streets in Europe," and as a haunt of grandees. (The Byron family owned number 15.) By the late eighteenth century its reputation had slipped a little, and it was favoured by artists of one kind or another, rather than by aristocrats. Haydon lived at number 47 from 1818 to 1827, and a harp-maker was at number 18 in TGW's time.

Number 49 (which was later renumbered 53, and demolished in 1953) was divided into four compartments, as described in the *Survey of London* (vol. XXX, 1963), p. 264. The front was four storeys high and five windows wide, and the original plain brick façade had been rendered with stucco. The "finest internal feature was the staircase, which rose in three flights round an oblong well with a gallery landing on the first floor" (where it seems the Wainewrights had their rooms). The balustrade of the short first flight was swept out at the bottom in a bold quadrant curve, and the face of the landing at the level of the gallery was treated as an entablature, having an enriched architrave and an ogee-profiled frieze. The effect was at once grand and voluptuous; no wonder TGW liked it.

The fact that Mrs. Siddons had once lived in the same building made it even more appealing to him. She had moved there in 1792 with her husband William and their two sons. Their two daughters followed a year later, bringing difficulties with them; it was here that Sir Thomas Lawrence fell in love with the two girls simultaneously, could not choose between them, made and unmade his mind, and generally "behaved like a madman" (Mackenzie, p. 106). They stayed until 1804.

3. Following Scott's death, the future of the *London Magazine* hung in the balance. Its proprietors—Robert Baldwin, Charles Craddock and William Joy—eventually sold it to the publishers John Taylor and James Hessey for £500 on 26 April 1821. Taylor briefly considered making Cary editor (thinking "the Name of the Translator of Dante will do some good"), then took over himself in July, hiring Reynolds and Hood as his "valuable co-adjutors," and working from his office in Fleet Street. Since setting up business together in 1816, Taylor and Hessey had established themselves as the best literary publishers in England—eager to exploit the emerging middle-class market, but also keen to produce good-quality books by good-quality names. Their list eventually included Keats, Lamb, Clare, de Quincey, Hood, Coleridge, Reynolds, Carlyle, and Cary.

Taylor and Hessey saw the *London* as a showcase for their existing authors, and also a means of attracting new ones, and since their tastes were close to Scott's, there was no hiatus between the old and the new regimes. During the early years of Taylor's editorship, the *London* continued to promote a strongly collegiate and liberal ethos, which depended greatly on contributions from Lamb (for "Elia"), Hazlitt (for "Table Talk"), Cary (for his continuation of the "Lives of the Poets") and Hood (for the "Lion's Head"). TGW's contributions were erratic, but Lamb, Hazlitt and Leigh Hunt (in the *Examiner* on 22 July 1821) all defended his reputation, and a piece by Cornelius Van Vinkbooms on the current exhibition at the Royal Academy appeared in Taylor's first issue. (Van Vinkbooms published three more articles in 1821; Janus Weathercock four in 1822 and two in 1823. All of them except the last—Janus's "Farewell"—dealt with the same themes as his pieces for Scott, and all were written in the same flamboyant style.) The rates of pay compared favourably with those offered by other magazines (16 guineas a sheet); sales held steady, and for a while the magazine was a model of its kind: intelligent, fun, staunch in its views, and mutually co-operative.

Taylor and Hessey could not ride their success for long. By mid-1823 many contributors felt, like Lamb, that "the *London*, I fear, falls off" (Blunden, 1933, p. 150), and like Hazlitt that "the articles seem thrown into the letter box and . . . come out like blanks or prizes in a lottery" (Bauer, p. 76). This same year, the offices of the magazine moved from Fleet Street to Waterloo Place, off Pall Mall, and the decline continued. Two years later, Taylor and Hessey sold out to Henry Southern, a book-loving lawyer, whereupon Lamb wrote to his friend Barton, "Taylor has dropped the *London*. It was indeed a dead weight. It has got in the Slough of Despond. I shuffle off my part of the pack, and stand the Xtian with light and merry shoulders. It has got silly, indecorous, pert, and everything that is bad" (Blunden, 1933, p. 157). During his four years as editor, Taylor lost about £2,000.

4. Taylor's editorship of the *London Magazine*, as Blunden says, "implied a social as well as a literary gathering" (1933, p. 136), and the monthly dinners he held in his Fleet Street rooms, and later in Waterloo Place, were obviously very entertaining. When TGW was installed in Great Marlborough Street, he organized similar get-togethers. On 24 May 1822, for instance, in one of his few surviving letters, he writes to H. F. Cary,

> Dear Sir,—On this next Monday several friends have agreed to eat their dinner with me, at half-past six *precisely*. Their names are Chas. Lamb, Taylor and Hessey, Cunningham, Clare, and the Ode to Dr. Kitchener [Thomas Hood]. From Mr. Taylor I learn that the first of these is as yet *personally* unacquainted with you—Overlook then the mental distance between the English Dante and the Jack-puddin of the L. M. and allow me to become the much honoured instrument of your mutual introduction. We have an airy bedroom and *well-aired* bed, quite ready for your service. I remain, Dear Sir, With Great Respect your *'Constant Reader'* T. G. Wainewright.

(This letter is quoted in R. W. King, p. 138, and elsewhere.)

5. Lamb refers to his "madness" in a letter to Coleridge written on 27 May 1798, after spending six weeks in a lunatic asylum in Hoxton, following the end of his love affair with Ann Simmons. See *Selected Prose*, p. 56.

6. The *Liber Amoris*, Hazlitt's account of his tempestuous affair with Sarah Walker, appeared anonymously in May 1823, but he was revealed as the author within eight days of publication. Hazlitt himself said the book "exploded a mine under my feet."

Hazlitt (1778–1830) first met Scott when visiting Leigh Hunt in gaol in 1814—along with Thomas Barnes, Haydon, Lamb and others. He contributed to the *Champion*, and when Scott began editing the *London Magazine*, became its star author, remaining so for a while under Taylor—both as "Mr. Drama" and as the author of "Table Talk." (This series started in June 1820 and was first collected and published in 1821. Like all Hazlitt's best work, it has what TGW called "discrimination, gusto, raciness, poetical feeling, and power of language.")

TGW's "quarrel" with Hazlitt has been described as a serious row which shows "the vanity and shallow temerity, the vulgar and impertinent superciliousness of the pseudo-critic [Janus]" (Thornbury, p. 327). Actually it was a typical example of the way *Londoners* treated each other, always teasing and provoking. In March 1820 Hazlitt wrote an article advising his readers to "hover over the Surrey Theatre or snatch a grace beyond the reach of art from the Miss Dennetts at the Adelphi; or take a peep (like the Devil on Two Sticks) at Mr. Booth at the Coburg" (*Selected Prose*, p. 297). In June, Janus Weathercock playfully criticized the vulgarity of this advice: "He entertains serious thoughts of the Royal Coburg Theatre—which we find, by reference to the picture of London, is situated in the borough of Southwark!—faugh!" (*Essays*, p. 73). In a footnote, Scott warned Janus that he was "entering on ground where 'angels fear to tread'" (ibid., p. 74), and in July Hazlitt duly retaliated, defending his admiration for the three "Miss Dennetts" and saying "our friend and correspondent Janus . . . is afraid [even] to trust himself to Sadler's Wells, lest his clothes should be covered with ginger bread, and spoiled for the smell of gin and tobacco" (ibid., p. 74). In December, however, Hazlitt referred amicably to "facetious and biting Janus, of versatile memory," and in May 1823 Janus also remembered their correspondence affectionately. This seems to prove that the whole exchange was essentially good-natured—though it has to be said that in his essay "On Vulgarity and Affectation" (1821), Hazlitt rebukes Janus ("a Bucolic Juvenile") severely. Just for a moment, Hazlitt "seems to have forgotten that Janus was writing with his tongue in his cheek" (Curling, p. 183), and to have lost his sense of humour.

7. See Curling, pp. 159–60. The account given here conflates two versions of the same episode, one by Hood, one by J. C. Hotten in the Preface to Dickens's *Hunted Down;* it refers to a dinner Clare had with TGW in May or August 1824.

8. John Clare (1793–1864) was the son of a Northamptonshire peasant; his *Poems Descriptive of Rural Life* (1820) became a bestseller. Subsequent volumes did less well, and Clare went insane in 1837, spending the last part of his life in Northampton Asylum. He first met his London publishers Taylor and Hessey in March 1820, dining with them several times this month, and meeting many of their friends—including TGW—all of whom treated him as an exciting curiosity. TGW first mentioned Clare in one of his articles in June, referring to his "sylvan muse," and as Van Vinkbooms he later praised the "natural and characteristic" portrait of Clare that had recently been painted by William Hilton: "Observe the thigh caught up consciously by the

hand! It does Hilton's penetration credit to have arrested that most un-sophisticated and speaking action."

When Clare was back in London again in May 1822, TGW invited him to dinner with Lamb, Taylor and Hessey, Cunningham, Hood and Cary; he genuinely admired him. Clare's feelings for TGW were more cautious. As Hood said, "The fact of fustian and corduroy, accompanied by a strong Midlands accent, finding a seat on the satin damask of the drawing room of his exquisitely scented and lisping master, staggered all [Clare's] previous experience of life" (Broderip). Clare himself wrote,

> Wainewright is a very comical sort of chap he is about twenty-seven & wears a quizzing-glass & makes an excuse for the ornament by complaining of bad eyes. He is the Van Vinkbooms, Janus Weathercock, etc., of the Magazine. He had a picture in the [Royal Academy] exhibition of "Paris in the Chamber of Helen" & the last time I was in London he had one there of "The Milkmaid" from Walton's Angler—both in my opinion very mid-dling performances but my opinion is but of itself a middling one in such matters so I may be mistaken. He is a very clever writer & some of his papers in the Magazine are very entertaining & some very good (*The Prose of John Clare*, pp. 91–2).

TGW's last meeting with Clare was in 1824. Early in 1830, Clare wrote to Cary asking after Lamb and "that facetious good hearted fellow" Janus; Cary replied, "I have not seen either Lamb or Wainewright since last sum-mer, when the former spent a day with me here [at the British Museum], and another day we all three met at the house of the latter, who now resides in a place he has inherited from a relation at Turnham Green."

9. H. F. Cary (1772–1844) was a man "of almost extreme modesty and sen-sibility." He was educated at Rugby and Oxford, took Holy Orders in his twenties, and after working in various Midlands churches, became curate at Chiswick in 1814. This same year his translation of Dante was published, at his own expense. In 1819 it was republished by Taylor and Hessey (on the recommendation of Coleridge) in three handsome octavo volumes, and immediately acclaimed as a masterpiece. Cary later translated other Greek and Latin texts, and wrote regularly for the *London Magazine*. Living in Hogarth's old house in Chiswick between 1814 and 1826, he was TGW's neighbour, as well as his friend. They often dined together, they both had a "vulture-like appetite for books" (R. W. King, pp. 75–6), and they were

united in their strong admiration for Blake. (TGW probably introduced Cary to Blake, who used Cary's translation when he began making his illustrations to the *Divine Comedy* in 1825.)

10. Bryan Procter (1787–1874), who published lyric and narrative poetry under the name of Barry Cornwall, was a regular contributor to the *London Magazine,* and one of the last people to visit Keats in England. TGW saw a great deal of him during the 1820s, and met him at a dinner in Linden House with the painter Richard Westall (1779–1836) and others. As a young man, Procter practised as a solicitor; in later life he was made a Commissioner in Lunacy.

Thomas Noon Talfourd (1795–1854) was a successful barrister (eventually he became a judge, and Justice of Common Pleas), and a belletrist and playwright. He was good friends with the *London* set in general and Lamb in particular—later becoming his executor and editor. He reviled TGW in *The Final Memorials of Charles Lamb* (1848), saying that his "tastes appreciated only the most superficial beauty, his vanities were the poorest and most empty; yet he fancied himself akin to greatness." As a High Court judge, he seems never to have forgiven himself for failing to read TGW's criminal character, and so trashed the friendship they had previously enjoyed. But while his criticisms of TGW "luxuriat[ing] in artistic impertinence" make him sound a prig, he may have had better reasons than most for his condemnation. According to the agent of the Eagle Insurance Company, H. P. Smith, Talfourd was one of the very few people to see the "diary" of TGW's various crimes, which was discovered among his papers in France. (For more details, see pp. 256-7.)

Thomas Hood (1799–1845) is best remembered as the author of "The Song of the Shirt" (1843). He was made "a sort of sub-editor" (Bauer, p. 84) of the *London* in June 1822, and took over the "Lion's Mouth" page. His witty articles and poems lit up the magazine—and in company, according to Cornwall, he also "possessed good spirits . . . [which] exhibited themselves in frequent puns and sly jokes." He and Taylor between them were responsible for commissioning and editing TGW's articles for the *London.*

Allan Cunningham (1784–1842) wrote an influential *Lives of the Most Eminent British Painters, Sculptors and Architects* (1829–33), but was also well known for his songs—among them, "A Wet Sheet and a Flowing Sea." He often contributed to the *London,* and saw TGW frequently.

John Hamilton Reynolds (1794–1852) was the main theatre reviewer for the *London* after Hazlitt had given up the job. He had middling success as a poet and as a lawyer, but had a close and intensely rewarding friendship with Keats. His sister Jane was married to Hood.

At their only meeting, in November 1821, de Quincey thought TGW showed "a tone of sincerity and of active sensibility, as in one who spoke for himself." Later, he changed his tune, saying, "It was easy for a man of any experience to read two facts in all his idle *étalage:* one being that his finery was but of a second-rate order; the other, that he was a *parvenu,* not at home even amidst his second-rate splendour." (See *Collected Writings,* vol. 5, pp. 246–51.) This shift is also evident in de Quincey's essay "On Murder, Considered as One of the Fine Arts." In the first version of the essay (1827) there is of course no oblique reference to TGW among the various criminals who are subjected to de Quincey's wittily aesthetic criticism. In the revised and expanded version (1854), the notorious murderer Williams (who had committed his crimes in 1811) is transformed from a brutal and unsophisticated villain into someone whose dandified dress and manner distinctly recall TGW.

It is more nearly certain that TGW met Coleridge than Keats, but his essays certainly prove that he admired Keats's poems. In one place TGW describes a print by Giulio Bonasoni and says,

> We think we know one bard, an ardent admirer of nature, animate and inanimate, yet no lover of underbred, colloquial, city vulgarisms; in short, a *genuine* descendant from the Elizabethan stock, who will thank us for introducing this elegant stranger to him (if indeed they are not already acquainted).

Elsewhere TGW compares lines from the "Ode to a Nightingale" to Stothard's "glowing design of the vintage," and remarks that stanzas 32–36 of "The Eve of St. Agnes" "harmonize sweetly" with "the sentimental manner of Correggio." Elsewhere again, he says that the description of the sleeping youth in *Endymion* "illustrate[s] the precious Florentine gem" representing "a hermaphrodite figure." (See Jack, pp. 258–9.) This depth of knowledge and enthusiasm for Keats's work is striking, since the audience for Keats's writing at this time was very small. A further reference "leaves open the possibility that Keats and TGW may have met" (ibid., p. 259): "Should our choice gain the mede of his approbation, we should not heed a jot the blind gabbling of a million of cold-matter-of-fact critics, or soi-disant artists."

10

WHAT IS MINE

I magine a man walking in a wild countryside. He sees before him a peak which marks the summit of everything around, and which—if he climbs it—will give him the superiority he requires. He approaches this pinnacle with great labour, through grasping heather and biting streams, yet when he draws near his goal, he finds beyond it another and higher mountain rising into view. He consults himself, hears the clamour of his over-taxed heart, and decides that he cannot continue his journey.

My own life appears in this picture. I spent my former days—my *London* days—believing that I would soon reach a secure destination. (Let me call it Fame, and not blush at my presumption.) Yet the more eagerly I pursued my prize, the more nervously it retreated from me—always drawing me after, so that I soon fell into a state of confusion and weariness. The name I had made for myself, the triple-headed name of Janus–Vinkbooms–Bonmot: it enabled me to pay my butcher and tailor now and again, and it brought me friendships I valued more than gold. But beyond these? Beyond these, my existence was uncertain, hurried on its way by force of circumstance and my own desire to please. I had learned how to prove my delight in earthly existence, but my dreams of immortality went unrewarded.

The same disappointments afflicted my life as an Artist. Such a host of new faces crowded upon my canvas in my last chapter, and most of them authors, that I have neglected to mention the hours I spent in my Painting Room during the year 1821 and a few others following, and the works I created there. Yet it was during this same time in which I established myself as a critic, and as a host, that I also showed at the Academy (which I modestly forbore to mention in my articles), and even received the praise of that fraternal genius William Blake. [1]

If I am vain today about my success, it will avail me nothing—and lose me nothing. I shall therefore permit myself once more to enter the wide courtyard of the Academy, to pass through its imposing doors, and to feel— as though for the first time—the breath squeezed from my lungs by the splendour of the display. The walls are a lustrous strawberry red, and hung upon them almost from floor to ceiling are the pictures, arranged like the pieces in a jigsaw puzzle. *Six rows,* perhaps, of the smaller works! An impossible busy-ness of paint. A cruel load on the brain, as it flits from frame to frame, labour-ing to wipe itself clean and judge everything afresh, according to its merits. And when this is done (or not done), then it is on to the full-lengths which hang "on the line." If there be a figure in any of them, the toes of the boots will probably be on a level with my eye, and fairly kick it out of my head.

For nothing but strong colours, large gestures, trumpet notes may be noticed in a display of this kind. Which in turn means that the honour I crave—the honour everyone here craves—turns out to be nothing more than the fate of being squashed and squeezed into invisibility, jostled and jangled into blindness, seen and not to be seen. It is a mad world, yet I wel-come it, taking it upon its own terms, in as much as the figments of my imag-ination may rub their shoulders against those created by my Masters: by our Professor, by Holst, and by Master Ruddicombe himself.

Allow me, then, to find a way through the throng towards my portrait of *Undine.* The story is familiar: how the lady (a water-sprite) was raised by an ancient fisherman, but fell in love with the knight Hulbrand, whom she mar-ried, and thereby gained a soul. Her happiness was of course terrific—but soon shaken when she discovered that Bertalda, the first love of her hus-band, was the daughter of the fisherman who raised her. Then, when all three repaired to the gloomy magnificence of Castle Ringstetten, where Hulbrand's love for Bertalda was rekindled, such little joy as remained to our lady was altogether ended.

It is the pangs of Bertalda's conscience that I show in my picture—her fair form surrounded by insinuating tongues and fingers, by starting eyeballs and grinning jaws. Is not the scale and finish admirable? Is there not a breathing terror and remorse? A tempest of rebukes? And is not the speechless alarm of Bertalda also very fine—does it not prove her guilt? My Eliza stood patiently for long hours, dressed magnificently in scarlet, so that I could capture this effect precisely. Stood with flowers braided in a corona upon her head, her hair rippling over her shoulders. Stood while her innocent sister Helen (in the person of Undine) looked pityingly at her from beneath a half-veil. Stood while I gazed into her eyes and saw—but I have said enough. [2]

No, I shall say more. In my representation of Bertalda, I looked more deeply into the soul than I had ever managed to do previously; and the more deeply I looked, the less certain I became of any such thing as essential char-acter. I do not mean that I discovered love and sympathy were a sham. I mean that I began to ask myself what lengths one person might go to for another, because of love.

Yet even this is not perfectly honest. I have dragged my masterwork of Bertalda out of the dark backward and abysm of time. I have stood back and admired Eliza once more in her scarlet dress, with her arms crossed over her bosom and her eyes wide enough to show me the way into her soul. And I have done so for what? For more than the need to dignify my work. I have done so to prove how diligently I laboured to earn my living.

I shall immediately withdraw from the heat of particular money-memories, so as not to seem too pressing about a pressing business, and give a cool general impression. It will be recollected that my grandfather at his death had left me £5000 in a Trust which was administered by two uncles (one a Foss, one a Wainewright), and by a cousin (Foss the second). When I was still a child and young man, the interest which accrued to me from this Trust was tipped back into its well, or drawn off and used to pay for my schooling and apprenticeship, etc. Since gaining my maturity, I had been compelled to live off the interest entirely, with the supplement of whatever I might earn by my brush or my pen.

It will surprise no one to hear that I had found this impossible. My notion of a gentleman; my reverence for all that is good and uplifting; my wish to clothe Eliza in finery as she desired and I approved; my good nature with my friends: all these made my inheritance seem a niggardly nothing. Or rather, not quite a nothing. I imagined it as a small greasy creature, a kind of slippery, new-born mouse, lying in the gloom of a skirting and making occasional feeble life-struggles. I depended upon it, yet I despised it—which I dare say is explained by my sense that it was rightfully mine, although in law I was not entitled to claim it entirely.

This rankled with me; the recollection of it still rankles. From the fastness of Great Marlborough Street, I relished the sweet life of colour around me (which was the life of my soul), while in the street below me milled the swelling gang of my debtors. The butcher's boy, who carried messages from his master threatening I cannot say what kinds of torture. A milliner favoured by Eliza. My shoe-maker. I shall not extend the catalogue, it is already enough to prove my argument. Which is simply this: if I had been able to put my hands on the whole amount left to me by my grandfather, I should have been able to satisfy my tormentors, and begin my life again from a new position of authority.

The desperate times in our existence fill us with terror, yet our fear becomes like a dream as it passes into history. Our self-dislike is too extreme to be preserved at its original strength, and likewise our relief. With this in mind, I have to admit that I cannot quite recapture, and feel as painfully as I once did, the anxiety which gnawed at me while my debts increased. I can only show how urgently it drove me to seek a solution—at my peril.

During the summer of 1822, my Inheritance gave one of its intermittent life-like shudders. Its Trustees, believing they knew my business better than I did myself, converted the entire amount of my £5000 from Navy 5 per cents to the New 4 per cent Annuities, and in the process added to my fortune by the princely sum of £250. (Enough for you there, Sir Butcher; and a little to spare for you, Madame Milliner.) I was a witness to this transaction, and watching my cousin and uncles scratching away at the necessary documents—a delicate light falling on to their pink hands from a rose window set high in that part of the Bank of England where we had gathered—a new thought leapt suddenly into my breast. If I could write their names exactly as they wrote them themselves, the Bank would become my servant! I might at last become the master of my own life.

It may be wondered that I did not pause here, and consider more carefully the likely outcome of my plan. But in truth, my need was so urgent, I judged this to be a time for action, not reflection. Accordingly, I devoted the next several days to practising the signatures of my Trustees, which was not difficult, since I had letters from them all in my possession. So as not to draw undue attention to my case, I reckoned it sensible to take a lesser part of the £5000 in my first attempt, and then if successful—and if the need arose—to return at some later date for the remaining sum. When my hand was steady in its new trade, I applied to the Bank, entered its stony and ringing heart at the appointed moment, flourished my pen expertly, handed across the document, and left—having secured in a few moments the means of living in comfort for several months or more. [3]

Did I crow like a cockerel in my triumph? I did not so much as whisper. I may love a long neck, but I have never wished my own to be extended beyond its natural measurements.

To contemplate the penalty for forgery with such facetiousness does me no credit. Yet—as I have sometimes said before, and cannot repeat often enough—I am not able to recognize my crime. The best I can do is to insist that because I considered the money my own, to dispose of as I chose, I did not think it wrong to grasp it in my own hands. And because I did not think it wrong to do this, I did not suppose—alas, foolish Janus!—that a punishment was likely. I merely slipped the bills into my breeches pocket and went on my way rejoicing. Throw open your doors, Mr. Colnaghi! Vintner, put forth your finest! Roll up at my door, you jarveys, mud-spattered in your master's haste for my company!

Since then, I have often considered my deeds, and the consequences of my deeds, and felt incapable of linking one to the other with any sensible arguments. I have remembered the man I was, and compared him to the wretch I have become, and found no reason to associate the two. Where is he, the man I was? Dead but not buried; he is a breathing ghost.

Then again, in my sad posthumous life I have sometimes wanted to defend myself by a different kind of argument. All of us who live in the house of forgery are relations. In this sense I have Horace Walpole as my father, and confess that I have lingered for many days and nights among the mysteries of his *Otranto*. My cousin is that ingenious imposter Chatterton, whose Rowley made him immortal. I have William Ireland as another companion, and should willingly play a part in his *Vortigern* to serve his cause. I will go travelling with my friend George Psalmanazar, and report on the inhabitants of Formosa, so that I may prove the imagination equal to history. My uncle is that shaggy and delightful deceiver Macpherson. Etc. Etc. These men knew the shame of revelation—and Chatterton, the most marvellous of them all, a worse fate still, as though to be a marvel meant that he must suffer most. Yet were any of them threatened with the gallows? They were not. Were any confined in stinking darkness, then driven out like cattle into desolation? They were not. Where is the just God who is able to explain these differences? Where is even the lawyer who can give a satisfactory answer to my question? [4]

I should not speak thus, knowing all my arguments are useless. I shall therefore put matters plainly, as I have promised to do: I laid hold of my capital in the hope that it would prolong the existence I enjoyed, only to find that as my pockets became more comfortable, my conscience felt less easy.

But this pricking, or prickling, was soon forgotten—not because I habitually neglected what is right, but because the Bank had hardly closed its doors behind me when I encountered a new and more engrossing obstacle to my happiness. I mean: requests for my articles in the *London* began to dry up. At first I could not believe this was intended, and supposed the silence of my editor was nothing more than evidence that he was immersed in various other labours. But as his hush lengthened, I heard it turn from distractedness into actual neglect, at which point I myself felt compelled to make a noise, since no one else seemed willing.

Were my frivolities so brilliant, I demanded to be told, that no one saw how seriously I weighed my arguments? Was I so preoccupied with ideas, that no one understood how deeply I cared for humans? Was I so purely and simply "Mr. Fine Arts," that no one felt my admiration for the *London* in general? *In his own pages,* I had advised Taylor to find a larger audience for his magazine, which would allow him to advance his outposts still higher up the mount of green-flowering Helicon. And what was my reward for this good advice? First, as I say, the abominable curtailment of my efforts— then, complete banishment.

Banishment!

The certainty of my censure, when I eventually understood it, overwhelmed me. It was no consolation that my outward life was now easier than it had ever been—my credit greater, and also my power to own what I admired. Without a voice to champion my causes, and win the approbation of those I held in high regard, my inner world (if I may call it that) felt like a desert. But the silence into which I sank was not the silence of vacancy; it was the silence of urgent thought. My brain whirled with recriminations, and I intended a most poetic justice; my heart brimmed with passion, and I planned a most intricate revenge.

For weeks I languished in this same state, feeling at once full and empty—but when the mood at last broke I surprised myself. I did not respond to my treatment in kind, with severity and anger. Not at all. I was nothing but gentleness and grace. In my first and last word on the subject of my own death, my *Janus Weatherbound* (which I published the year of our Lord, and my disappointment, 1823), I merely described myself as "Steadfast for Lack of Oil," pointing in one dreary direction when it had always been my delight to swing in many. And then, with no more heat in my argument than this, I bade a sad GOOD-NIGHT TO ALL. Good night to my pen, rattling in its dry well. Goodnight to my fancies, hung high on the walls of galleries where no eye can penetrate. Goodbye to my pride, in being a man as generous as he was amiable. Goodbye to my dear *Londoners,* and to Lamb in particular. Eheu! Elia! Vale! [5]

I shall not rehearse my sorrow in greater detail. My farewell was printed; it stands; and whoever chooses may read it, while there is still light shining in the world. Suffice it to say, I complained that when I had scarcely entered the spring of my life, and done no more than glimpse the sweet flowers of success blossoming around me in glorious profusion, an unseasonable frost had struck at the root of all my hopes, and left me comfortless. And with that, for once in my peculiar career, I shall immediately be as good as my word, and cease. Hold my tongue. Break my staff. Drown my book. Stare upon the closing day and keep my peace. Yes, truly. Keep my peace.

1. TGW exhibited five paintings at the Royal Academy between 1821 and 1825. They are now all lost or misattributed, but their "titles and accompanying literary quotations indicate that while TGW was working in the eighteenth-century genre of 'Historia,' or Narrative Style, he used this manner to express nineteenth-century Romantic ideas" (Kerr, p. 827). The titles of his five paintings were: *A Subject from the Romance of Undine* (July 1821); *Paris in the Chamber of Helen* ("Then Jove-loved Hector entered") (July 1822); *The Milkmaid's Song* ("Come live with me and be my love," from *The Compleat Angler,* Walton and Venator listening) (July 1823); *Sketch from La Gerusalemme Liberata* (canto VII, stanza 27) (July 1824); and *First Idea of a Scene from Der Freischutz* (July 1825).

Not only have these paintings vanished, there is virtually no contemporary appreciation of them either. One of the few that received any attention was *The Milkmaid's Song*. During the late summer of 1823, William Blake and Samuel Palmer went to the RA and Blake pointed out TGW's picture (which was 5'7" × 4'7") "near the ceiling" and pronounced it "very fine." Palmer, however, was more interested in his companion than the painting. He later remembered "Blake, in his plain black suit and *rather* broad-brimmed, but not Quakerish hat, standing so quietly among all the dressed-up, rustling, swelling people, and myself thinking, 'How little you know *who* is among you!'"

2. In *The Romantic Art of Theodore von Holst* (1994), Max Browne published two illustrations (one on the cover) of Holst's *Bertalda Frightened by Apparitions*. In a review in the *Burlington Magazine,* Martin Butlin suggested this work might in fact be TGW's missing *Subject from the Romance of Undine*. The suggestion cannot be proved, and is repudiated by Browne himself, but it remains an interesting one, since the picture is not cited in Holst's list of exhibited pictures. It shows, if nothing else, how close TGW, Holst and Fuseli were to one another, and how similar their techniques. The Undine story (which existed in several forms, and was taken from de la Motte Fouqué's *Kunstmärchen,* first published in 1811) was a particular favourite: it combined lubricious sentimentalism with erotic Gothicism—and a frankly greedy voyeurism.

3. The £5000 Navy 5 per cent stock, which TGW had inherited from his grandfather, was converted to £5,250 New 4 per cent Annuities on 5 July 1822. In order to lay his hands on £2,250 of it, TGW gave a Power of Attor-

ney to the Bank of England ten days later—the document bearing the forged signatures of Edward Foss, Robert Wainewright, and Edward Foss (junior). He committed his second forgery on 17 May 1823, and collected the remaining £3000. The Trustees took so little interest in their responsibilities that the Bank did not discover the fraud until January 1835. But it is difficult to believe Eliza was kept in the dark, and correspondingly easy to think she must have encouraged TGW and helped him.

4. Horace Walpole's *Castle of Otranto* (1755) was first published as the translation of a manuscript dating from the eleventh or twelfth century. Thomas Chatterton poisoned himself with arsenic on 24 August 1770, aged seventeen. His Rowley forgeries caused a sensation during the 1760s, but were exposed by Edmond Malone in 1782 (though Malone continued to think Chatterton was the greatest genius England had produced since Shakespeare). William Ireland's fake Shakespeare play, *Vortigern and Rowena* (1795), was produced by Sheridan but immediately discredited. George Psalmanazar (1679–1763) wrote a bogus *Description of Formosa* (1704). Macpherson's *Ossian: Fragments of Ancient Poetry Translated from the Gaelic* had a terrific success in the late eighteenth century, and was finally exposed as a fraud by the Highland Society in 1805.

These are just some examples of the many forgeries circulating during the early Romantic period, and they provide an interesting background to TGW's deception. Although their aims were artistic, and his venal, they show a similar disrespect for inherited systems of law and truth, and a similar wish to advance the cause of the self by indirection. Hazlitt recognized the link when he said,

> I conceive that words are like money, not the worse for being common, but that it is the stamp of custom alone that gives them their circulation or value. I am fastidious in this respect, and would almost as soon coin the currency of the realm as counterfeit the King's English.

5. Lamb's "Elia" essays were first collected and published as a book in January 1823, whereupon Lamb wrote an article for the *London,* in his own person, which announced the demise of his alter ego: "To say truth, it is time he were gone. The humour of the thing, if there was ever much to it, was pretty well exhausted; and a two years' and a half existence has been a tolerable duration for a phantom." Various *Londoners,* including TGW, then wrote elegies for Elia, but two months later Lamb revived him, saying that

"Janus's" account was a "sham." (Elia's *Last Essays* were collected in 1833, when Lamb and Taylor quarrelled about copyright.) The whole episode was typical of the way *Londoners* played with true and false identities—and would seem entirely good-natured had it not coincided with the actual departure of TGW from the pages of the magazine.

11

ALL BULL'S-EYE

*P*ity me. I had always loved indirections; then in my tumble from the pages of the *London* I was forced to look at things straight. Pity me. A creature of here-and-there, suddenly transfixed and still.

Yet I was not wholly at a loss, and in the days (I say days, but I mean years) following my change of fortune, hardly an hour went past without some attempt at resurrection. I was known as a collector of prints, and continued to earn the gratitude of Colnaghi's. I burnished my name at the Academy, and even at the British Institution, where I showed my *Milkmaid's Song* to general applause. I entertained the companions of my soul—Fuseli and Holst—and other kindred spirits: Blake and Lamb, whom I have already celebrated. None of them understood the true state of my affairs, any more than strangers did, who saw me on my park promenades and suchlike, smiling and raising my hat to the world. Indeed, I almost convinced *myself* that this seemingly careless existence could lengthen *ad infinitum,* like a day in summer when the sun sinks by slow degrees, from red, to gold, to bronze, to russet, to purple, and the nervous heart is soothed, dreaming that darkness will never come. [1]

But our fictions cannot sustain us for long, and in due course life lost patience with itself and me. The languid current that had carried me smoothly, scarcely a ripple distressing its surface, drove without warning into a narrow and dreadful channel. I was so sadly tossed from side to side, and so repeatedly, that I suspected a malign fate was conspiring to shipwreck all my remaining cargo.

The first of these blows was: the death of Fuseli, in the disastrous year 1825. I had in my previous career lost friends to whom my success would have been a cordial, but the passing of this great man blasted all the romantic yearnings of my youth. My grief was only a little allayed by the request that I should be one of those charged with the honour of escorting his coffin from Somerset House to its final resting place—the vault of St. Paul's Cathedral. [2]

It was a splendid procession, and a fitting one. Walking before the flower-covered bier went pages bearing black feathers, and four porters in silk dresses. Next came eight mourning coaches, each drawn by four horses. In the first travelled his two executors. In the remainder came the President, Secretary, Treasurer and Council of the Academy—and assorted private friends. Among them, sharing the sorrow of my poor self, were Haydon and Samuel Rogers, the banker-poet. Also Robert Smirke, the great architect, and my own quondam Master, Mr. P. The hearse itself was drawn by six horses caparisoned in black velvet, each with a nodding plume.

Solemnly we crossed over the river—the weather grey and misty as though the heavens themselves were grieving. Solemnly we passed through the hushed City. Solemnly we took down the coffin and went in under the great dome of the Cathedral, and thence to the vault. I cannot forget the shock of seeing real and ordinary earth, where they had lifted the floor slabs, since in that place it seemed as though the work of human hands must have shaped everything to a tremendous depth and made it sacred. Likewise, I shall always remember the pride of seeing my Professor lowered between his friends Opie and Reynolds, with whom he could now speak for eternity.

I shall not rekindle here my habit of making fresh farewells. I shall merely observe that this death gave me more sorrow than others I had known, and seemed to clear a way for life to hurl down further offences upon me. In the summer of this same year, before the carving of my friend's memorial was complete, Messrs. Taylor and Hessey sold their interest in the *London,* so finally removing any hope that I might one day renew my career with them as an Author. At almost the same moment, my uncle sold the *Monthly.* It is true that I had never allowed myself to appear in his pages, yet the instant they passed beyond my range, I could not help thinking that a chance had been lost. Now on my visits to Linden House, when I saw my uncle pleasing himself in his garden at all hours, his leisure stung me by seeming so obviously a reward for labours he had previously undertaken. How could I expect similar benefits, since I had not made similar exertions and investments?

It was such questions that spurred me, during this same fatal period, towards my greatest effort at resurrection, which was also my cruellest test. I offered myself to become an Associate of the Academy, with some forty others—and was rejected! The same doors which had swung wide for the Professor were bolted against his most ardent disciple. The floors which had echoed to his footsteps would not receive the weight of my own. The walls on which he had revealed the most sublime heights of his imagination, and its most terrible depths, would not support a single line of my pencil or a gesture of my brush. As I returned to Great Marlborough Street carrying the news of this decision, I wished the earth beneath me might open as I had seen it do in St. Paul's, and receive me immediately, for my spirit was already crushed out of me.

I must immediately add, and with pride: I did not altogether surrender to my disappointments, but rather endeavoured to transform them—as an Author. This ambition, however, proved my last throw, since in the eyes of the world my publication was a mere curiosity. I am speaking here, as too few will understand, of my *Egomet Bonmot.* [3]

It does not become a gentleman to defend his own productions, or explain the meaning in any book he writes. Art should proceed through the world like a dandy in a starched collar, which makes it impossible to look down at the antics of critics—as my late friend Bonmot well understood, and took the trouble to express as follows:

> *A pretty thing, forsooth, to dream that I*
> *Would ape the sign-post bungler who constrained*
> *—For his ill use of colours, light, and shade—*
> *To seek in language an ally of paint,*
> *Scrawled underneath his daub—*This here's a house.

Notwithstanding such warnings, I must explain something about this volume of mine, lest its very existence be forgotten. It is a satire, and recognizes the following fact: when a man arrives at the age of thirty, he hears a disappointed crowd jeering behind him, and the field for delightful hope (which in youth had seemed extensive) dwindled to a mere span before him. Thus it was with Bonmot, who I had always hoped, in my days on the *London*, would represent the best of my aspirations. I intended that he should be a fanciful and free spirit, yet also a glass through which I might pursue myself to my own dark corners, and see into my depths.

I endeavoured to make this plain to the simplest fool in my Introduction, which like all the rest that followed was so ably edited by that nonpareil Mr. Mwaughmaim:

> *What's here?* [I wrote] *Myself and I—I and Myself?—*
> *He talks of little but himself.—I' faith*
> *I see it now;—a right broad target this*
> *For ridicule:—my aim upon't he'll hit*

All Bull's-Eye

The very spot sans aim,—for in these days
That Butt is all Bull's-eye.

That is as clear as the nose on a face, is it not? And if I am wrong (which has sometimes been known), then I appeal: was there not also PROSE, plain prose in my production, to give my readers satisfaction? Plain prose to relate the history of my friend, and tell how he had been a person of considerable attainments, which made him an agreeable companion? But I jump ahead of myself in asking such questions, and must double back, and begin my story at its beginning. Through his early years, Bonmot was a hopeful man; yet, when he came to London, dreaming of literary eminence, he suffered a series of disappointments. Grave as these seemed, they were at first unable to disturb a certain equanimity which then distinguished him. It was not long, however, before his setbacks provoked him to decry the adequacy of critics to pass judgement on his works. Accordingly, he grew boisterous in his own praises, and vaunted himself on his descent from an illustrious ancestry, whose dignity and consummate knowledge he now boasted were worthily confined to his competent keeping. Nor did his changeableness end there. From the birth of this new pride, Bonmot resolved to adopt the invincible spirit of *bounce,* and published anonymously a hundred works. It was the strangest medley—everything by fits, and nothing long; changing not with the phases of the moon, but with the minutes on the clock.

Literary distinction, when at last obtained after the varied struggles of years, often falls upon battered and blunted feelings. The romantic longings of youth are sobered down into mere matters of fact; the morn of life no longer glitters in the orient sun; the world has laid its paralysing paw upon the acuteness of our sentiments; an analysing spirit creeps over us; experience unconsciously mocks us to dissect things which in former years we simply used to worship for their exterior beauty; the wine of life is drawn and nothing but the lees remain; an icy hand is upon us and the genial current of the soul is frozen; many friends, too, are lost—hid perhaps in the grave.

This was the fate of Bonmot, as I know myself, who suffered with him at his deathbed, and propped him through his final agonies. Like Socrates, he desired that his last moments should be spent in instruction. Furthermore, he determined to make a swan-like end by returning to his original genius, and delivering what he had to say in rhyme. I do not propose to rehearse the whole of these verses once more—though I shall give odd fragments, to add to those I have already remembered. All in all, they swelled the plaint of the Introduction, adding further details of love found and failed, a marriage desired and done, works lost and works published—rising, as they combined, towards an entire justification of the sad mood which latterly afflicted my friend:

> *Important epoch!—when we hit the vein*
> *Of sarcasm, with its cutting, biting train*
> *Of epigrammatic bitters sharply pointed*
> *And style colloquial, striking, bold, disjointed—*
> *Of all the taking styles give me "the disappointed."*

There is no cause for surprise here. It was the disregard of the world that drove Bonmot to centre everything upon his Self—an intimate conviction, to which probably might be traced similar endeavours made (*haud passibus aequis*) by others of the confraternity of egoists who lift up their heads these days. But what was this Self, which—as the cunning editor Mr. Mwaughmaim permits us to see—was the quintessence of my friend? I shall not give an opinion in my own words, but in his, as befits the subject. Our poor hero suffered from the conviction of something abhorrent to humanity in his own breast, and see! rather than seeking to expunge it, he welcomed it as though he were Lord Byron himself, intent on turning sin into a source of riches:

> *In short, what's easier than that thing in vogue*
> *An honest rascal, or a noble rogue;—*
> *What's easier than by help of lurking hint*
> *To show a villain virtuous in print;*
> *And, by a second hint's ingenious fetch*
> *To nourish pity for this misused wretch,*
> *This hapless victim of a dismal doom*
> *Whose withered heart's, alas, a thing of gloom:—*
> *Then, with one dark hint further, clench the nail,*
> *And who is then the hero of the tale?—*
> *Why, in the bard's own person we shall find*
> *The wandering outlaw of his own black mind!—*
> *I say (except myself) there's scarce a wight*
> *"Sings darkling" nonsense about "bosom's blight,"*
> *But thinks 'tis nice to place before our eyes*
> *Things of disgust at which men's gorges rise—*
> *Yet—as 'twere false to swear an oath downright*

That he is wretched, liver, heart and light,—
(False as that place not named to ears polite)
Dark mystery—great source of the sublime,—
Just saves his bacon from a real crime.

Just saves. And yet there was no dignity in Bonmot, no control or intelligence, which could save him from every evil that lay within him. Once again, this may be offered as a general truth. The seed of our own destruction exists in all of us, warmed by the exertion of our days until it is stronger than the body that contains it, whereupon it suddenly becomes dominant. Bonmot was on just such a course to destruction, resolving that some form of iniquity—real or imagined—would be his salvation in the world (however it affected his standing in the next). Yet I believe that his gentle readers were apt to forgive him, knowing his sins were merely expedient, and not the consequence of some great flaw in his nature.

At any rate, they would have been willing to forgive him, had they been given the opportunity. But Time, which is merciful as well as harsh, interceded—so that Bonmot was transported beyond the reach of forgiveness, and of everything else besides. To be precise: the poor fellow was seized by an affliction which soon hurried him from his study to his deathbed, where, as I have already shown, he was attended in his final hours by Mr. Mwaughmaim, who faithfully transcribed his final notions, his "Century of Thoughts," his *De Rebus Omnibus* (which transcend in importance, as they do in variety, the *Pensées* of great Pascal himself), and also his last words. These (as every one would expect in a man of principle) honoured the interest which had guided him through his entire experience. "I; I," he breathed softly, and expired. [4]

I shall not surmise how Bonmot's Confession was a record of my own Self during this turbulent time. Nor shall I sift through it for memories of my lamented Professor, and other losses I had recently suffered. As I have already indicated: such enquiries are not becoming. In their place, I shall merely say: thus does the world grow more drab and dull. With such rewards are the brightest spirits cheered on their passage through this weeping vale. With calumny and bitterness. With neglect and ignominy. My friend was a martyr to the cause which every aspiring heart must recognize and call its own. I salute him, and commend him to the care of all nations, as he undertakes his voyage into posterity. He made himself a monument *aere perennius*, and though it is his works, formed to outlive the sculptured marble, that deserve in fact to be the true conservators of his fame, yet according to his desire, this Epitaph, on which he had expended so many hours, has been engraved on his stone. It is plain, expressive, touching, this:

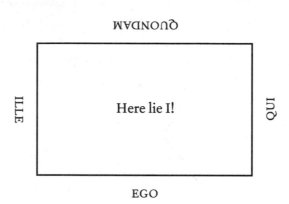

1. We know very little about TGW's life between his last *London* article (May 1823) and the funeral of Fuseli on 25 April 1825. He seems to have continued seeing his friends, done a little painting, involved himself in print-dealing (corruptly, according to some sources), and certainly to have run up serious debts.

2. Fuseli died on 16 April 1825 and was buried nine days later. "By a special resolution of the Council of the Royal Academy," the funeral "was a private one, attended only by Members of the Council and, by express invitation only, a few intimate friends of the deceased." Included among them were the Duchess of St. Albans; the Countess of Guildford; the Marquess of Bute; Lord James Stewart; Vice-Admiral Sir Graham Moore, KCB; the Hon. Colonel Howard, MP; Sir Edward Antrobus, Bt; and—odd man out—TGW.

3. *Some Passages in the Life etc. of Egomet Bonmot Esq, edited by Mr. Mwaughmaim, and now first published by Me,* which appeared in 1825, is in part an elegy for lost youth, and in part a howl of disappointment. It derives from Lamb's *A Character of the Late Elia* (1823) and contains several close echoes of mood and phrase: Lamb, for instance, says of his pseudonymous creation, "My late friend was in many respects a singular character," and TGW says of his, "My late friend was a gentleman of considerable attainments—he had, besides humour—sentiment—cleverness—and an original turn of thinking." Both texts, too, play fast and loose with the facts of their writers' lives—Lamb saying he has been raised in the country, and TGW alluding to an unlikely love affair with one "Polly," to a play he has written and seen performed, to poems he has written and destroyed, to a "Century of Thoughts—all leading to nothing," and so on. Despite these debts, though, *Some Passages* has an original and peculiar fascination. It is full of vain boasts (about TGW's own work, real and imagined), of stinging criticisms (of contemporary magazine culture), of neuroses (about women, fame and the fear of failure), and of surprisingly unembittered zeal—especially in those parts, numbering several hundred lines, that are written in rhyme. While projecting the picture of a mind dangerously close to hysterical collapse, it also proves TGW's resilient energy, and his enduring good spirits. Furthermore, it makes a more direct address to the Self—and to the question of multiple Selves—than anything else produced by the *Londoners*.

It is a portrait of someone cracking up, which analyses the means of staying in one piece.

4. Bonmot's "noncupative will" bequeaths everything he claimed to have written to the public: a "wondrous tale," eleven novelettes, various plays, his anonymous writings, and his "Century of Thoughts." Like the rest of *Some Passages,* it wants to make a joke of disappointment, and cannot quite manage it.

12

TRUE NATURE

*O*ur life on this earth is a desperate confusion. With every new dawn, we suppose we may begin afresh—fulfilling our hopes and achieving our ambitions. Yet as the hours of daylight pass, impediments rise up before us, and difficulties rain down upon us, so that by evening we are the same bowed and exhausted creatures we were yesterday.

Nor do these blows fall equally. Some lives, although full of malice and wickedness, escape punishment. Others suffer for no reason, except their cowering faces invite injury. Another sort exist in a middle way, observing that their deeds and their rewards are not well matched: namely, one man tunnels underground in the utmost misery and hardship, and comes up with a pittance, while a second twiddles his thumbs and grows rich doing nothing. I am a man of this middle sort. I have given my best energies to perfecting the mere fact of my existence, and been condemned to live like a dog. I have made it my chief delight to enjoy the company of like minds, and been cast into desolation. I protest: my sole intention was the pursuit of beauty!

But to return where I was: to myself as a despairing Author. One part of me—a giddy part, I admit—hoped that the last gasps of my friend Bonmot would harden into gold and fill my pockets. No such alchemical transformation occurred. A far larger part of me knew that the death of my Professor, and all those other sorrows which followed hard upon its heels, marked a premature end to my career as a gentleman, and the commencement of a much more unhappy era.

I nerved myself for the turnabout so well that I became entirely made of uncertainties—and did nothing. I lived in a miasma, ground by the mill of days. In the bower of my library, a portfolio might still warm my heart, and the shining firelight make my eyes sparkle. But these were precarious pleasures, and I could no longer believe that what appeared to be mine was mine in fact. I felt like a man on a high mountain, who knows that the paths down to safety are all impassable, and who in the terror of his predicament prepares to throw himself into the abyss. I had become my own worst enemy.

It was my fragile nurse who saved me, my Eliza. Taking her accustomed position at my shoulder, she explained that if my place in the world had been undermined, it did not prevent me from establishing another elsewhere—by which she meant leaving Great Marlborough Street, and returning to Linden House. In this same fit of planning, she imparted a different and more blessed piece of information: that I was to have an heir. I confess that after many sunnier years of marriage, to have such a thing at such a moment seemed a turbulent joy.

When my uncle was informed of our intention, he welcomed it immediately, although we could not repay his kindness by explaining all our motives to him. In this respect, our arrival under his roof was a sort of deception. He believed that Eliza and I were impelled by nothing other than natural affection, and concern for his old age. [1]

To give solidity to these thoughts, I disguised the hurt that I did myself in leaving Great Marlborough Street, which was during the autumn of 1826. Taking my last look round the rooms which had been the theatre of so much pleasure, printing on my mind for ever the impression of those bare walls, those dusty floors, those scraps of unwanted paper, and all the other signs of our removal, I felt that I had been transformed from my corporeal self into a ghost.

Settling such items as came with us to Linden House, I discovered a distracting novelty. Yet this latter-day house-making could not entertain me for long. When Eliza and I had done everything necessary for our peace, we found ourselves in a mood of great strangeness. Hers was understandable: she was easily wearied, and required to rest for many hours of each day. Mine was less happily explained. I had returned as a man to the scenes of my childhood—not as someone full of the glory he had achieved on his adventure through the world, but as a sorry traveller in need of refuge. Each day I loitered under the autumn trees, or sat within the library, or comforted Eliza in her idleness. In every case, I tormented myself with vanished pleasures. I was in a place I loved, yet not of it. I was in a condition to be grateful, yet could not feel it. Watching my uncle go about his innocent business, I resented him when I should have fallen on my knees and given thanks.

I can assure anyone who cares to know: although these contradictions excited a painful storm in my breast, I would much more willingly have endured my distress than permit any pain to afflict my uncle. By one means or another, he had been my defender since my youth—guiding my hand, paying my way. What could I feel for him, except obligation? Yet I must sorrowfully report that within only a few months of my arriving in Linden

House the old man took sick and died. It was a most unexpected tragedy, as everyone agreed, and I well remember the sobs of the maid Sarah Handcock, as she came into the library to inform me of his passing. (This poor woman, who had been with the family for many years, now feared for her future employment, as did her companion in service, Harriet Grattan. I wasted no time informing them both of my intention to keep everything as before, but received only trouble for my solicitude, as I mean to show in a while.)

It was a consolation I could have predicted, but did not in the least look for, or presume upon, to feel my grief assuaged by the knowledge that I was now the owner of Linden House.

I shall interpose, before coming to the other and purely circumstantial results of my uncle's demise, some thoughts that struck me at the time—thoughts concerning death in general, and unexpected losses in particular. My life, and the lives of all my circle, had been much afflicted by grief of one kind or another. Elia himself knew how tragedy, like water seeking a passage through rock, will trickle this way and that until it finds a way ahead. The torrent had cascaded into his own house—when his poor sister, in a fit of insanity, had been the murderer of their mother, and then a constant though never-complained-of burden to her brother, who became her most kindly gaoler. I have heard him say, in his "Witches . . ." and elsewhere, that this made him painfully alive to nervous terrors, so that he would often lay his head upon the pillow in expectation of seeing some frightful spectre.

This was a dreadful trouble for my friend yet it created sympathies in him which he might not otherwise have owned—sympathies with the poor and the oppressed, with the dejected, even with criminals or the insane. This in turn (extending the original terms of my digression) leads me to ask: which of us may certainly say, such a man is a criminal, such a man virtuous; such a fellow mad, such a one sane? There is, in the stretch of human suffering to the utmost endurance, severe bodily pain brought on by strong mental agony, the frightful obstinate laugh of madness—yet those who never were witness to madness in real life, they may see nothing but what is familiar to them in this face.

So it is with crime. I have only to think of other men I have known to be certain that no one comprehends the whole extent of himself, and what good or evil he might do. To think of Hazlitt, for example, who well understood that real character is not one thing, but a thousand things; and reminded his readers that actual qualities do not conform to any faculties which are standard in the mind, but rest upon their own truth in nature. I have heard him say on one occasion that the greatest hypocrite he ever knew was a little, demure, pretty, modest-looking girl, with eyes kindly cast on the ground, and an air as soft as enchantment; and on another occasion that we can hardly pretend to pronounce magisterially on the good or bad qualities of strangers; and, at the same time, that we are ignorant of those who are our friends, our kindred, and our own. His most energetic and marvellous description of "The Fight"—in which Hickman and the other pugilist appear like figures in the Inferno, their eyes filled with blood, their noses streaming blood, and their mouths gaping blood—is a proof of how our imaginations may transform us into the very things we would condemn. So also does his *Liber Amoris* show the power of ungovernable feelings—his *hysterica passio*, which unhinged his reason.

I say again: if a particular individual were merely the wretch we read of, or conceive in the abstract, he would not disappoint the spectator, but would look like what he would be: a monster! Yet he has other qualities, ideas, feelings, nay, probably virtues, mixed up with the most profligate habits or desperate acts. This need not lessen our abhorrence of the crime, but it does of the criminal; for it has the latter effect only by showing him to us in different points of view, in which he appears a common mortal, and not the caricature of vice we took him for, not spotted all over with infamy.

I am almost at the end of my examples, but cannot neglect mentioning the Opium Eater in such a company as this. He was a man whose midget looks were at variance with the rest of him; who understood that in the murdered person all strife of thought, all flux and reflux of passion and of purpose, are crushed by one overwhelming panic—and yet who also knew the folly of removing the murderer himself from the region of human beings, human purposes, human desires, if we are to comprehend his aim and impulse. I will say no more about him here, only wish him well in his career of criticizing others, and invoke in his stead a universal law upon which I may rely for support. Any man who is devoted to the whole world of his imagination, as I have been, will understand the necessity of embracing moods more black than his own, and desires more deadly. I have lived in my fancy with devils and incubi, with murderers and lunatics, with melancholy and wide-eyed despair. Why should I stop all my sympathy when I turn from these imagined lives to Life itelf? Are they not intended to cross from one to the other, with all their flawed humanity intact? That is the end of sublime Art: to show us our entire selves in a mirror whose distortions are the truth.

With that, I shall return to the deathbed of my uncle. He lay in the same delightful house, in the same pretty room, with the same north light falling upon his empty face, as my grandmother had done many years before. As I stooped to take my last farewell (Handcock looking on—eagerly, as I now think), I recollected the softness of her temples against my childish lips, and also that the touch meant nothing to me. Now, with a grown man's cares upon me, and a more certain knowledge of our common lot, I felt more profoundly, and grieved that all flesh is grass.

Nevertheless, I had hopes that once the flood of my sorrow was spent, I should find myself in a condition which allowed for the resumption of my happiness. A mere month after my uncle had been buried, the little creature who should have been his great-nephew was born: I mean my son, named Griffiths with all due honour. I wish that I could immediately add a sign of my pleasure that he grew up conscious of his inheritance and its advantages, but I cannot. The plain fact is: I cannot add a sign of anything about my son. He was in effect the child of Eliza for the short time that we lived together under the same dispensation, and when that dispensation ended: all is a blank to me. Such an admission will seem unkind, but if the truth is plain it had better be admitted. The best that I can say is, I would have loved my son, had I known him. Wherever he now lives in the wide world, under whatever name and with whatever business, I wish him nearer to happiness than his unfortunate father—who feels the shame of our connection, I trust, more heavily than he does himself. [2]

By contrast, my other hope for happiness was as plain as daylight. Although my uncle had never been so intimate as to give details of his financial affairs, nor I so bold as to enquire after them, the gentleness of his attitude to work, and his pleasure in adding parcels of land to our plantation, had persuaded me that once I was the proprietor of Linden House, my anxieties about the management of life would be resolved for ever. Therefore, in the days after his unfortunate demise, I found a new enjoyment in patrolling the ample chambers of the house, and in taking the spring air in the gardens. These were the rituals I had kept since earliest childhood, living always on the charity and indulgence of others. Now I was the monarch of all I surveyed, and my heart lifted like an eagle, spreading golden wings, while I looked down at the delights which were mine.

I will not describe the works I planned, what exceptional monuments and imperial rustications, what new ranks of sumptuous bindings, what profusion of prints; neither will I give details of the efforts I now suddenly demanded of myself, in order to be worthy of my new station—the gates of my imagination flung open, and all its contents spilling out in abundance.

Why will I not do these things? For no reason other than that it would add a fresh burden to my spirit, and I do not believe I have the constitution (as I have indicated before) to suffer my losses a second time.

I will therefore be brief, and say this. After no more than a few days of imagining the existence I considered mine, I discovered that my hopes were all built on sand—since the size of my uncle's estate was much less than I had supposed! The security of a full account at the bank; the smiling look into the eye of a tradesman who knows he will be paid eventually; the freedom to rise late and not concern myself with reward! *All these things were an illusion*. I thought of that lamented king, Midas, as I moved quietly through the rooms where I had lately rejoiced. Their objects of beauty were suddenly a heavy weight to me—insupportable. To gaze upon a print burned my eyes. To handle a precious volume scorched my fingers. When I tugged open my curtains on a morning, and looked between the bare branches towards the end of my plantation, I saw only loss and anguish where I had expected there would always be plenty. [3]

It may be wondered, by timid souls, why I did not immediately resolve my situation in the sale of Linden House, before the load of my disappointment crushed me. Braver hearts will not need an answer. When I examined my life, I saw that it had been entirely a preparation for this moment of inheritance. I could not allow what was mine to be snatched from me, in the very instant that it was given. Besides, I was not an innocent in the matter of shifting and scraping and had—if I may say so—with the passage of the years, acquired a certain skill in the delicate business of making ends meet. It is a disagreeable subject, viewed from this angle, but the plain truth is: life is a matter of appearances, and when these are well maintained, credit is forthcoming. I had a certain acquaintance named Atkinson, to whom I was already grateful, who now obliged me generously with a loan. Another man called Sharpus (whose name suggested I shall not stoop to say what) also understood my case. Thanks to these two, and the forbearance of others, I squeezed some sweetness from the bitter fruit I had been given, and found some light in the darkness which gathered round me.

Did I convince myself that the recovery of my financial health might become permanent? I cannot remember. The mind plays tricks with our happiness, as it does with our unhappiness, and persuades us that what we felt so urgently at one particular moment was in fact a mere nothing. My present state is so much more unfortunate than anything I knew then, I am inclined to think that I carried my cares lightly. I recollect myself strolling under the trees with Eliza on my arm, and our infant brought up behind by some cooing nurse: I am the very image of a man of property and rectitude. I see old familiar faces round my dining table—not as numerous as before, and not as frequent—but still there! still eager and smiling! [4]

Yet no sooner do I revolve these images, expecting another comfortable scene to rise before me, than they become a painful jumble of fragments and hysterical oddments. It is the pattern of my own giddiness that I see at these times, the broken shape of hours alone in my library and elsewhere, when I am doing nothing, letting my thoughts drift in a gloomy paralysis. In such moods, a man may not know the limits of his own mind. He may encounter a darkness in himself which makes him capable of ideas he would not dare to entertain in better times. And these ideas might in turn encourage him to plan actions that he would be ashamed to call his own—if he were in his true mind. But he is not in his true mind—and when the truth goes, all other human honesties are swallowed after it, into a region where no man may be trusted, however amiable he seems, and no confession may be believed, however heartfelt it appears.

1. It is likely that the second tranche of TGW's illegally gained inheritance had been spent by 1826, since during this year he entered into a grim deal with a loan shark named John Atkinson. Their agreement stipulated that TGW would pay Atkinson (and various of his relatives) a total of £150 a year for the duration of their lives "and the lives of the last survivor" (Hammond, p. 8). This was in repayment of a loan of £3000 that Atkinson had already made to TGW, plus a new loan of £1,500. The security for these two loans was "some unspecified books, engravings and pictures which had to be insured at [TGW's] expense for £1,500 and kept in boxes by Robert Shank Acheson, a solicitor and associate of Atkinson. Besides lending [TGW] the further £1,500, Atkinson agreed not to pursue a judgment against [him] in the High court for debt" (ibid.). These dealings tell us that TGW had spent at least £8000 in the previous five years—at a time when a professional man could live reasonably well on £400 a year.

2. Virtually nothing is known about TGW's son, Griffiths. He was baptized on 4 June 1825, two months after George Griffiths died, and eleven years after TGW and Eliza were married. This long gap led some of TGW's enemies to suppose the boy was illegitimate. Barry Cornwall, for instance, said "scandal whispered" that he was "the son of a dissipated and impoverished peer" (Procter, p. 190). There are no solid reasons for believing this—or Cornwall's other claim: that TGW "seemed to have little affection for the boy."

3. George Griffiths died in 1828; the administration was granted on his Estate on 5 February, and the whole passed to TGW, his "lawful nephew and only next of kin" (information from de Chantilly). However, the total value of the Estate was only £5000, and (in W. C. Hazlitt's estimate) Linden House cost about £1000 a year to run; this, combined with TGW's existing debts, meant that the inheritance TGW hoped would stave off disaster only brought it closer. Within a few months he was living almost entirely on credit, owing large sums to the local butcher, baker, grocer and coal merchant. On 8 July, as Curling points out, "He was obliged to grant a bill of sale on the entire furniture and effects of Linden House; his creditor was a crockery merchant of Cockspur Street, named Sharpus, who ran a money-lending business on the quiet. To the same person, [TGW] was also indebted, under a warranty of attorney, for £610, which was to fall due in August . . . In addition, he owed about £200 to a friend, a Piccadilly auction-

eer named Wheatley" (pp. 231–2). In May 1829, TGW went back to John Atkinson, from whom he had already borrowed heavily in 1826, and "mortgaged Linden House and its estate as further security for the annuity of £150 (which it is difficult to believe he had actually been paying), and for a further £2000 which had been lent to him by Atkinson. Once again [TGW] received a further £1,500 loan as part of his transaction" (Hammond, p. 8).

4. Lamb and Cary visited Linden House in the summer of 1829, and probably at other times as well. Cornwall also dined there with Richard Westall in 1830, and remembered the evening in his autobiography. He gave a clear view of TGW's desperate scrambling for money at this time:

> Mr. Westall and I found that he had contracted intimacies with some German art students, and that he had been buying and dealing with scarce old prints and etchings to a great extent. Among these were some very costly engravings after Maro Antonio and Bonasoni, which he had purchased from Mr. Dominic Colnaghi upon trust, and parted with by mortgage or sale immediately afterwards. Subsequently he purchased very cheap copies of the same prints, and placed these on the cardboards, which had large prices noted on them in Mr. Colnaghi's writing, and from which the expensive specimens had been removed . . . Besides this mode of obtaining money for his pleasures, [TGW] had recourse to loans. Amongst others he applied to me for a loan of £200, which it was not convenient for me, at that time, to advance (Procter, p. 228).

13

BILLS OF SALE

*W*hen we read the stories men tell of their own lives, we often find them describing the blessing or catastrophe which gives a shape to their entire existence—and failing to make it vital for us, their readers. This is not because they miss the importance of what is large; it is because they neglect the value of what is little.

I shall explain what I mean in my own case. The events I am describing, the death of my uncle, etc.: they represent what is of interest *to the world*. They are the stuff of gossip and study, and have already won me a certain sorry immortality. What is of value to *me*—to my own Self—bears no relation to any of them. I am thinking here of such profound but unnoticed pleasures (unnoticed by others) as the rain on a spring morning, shaken off a branch when a thrush settles there and starts its melodious lay; the brilliance of a glass fragment, lost in the dust of a pathway until the sun happens to strike it; the luxurious curl of a water eddy, glimpsed in a stream for an instant, then lost.

My conclusion is clear. What the world sees when it looks at a man is a sort of nothing, if all it sees are the busy moments in his day. It is a simplification of the truth. It is the rind of the apple, not the flesh and the pips; the shell, not the sweet nut within; the visible top of the iceberg, not the gloomy, vast and sub-aqueous mass.

And with that said: to business. In the sad year following my uncle's death, in which my grief at his passing, and my pained gratitude for his kindness to me, were eased only by knowing that my daily devotions did honour to his monument—Linden House—in this sad year I strained myself as never before to embrace my ideal. It was a doomed endeavour. My whole energy was given to maintaining the appearance of a gentleman, but whereas this had once been a careless delight (careless yet manufactured with care), it was now a continual anxiety. I looked upon tradesmen as though they were devils. I did not often entertain my friends at home. My trusty nag Contributor stamped in his stall, and yet I could not frequently give him his exercise, for want of a regular fellow to be of service to me. My equally trusty New-foundlander, Neptune, when he laid his heavy muzzle upon my knee, groaned aloud for the bitterness he could read in my heart. Even Eliza and our little one kept from me, fearing the wrath which is nourished by despair.

Yet the beauties which still surrounded me were not all wasted. Indeed, my delight in their power was a continual goad, urging me to begin my recovery. By recovery I do not mean, simply, my efforts to resolve my business with Sharpus, Atkinson and suchlike. I mean some other plan, which would allow my life to remain within my own control.

It was shortly after I began contemplating my new scheme, that an unforeseen event disturbed the course I had set myself. Eliza's mother, Mrs. Abercromby, having encountered difficulties of her own, and being of an age which made them especially arduous, declared that she could no longer maintain her lodging house in Mortlake, and would be grateful for accommodation in Linden House—herself and her two daughters, Helen and Madeleine. [1] This news made me, in the ship of my thoughts, summon all hands on deck, haul in the sails, toss an anchor over the side, and hope to catch fast on something solid. I believed (not to put too fine a point upon it) that it represented the end of the plan I was formulating—which filled me with indignation, until I considered everything again, and saw something to my advantage in the altered circumstances.

Mrs. Abercromby had shown kindness to me during the early days of my marriage. But even then, when my ability to live as a gentleman was sorely constricted, she frowned upon my aspirations. She was a woman well acquainted with poverty and hardship, and the opposite filled her with apprehension. Over the years, I confess, she became a little shrewish with me. Of her daughters, Madeleine the younger was the most like her mother—a slight, fair, trembling creature, who desired strong opinions and strong characters around her so that she might know her own mind. The elder sister, Helen, was a beauty, as even that fierce judge the Professor had seen, calling upon her to model for him as I have said, and extending his kindness into many real conversations with her. I sympathized with his interest, having made Helen a part of my own life on occasion. She had dined at my table and been entertained by my friends. She knew the hopes of my heart, and in the temple of her beauty had remained knowledgeable enough about the world to understand that her privileges must be paid for. This loyalty to my own ambitions made her precious to me. [2]

Had I been a cynical man, I should have smiled to think how Linden House must have seemed to those gazing from the Mall across its spreading lawns. A place of bustle and quickness; its scintillating windows ajar in the daylight to admit the fresh spring scents, and glowing at night with a glimpse of a Bonasoni here, a Lewis there. Yet at any moment, everything might crumble and disappear—the prints be ripped from the walls and the book torn from my hand—unless I could sail onwards again and effect my own rescue. Away from the brightness and the business, I called my Eliza up on deck beside me, and eventually Helen.

When a secret has been announced to the panelled pomp of the Old Bailey, and when it has flown up against its mullioned windows—longing to escape into the open air and be lost for ever—and when it has found no release but instead sunk down wearily again into the ears of the common mob—then it may safely be assumed to be a secret no longer. Having watched the process myself, and suffered the fate consequent upon it, I have no hesitation now in giving the details of the new plan I have been mentioning, seeing that it has long since been dragged into the light of common day. In mitigation of myself, I will only point out how my wife Eliza and Helen both drove it forward eagerly, and without threats from me.

Soon after arriving under my roof, Helen came of age (that is to say, in the spring of 1830). An even shorter while after this, she took herself with Eliza to the offices of the Palladium Insurance Company, and requested a policy on her life. She subsequently visited a number of other such establishments, saying what was necessary, and omitting what was not, until a veritable fortune had been amassed on her pretty head. It was a tedious business, and also an anxious one, and I well remember her returning from town with the grime of the high road disfiguring her cheek, and a look of weary confusion in her eye. On each occasion, I was able to recover her spirits by reminding her how parlous our condition would shortly become, were it not for her courage. At this intelligence, Helen lifted her face and strengthened herself for a fresh battle on the morrow. Truly, I never admired the admirable creature more than during this summer, nor my wife either.

My enemies have always supposed it inevitable that Helen would be sacrificed on the altar of my intentions. To this I can only ask: what person would be a party to plans resulting in their own destruction? The question does not deserve an answer—though I shall provide one. Helen understood that once our arrangements were complete, we would be quitting England, discreetly, for a place where all our family would prosper, and learn to accommodate in our comfortable bosoms the uncomfortable loss of our former home.

When I allowed myself to dream of our life to come, my imagination was filled with long views: scenes from lofty mountain tops, such as the Professor might have created; dizzy prospects over golden meadows; the free passage of a breeze across open water, teasing the surface into bright curls and crests, so that the idle onlooker might mark its progress. What I discovered, in fact, was dismal narrowness and constriction. At all times in my previous existence, even during my apprenticeship with Mr. P., and especially when I came into my own as a *Londoner,* I had spurned any thoughts of littleness. I had woven wings for myself, and flown high above the mean things of the world, getting and giving splendour. Now when I fluttered and skipped, straining for the heavens, I remained earthbound. With each day, it seemed, some new creditor appeared on the steps of my home, wringing his hands and my heart. When I patrolled my plantation, the cool rustle of leaves did nothing to soothe the jangling of my nerves, or to ease the ache that had taken a grip around my brow.

It is a commonplace to observe that any succession of happy days must end with a time of sorrow. The sun shines upon our faces, but even as it warms us, vapours are being drawn out of the earth, and turned into clouds beyond the horizon, which at any moment will roll towards us and blight our hopes. But what of the man such as myself, whose life is already unhappy? May he expect the process vice versa? No, he may not. The man who is already full of woe must expect his misery to deepen. Life snatches at its unfortunates like a cat seizing upon a mouse, plays with them all-powerfully while they struggle to regain their freedom, and at the end crushes them.

I shall show what I mean. During this summer, my business with Helen and Eliza had given me some cause for joy; yet it seemed that I had only to suspect fortune of considering me kindly for me to be cast down again. Sharpus came at me with his teeth flashing and nipping, so that it was only by the most strenuous exertion that I turned him aside. Much worse than this, I was compelled to grant a Bill of Sale on the furniture and effects of Linden House. [3]

This was the heaviest blow to fall, though by the time it struck, my senses were so numb with grief, I could scarcely feel the shame of my predicament. Ever since I had first opened my eyes on this world, the sky that I had seen brighten and darken, the trees I had watched clothing themselves in green, then standing bare, the voices of all the creatures I had known in God's kingdom—the wrens and squirrels, the jackdaws, and the simple sparrows, the thrushes and the lovely liquid nightingales—all of them had seemed to derive from the one source and be sanctified by their origin. Moreover, everything that was man-made had been blessed in the same way. Linden House was not the grandest mansion in the land, but it was a whole kingdom to me: the apogee of my dreams, and the very definition of my desire. To have it now, at last, in my grasp, and to lose it within a few paltry months! To think of a stranger's hand creeping across the pages in my library, then pointing out the twist of a hair, or the throw of a cloth, in some drawing which my own eyes had made holy by contemplation! To imagine some other fingers stumbling through my drawers and cupboards, probing among my clothes, my papers, my sketches, my everything! Even now I cannot endure it. It is a desecration of the spirit, and a devastation of the Self.

Seeing me thus brought to my lowest point, Life then began its game of cat-and-mouse. In the spring of this year my uncle Foss died. It was not a loss that hurt me, though in my letter to his son Edward (which I have already described), I sympathized exceedingly with my good and pious cousins, insisting they would doubtless look for another meeting with their father in Eternity. My larger thought was that the old man, while still breathing, had been attached to the Trust I had taken as my own, and in death might become a kind of air-bag, dragging the papers towards the light. What I had undertaken with the signatures, etc., in order to possess my money, I had done many years previously: I could scarcely consider myself the same person now as then. Yet I still created the same silhouette. I still bore the same name.

On my uncle's death, therefore, I inherited nothing but greater cares in the world. And a short while after I had attended his obsequies, my wife's mother followed him into the blaze of Heaven's glory. I have heard it suggested, by the calumniator Sarah Handcock and others, that an unspeakable connection might be made between this unfortunate event and my own circumstances. I shall answer the charge, if charge it be, in the same way that I have done elsewhere. If my need was for money, why should I contemplate any action where no gain was conceivable?

As before, I have asked a question that does not merit an answer. Therefore I shall do no more than quietly close the old lady's eyes. She had been compassionate in times of past need, and the agonies of her decline were a trial for those who witnessed them. It is a sad truth that when all other ener-

1. Ralph Griffiths (1720–1803), founder-editor of the *Monthly Review* and TGW's grandfather-guardian. TGW thought he was mean-spirited; Josiah Wedgwood called him "impatient" but "a dear friend."

2. Linden House, Chiswick: TGW's gracious and inspirational childhood home, a place he would go to murderous lengths to inherit.

3. The Rev. Charles Burney, Jr. (1754–1817): TGW's schoolmaster, and "one of the best Greek and Latin scholars of the day."

4. Burney's school, at the foot of Croom's Hill in Greenwich, where TGW was a pupil. It was demolished in 1839.

5. John Linnell (1792–1882): Henry Fuseli's "little giant," William Blake's friend and TGW's first art master.

6. Thomas Phillips (1770–1845; self-portrait, 1820) to whom TGW was apprenticed when he left Linnell, and whom he later called "a great man of color."

7. The "Cloak Portrait" of Byron. Phillips first painted it in 1813, and subsequently made several copies; the version shown here was originally owned by Byron himself.

8. TGW's portrait of Byron, also painted in 1813, emphasizing its sitter's sensuality.

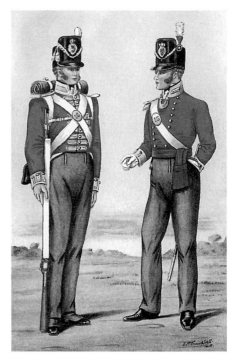

9. *The Bold Lover* (late 1810s?) by TGW. The scene illustrates Margaret of Navarre's *Heptameron, XVI*, to which TGW had been introduced by Henry Fuseli. It is typical of the mildly salacious work produced by TGW during his painting career in London.

10. Officers of the 16th Foot (otherwise known as the Bedfordshire Regiment of Foot), which TGW joined in April 1814 and left in May 1815. He was impressed by the regiment's uniforms, which allowed him to seem at once gallant and dandified.

11. *An Amorous Scene* (1821?) by TGW: another saucy work which also shows the influence of Henry Fuseli.

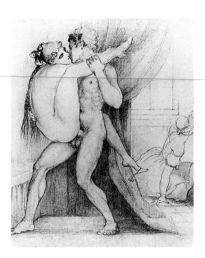

12–14. Three "melting love drawings" (c. 1820); 12 and 13 probably by Henry Fuseli, 14 most likely by Theodore von Holst. TGW is also said to have produced such images, but none of them survives.

15. Self-portrait by Henry Fuseli (1741–1825), TGW's friend and the "god of his worship," c. 1777.
16. William Blake (1757–1827) by John Linnell. In the 1820s, TGW bought
several important works from Blake.

17. Sketch for "A Dream after Reading Goethe's *Walpurgisnacht*": a self-portrait by
Theodore von Holst (1810–1844), TGW's brilliant and eccentric kindred spirit.
18. Sketch of TGW by Theodore von Holst, c. 1825. It shows how similar they were
in appearance and tastes.

19. Charles Lamb (1775–1834) by William Hazlitt.
20. William Hazlitt (1778–1830) by William Bewick, 1825.

21. Barry Cornwall (Bryan Procter; 1787–1874) by William Brockedon, 1830.
22. John Scott (1783–1821), the editor of the *London Magazine*, by Seymour Kirkup, 1819.

23. John Taylor (1781–1864), who took over as editor of the *London Magazine* after Scott was killed in a duel. By an unknown artist, c. 1820.

24. The Rev. H. F. Cary (1772–1844), after a painting by F. Cary, 1847.

25. Thomas de Quincey (1785–1859) by Sir John Watson-Gordon, c. 1845.

26. John Clare (1793–1864) by William Hilton, 1820.

27. TGW's portrait of Helen Abercromby, his wife's half-sister and his own victim, c. 1825.

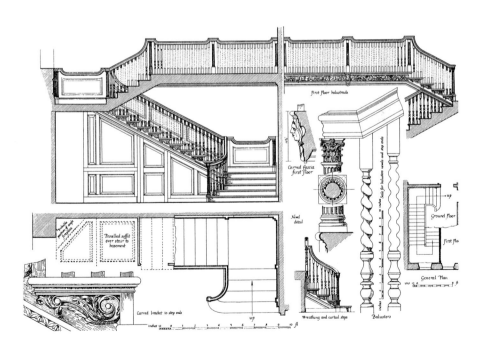

28. A plan of the staircase leading up to TGW's rooms in 49 Great Marlborough Street, where he lived and entertained extravagantly from 1821 to 1828.

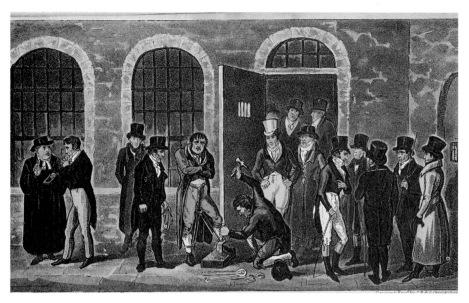

29. Newgate Prison, London, c. 1820, where TGW was incarcerated on his return to England from France in May 1837, and where he was glimpsed by Charles Dickens.

30. A prison hulk similar to the one in which TGW was held at Portsmouth between 23 and 29 July 1837.

31. Campbell Street, Hobart Town (showing the Theatre Royal and the Old Treasury) by Thomas Evans Chapman, 1840. When TGW arrived in Van Diemen's Land in November 1837, he was held in the Barracks on Campbell Street, and towards the end of his life he set up a studio near the theatre.

32. "Old Hobart Town chain gang, c. 1840." TGW was put to work "on the roads" for the whole of his first year in Van Diemen's Land.

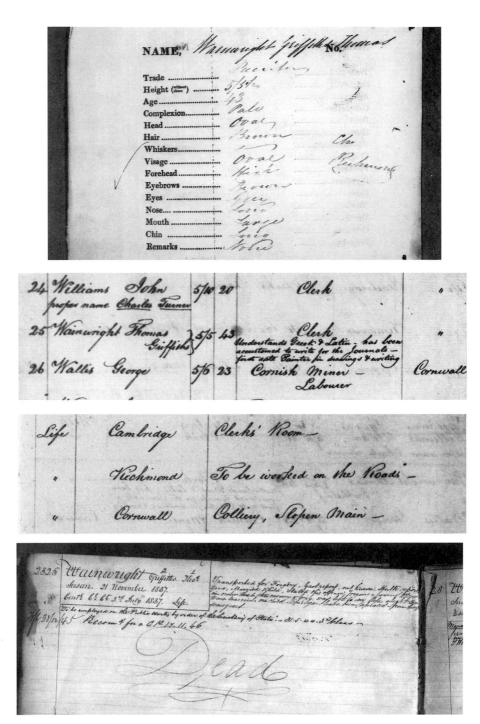

33–34. TGW's "mugging" document and further particulars, the latter taken when he appeared before the convict authorities in the Barracks on Campbell Street on the morning of 22 November 1837.

35. TGW's entry in the "assignment book" relating to convicts who had been transported on the *Susan*; "Dead" added later.

36. The young Hobart doctor Frederick Brodribb by TGW, 1840s.
37. Frederick's younger sister, Maria Brodribb, by TGW, 1840s.

38. The Superintendent of Schools, the Rev. William Bedford ("Holy Willie"), by TGW, 1840s.
39. Assistant Surgeon Robert Nuttall by TGW, 1840s.

40. Julia Sorrell by TGW, c. 1846: the daughter of the registrar of the Supreme Court and later wife of Thomas Arnold and mother of Mrs Humphry Ward.
41. Mrs Downing by TGW, 1840s.

42. The Cutmere twins, Jane and Lucy, 1840s.

43. TGW's self-portrait "Head of a Convict, very characteristic of low cunning and revenge," 1840s.

To His Excellency Sir John Eardly Wilmot. Bart.
Lieut. Governor of Van Dieman's Land, &c. &c

The Humble Petition of T. Griffiths Wainewright
praying the Indulgence of a Ticket of Leave — Susan (?)²

To palliate the boldness of this application he offers the state-
-ment ensueing. That seven years past he was arrested on
a charge of Forging & acting on, a power of Attorney to sell stock
13 years previous. Of which (tho' looking for little credence) he avers
his entire Innocence. He admits a knowledge of the actual commit-
-ter, gained tho', some years after the fact. Such however were their
relative positions that to have disclosed it would have made him
infamous where any human feeling is manifest. Nevertheless, by
his Counsels direction, he entered the plea not Guilty, to allow him
to adduce the "circonstance attenuante" viz. that the money (£5200) appro-
-priated was, without quibble, his own, derived from his parents.
An hour before his appearing to plead he was trepanned (thro' the
just but deluded Gov.ⁿ of Newgate) into withdrawing his plea, by a
promise, in such case, of a punishment merely nominal. The same
purporting to issue from ye Bank Parlour, but in fact from the
agents of certain Insurance Comp.ⁱᵉˢ interested to a heavy amount
(£16000) in compassing his legal non-existence. He pleaded
Guilty

44. The first page of TGW's petition for a ticket-of-leave, written in 1844, three years before he died.

gies have left the human form, and it is fit for nothing but sleep, it finds some secret reserve of power as it approaches the great and final moment of change. The last convulsions and apprehensions of Mrs. Abercromby were remarkable to behold. In the bosom of Heaven, may she sleep an untroubled sleep. [4]

Since the time I am describing, I have often had occasion to ponder the mercies of extinction. I have considered the sufferings that a body may be made to endure—the torments and deprivations, the longings and humiliations—until my brain seemed hot inside my skull. Then I have suddenly turned my thoughts to the contemplation of nothing, and felt all the heat and intensity pass from me, so that I seemed to be drifting, like a creature in the deep of the ocean, beyond all threat and harm.

Why, therefore, did not I dispatch myself before my sufferings became intolerable, since the gift to bestow or remove life lies in the power of each of us? The reply is simple. To have done so would have been to proclaim my guilt to the whole universe. I had rather suffer and be defiant.

Yet as the wheels of the funeral carriages rumbled through that year, and the bright days of summer gave way to the brief gold of autumn, then the dull state of winter, I believe that I did suffer death of a sort. When, in a different circumstance, Eliza and I would have been preparing for Christmas, my best efforts at cheer were all blasted. That most despised worm, that incubus far more demonic than any that haunted the nightmares of my most fantastical friends, that foul fiend the BAILIFF entered Linden House and took possession. He came stealthily, creeping in with a regretful air and a bad habit of fiddling his hat around in his hands, making sideways glances through the room at what would soon be his. For all his quietness, he might as well have broken down my door and stamped through my hall, noisily wreaking havoc. No Roman in the Capitol, watching the triumph of the barbarians as they took their liberties with his sacred city, could have grieved as I did over the arrival of this single predator. No innocent Trojan, alarmed by the fires of an enemy beyond his walls, could have moved around his familiar and endangered home with more sorrow. [5]

It was not an immediate departure. Yet since it was impossible for me to endure proximity to such a rude reminder of my shame, I cast about eagerly for lodgings apart from Linden House, and soon had success. (If success it can be called, to submit to such a loss.) As to the question of my collecting some belongings to take with me—it did not apply. "I shall depart as my essential self," I told our cuckoo-bailiff, "and with such life as I need within a single bag." I might have developed this thought in some diverting way, had I not seen that my language was more obscure than Greek to his ears. Whereupon I left him to his dismal business, and went about my own, which was to take my life apart like something that had offended me, and grind its fragments under my own heel. [6]

1. Mrs. Abercromby was in serious financial difficulties by the end of 1828. Earlier in the year she had borrowed £200 from her rent collector, James Stewart, and although he gradually repaid himself by withholding rents from her, he was still £40 out of pocket by the end of the year. In December her Mortlake house was sold for £200.

2. A number of people called Helen "beautiful." In a sketch of her by TGW, however, she has a bow mouth, solemn eyes and a stodgy expression. Maybe this tells us more about TGW's feminine ideal than it does about her actual looks.

3. The Warranty of Attorney due to Sharpus in August 1830, and worth £610, was deferred until 22 December. The Bill of Sale on the contents of Linden House was granted on 8 July.

4. According to most sources, including W. C. Hazlitt and Curling, Mrs. Abercromby was in good health when she made her will six days before she died, but her death itself, on 19 August 1830, was "sudden," and "in the most agonizing convulsions" (Curling, p. 232). Paul Hopkins, however, in a letter to the author (18 April 1999), points out that according to the Chiswick Parish Registers in St. Nicholas, Chiswick, she died in Mortlake "a full year earlier"—on 22 August 1829 (information from de Chantilly). The fact that the Confession is unreliable here is typical of TGW's behaviour as a whole; like many of his other lies, it mixes genuine forgetfulness with deviousness, guilt, and a love of playing games with his own existence.

5. A sheriff's representative was installed in Linden House in November 1830.

6. Until 1808, there was no way of investing money in life annuities that was "at once safe and profitable" (Francis, p. 199); although plenty of small insurance companies existed, the public tended to regard them with suspicion. In 1809, the government began dealing in life annuities, but this only made a bad situation worse, since the method used to calculate premiums was as dodgy as its predecessors. Even in the late 1820s and early 1830s, when TGW began planning his fraud, the whole business of life insurance was confused and irregular, which helps to explain why TGW managed to take out so many policies simultaneously, and why no one noticed that he was a virtual bankrupt and Helen was a healthy young girl who lived more or less entirely under his control.

Helen's movements during the late spring, summer and early autumn of 1830 are hectic but clear.

On 25 March, eleven days after her twenty-first birthday, she went with TGW and Eliza to the Eagle Insurance Company, where TGW applied for a life insurance policy on Helen's behalf. (It is possible that Eliza impersonated Madeleine at this meeting; see Curling, p. 385.)

On 31 March, the same people went to the Palladium Insurance Company for the same reason.

On 20 April Helen went back to the Palladium with Eliza, signed the policy, and paid a premium of £39 plus £4 stamp duty. Her life was now insured at £3000 for three years. Some lies were told during this meeting. Helen said she was twenty-two not twenty-one, and when the actuary, Nicholas Grute, asked why the policy was for only a short period, Eliza said "it was to raise money to enable them to get possession of property which would fall in within three years." When questioned about her reasons for wanting the policy, Helen said "she had been told it was proper to do it."

On 30 April, Helen and Eliza went back to the Eagle, where they paid another premium and stamp duty, and signed a policy worth £3000 for three years.

On 25 September TGW went alone to the Pelican Insurance Company and requested a life insurance policy for Helen for £5000 for two years.

On 28 September Eliza presented a Bill of Exchange at Jones, Lloyd and Co., intending to use the money she received to pay the premiums of future policies.

On 1 October Eliza and Helen completed the policy with the Pelican, seeing the Company Secretary, Monkhouse Tate, and leaving the premium to be paid at a later date. Also on 1 October, Helen completed the policy with the Pelican. She then went to the Globe Insurance Company and proposed a policy worth £5000 for two years on her own life. Shortly after leaving the offices, she returned to them with Eliza, who apologized for the confused state of her "half-sister" to the Company Secretary, John Denham, saying, "There are some money matters to be arranged. Ladies do not know much about these things." Denham accused Helen of insuring herself elsewhere, and refused to sign her up in spite of her denials.

On 5 October Helen and Eliza went to the Alliance Insurance Company, seeking a £5000 policy for two years. When questioned by the Company Secretary, Andrew Hamilton, Helen said "a suit was pending in Chancery, which will probably terminate in her favour, but that if she should die in the interval, this property would go to another family." She added, tartly, "I supposed what you had to enquire into was the state of my health, not the object for insurance." Hamilton explained that his question had been prompted by a recent case involving the murder of a client, and Helen replied, "I'm sure there is no one about me who could have any such object." Hamilton said, "Of course not," but still refused to give her a policy.

On 8 October Eliza and Helen went back to the Pelican, and paid a premium of £51 9s 2d plus stamp duty. Helen paid with a £50 note and a £10 note, which were later identified as those she had received on 28 September from Jones, Lloyd and Co.

On 15 October Eliza and Helen returned to the Eagle, seeking to increase the value of the policy there from £3000 to £5000; they were refused. On the same day they visited the Hope Insurance Company, seeking a policy of £2000 for two years, and the Imperial Insurance Company, asking for the same deal; Eliza said she wanted "to secure a sum of money to her sister, which she will be enabled to do by other means if she outlives that time." She went on, "But I don't know much about her affairs, you had better speak to her about it." Helen then told the Company Secretary, "That is so," and with Eliza denied that she was insuring herself elsewhere.

On 19 October Helen returned to the Hope, where she was passed fit by the medical officer.

On 20 October Helen went with TGW to the Provident Insurance Company, where she applied for a policy worth £2000 for two years. She was accepted, but took no further steps to clinch the deal.

On 22 October, Helen returned to the Imperial, where she was given a second tough grilling, and accused of insuring herself elsewhere. She said she "knew very little about the transaction and was acting on the advice of friends"—whereupon she was given her policy.

On 27 October the policy with the Hope was completed.

In other words, between March and October 1830, Helen had paid out premiums worth £220 (the money all coming from TGW and Eliza), and had insured her life with five separate companies for a total value of £16,000 for two (and in the case of the Palladium, three) years. All the officials who saw her agreed that she was, in the words of the Actuary at the Provident, "a remarkably healthy, cheerful, beautiful young woman, whose life was one in a thousand."

14

KNOCK, KNOCK, KNOCK

*H*ow does a person imagine his own brain? To one it might resemble a newfangled machine composed of rods and pistons, giving a whiff of steam as a notion is driven forward. To another it might be a calm lake, troubled only by the shadow of a cloud. To a third it might be a dreadful mine, which to enter is anguish, and where the least work is the hardest labour. To yet another it might be a series of chambers, each representing a different degree of thoughtfulness, and leading eventually to a comprehensive wisdom.

The idea that I have of my own mind is this: it is a labyrinth, in which every thought expects to be baffled, but is not deterred by the prospect. Rather, it feels nerved for the endeavour, and without this prospect might not produce any thoughts at all. By which I mean: in all the dire emergencies which beset me at this time, amidst all the miseries and losses, I showed no sign of wavering, but held a steady course. It is a sad truth: a man may discover his life even as he loses it.

I must admit, however: to order the carriage which would sweep me away from Linden House on that never-to-be-forgotten day (Sunday, 12 December 1830); to see it draw up with a confusion of snorts and jangles before my door; to climb aboard as readily as if I were keeping a dinner appointment; then to look back at the red-faced bailiff planted in the doorway—as these things came to pass, they tested my dignity to the limit. The sobs of Helen, in particular, were terrible to hear, and the silence of my Eliza—who held our infant in her arms the whole while, leaving our woman Handcock with nothing to do but dab her watering eyes—was more oppressive than a tombstone. [1]

The district I had settled on for our new home was no disgrace, being the same, almost, as I had enjoyed when I lived in Great Marlborough Street. But O! the contrast between those days and now. Then, at first, I had been free to look upon the passing world and not fear its returning gaze; now when I squinted through our tight windows into the street, I felt the least glance in my direction would scorch me.

For this reason, and because of what I am about to relate, I cannot remember that house with any degree of happiness. It was number 12 Conduit Street, which had a beneficial proximity to Warne's and Weigall's (so that my charges could enjoy the fashionable comings and goings at those two hotels), and also to Collins's Coffee House at number 19, where I might even be seen myself on occasion, if circumstances allowed it. Yet to my mind the quality of the place was marred by its being situated above the shop of a tailor—one Nichols. I have seen this poor man sitting in his window, plying his trade by the dim light of a winter sky, and reflected to myself that all our days are a kind of prison, whether we admit the fact or not.

I had little opportunity to dwell on such thoughts for long. No sooner had we settled into our rooms than the weight of business pressed me forward. Indeed the next ten days of my life passed at such a speed they seemed to squeeze all the breath from my body and leave me in a state which was neither entirely of this world nor of the next.

My first affairs were all legal, and related to the completion of plans I had made with Helen. In her excitement that our difficulties would soon be resolved, and in the sweetness of her courage, she seemed more beautiful at this time than any other. I thanked fortune that I had such a creature to help me. Yet as soon as my business was afoot, its main agent—I mean Helen herself—was afflicted with an illness which altered the course of our lives entirely. And since this illness soon proved grievous, and became the subject of my whole attention, I would be playing false if I did not now concentrate my memory upon it entirely. [2]

On the evening following our arrival in town, I had taken it upon myself to rally the spirits of my party by conducting them on a visit to the theatre. It was a taste of our former times together, and a flavour of other times yet to come—times when we would once again give ourselves to pleasure. It was our particular good luck, I recollect, to make a choice between Kemble at Covent Garden (Kemble who always carried the gentleman in every recollection), and Macready at Drury Lane (Macready whose inspiring countenance I had seen opposite me AT MY OWN TABLE in Great Marlborough Street).

I dare say my companions considered themselves happy to be in the society of one who had been intimate with these men. Helen, who was in something of a pother following her day's exertions, was especially tender with me about my opinions—which I afterwards remembered with an unusual delicacy of my own. She implored me, I recollect, that I should not make her decide between two superlatives, but allow her to see first one and then the other. And so it was to be. On that first evening of our new life we carried ourselves along to admire the commanding figure of Kemble, who carried *us* along exactly as we desired; and the following evening we put ourselves under the spell of Macready.

What better way to revive a heart sunk low under powerful emotion, and to recompose a mind shattered by beauty, than to feed it with ale and lobsters! That was our diet on the night of our first expedition; and then after our second: oysters and bottled porter. (Which I admit was against my usual custom, since porter is generally acceptable only in the country, where nothing else may be had.)

Critics may wonder why I descend at this point in my story to the dull cave of the stomach, and take up my abode there. But knowing what I am about to relate, I am bound to think it germane—as any man will agree, who has tasted these delectables, and then repented of his appetite. For on the morning following our return to crustacea, Helen did indeed pay for her pleasure. Within the confines of Conduit Street, it was impossible not to sympathize with her complaints, her groans being terrible and her silences far worse.

Little did I think they would not soon be over. Yet as hour succeeded hour, Eliza, Madeleine and I seemed to exist at her bedside in a sort of permanent twilight. Passengers would clop along the street below: they were nothing to us. Carriage wheels would roll and rumble: they were a dream. Our one reality was the fair head of Helen upon the pillow, her skin blanched to a deadly pallor, and her forehead sprinkled with the beads of her distress.

From the start of the wretched business, I took upon myself the leading role in attending to her needs. On the first morning, at the very earliest opportunity, I dispatched our woman Handcock to an apothecary near by, instructing her to lay hands upon a black draught. [3] To my own great discomfort, this did nothing to ease the suffering of my patient—who, though she showed strong control of her emotions, could not prevent herself from occasionally vomiting, and from twisting and untwisting herself in very much the same manner as her mother had done. (I remarked upon this to Handcock, who later turned it against me.) My own belief, which I shared with everyone who listened, was that the effect of the oysters, combined with the fact that it had rained heavily on our latest visit to the theatre, which meant that all my little ones reached home with their clothes and shoes half ruined by water—my own belief was that the illness lay upon her stomach.

~~This lasted until the Wednesday evening when, after watching over her~~ alone for some considerable time, I left Helen sleeping fitfully. I shall never forget the sound of her breathing in those quiet hours. With the grey moon-light falling upon her bed, and the unfamiliar shapes and colours of the rooms all around me, I sometimes fancied that she had died already, and taken me with her to some new place. I was not troubled by this notion. No; I believe that I allowed myself whole minutes of supposing all my anxieties were done with, and I was freed at last from the necessity to account for myself and my past life. But something would always break my reverie and drag me back. The bell of a clock sounding over the starlit roofs, a moan or some other small sound that escaped Helen's mouth. When I was fixed upon her in this manner, and upon each breath she drew in—it made me want to stop my own lungs from working, I was so filled with dread that she might cease to be.

On Thursday morning, seeing that no improvement had become evident during the night, I summoned a doctor—one Locock, of Hanover Square, whom I had known in my days upon the town. He was a good young man, observant, and considerate; in everything that followed, I had no reason to doubt his intentions. I remained at his side while he examined Helen, who was now sitting in her bedroom and complaining of a great headache, and of shooting pains about her generally. She felt, she said, a great weight pressing on her eyes, as if an invisible and heavy hand were attempting to close them (and had already made her half-blind)—whereupon Locock looked closely into her pupils, and noticed that they were uncommonly dilated. The con-clusion of this learned man was that her recent meals had indeed poisoned her system, as I had suggested to him, and that in spite of her pain, and of the labouring pulse he detected in her neck and wrist, she must needs raise her-self and endeavour to purge her system. He administered to her a little camomile and senna, as an aperient, and promised he would return on the morrow.

When it devoutly desires a thing, the human mind is easily able to deceive itself. One of the most affecting illusions I have suffered in my own time occurred during the night following Locock's first visit. I convinced myself that a steadier note could be heard in Helen's breathing, and a rud-dier glow be seen in her cheek. As I rose from my own bed the next day, refreshed by my hopefulness, I remained the victim of my deception—and so did Locock. When the doctor made his visit, he also pronounced her "improving," cupping her with a glass to speed the process of her recovery, administering a tartar emetic to steady her pulse, and ordering her to rise from her bed for dinner. Although it made us nervous to see how severely she shivered, lying upon the settle while we clanked away at a table near by, our delight at seeing our sister amongst us once more far outweighed all our other considerations. Before she retired again, I cheerfully gave her another black draught, as our doctor had instructed.

All the day following we kept our breathless watch, and the frail vessel of our patient seemed to hold her course towards health—looking into my eye with a brighter glance when I bent to bestow a kiss upon her golden hair; squeezing my fingers more boldly when I offered her my hand for encouragement. Her appetite, too, seemed restored, and she was able to take some soup. Yet just as I believed we were entering calm waters at last, when the storm seemed past and the sun once more fixed in the heavens, there appeared more terrible thunder-heads than any we had previously imagined. Late in the evening of Sunday, Helen began vomiting copiously, and continued all the night and the next day. It was a terrible thing to hear, and more terrible still to behold: the body of our sister no longer her own to control, nor her mind either—which, as the fever took her in its grip, began to wander wherever it chose. She imagined a young boy had come into the room, who she knew ought not to have been there, and therefore sobbed piteously at his continued stay, so that eventually he became a kind of miniature ogre for her. These and other ravings struck horror into all of us, and often, when she herself sank into exhaustion and silence, the tears of one or other of us could be heard elsewhere in the lodgings.

In my present existence—I mean my time away from England and familiar comforts—I have known men bid adieu to their own lives long before they have finished with them in fact. I have seen shadows going about human business (if it can be called business to break stones and cart sacks). I have shaken hands with rags. I have walked down a road with a scarecrow, and exchanged words with him. In every case, the vital spark was extinguished, and the purpose of action forgotten. But in those last days of Helen, I saw a determination for life which wrung my heart. Wrung it so painfully, I cannot perfectly remember the sequence of things which followed, only the moment which ended everything. Locock came and was attentive as ever, ordering a black draught as he saw fit. Locock shook his head and puzzled, commending Eliza and myself on the care we showed.

Locock gave Helen a camphor pill, and other intended remedies. Locock shook his head and puzzled again, with a longer face.

On Tuesday, after the doctor had made his morning visit, and once more been unable to give us the benefit of a happy report, Eliza and I held a consultation together, as we were wont to do at this time, for advice and comfort. We resolved that Helen would be better for another black draught, of which the nauseous flavour would be disguised, as usual, by administering it in a jelly. When this was done—the weather of the day being somewhat warmer than of late—we took a stroll in the nearby streets, leaving our old servant Handcock at the bedside.

Never was a moment for self-recovery worse chosen. At around two in the afternoon, according to the evidence of Handcock, Helen was thrown into dreadful convulsions—and while these held her in their grip, her beauty lost its form, the form which had delighted Fuseli and Holst, and had been a lamp to light me through the gloom of my recent days. Her face set in a desperate grin, as though she were being entertained by the very devil which undermined her. Handcock immediately sent her fellow domestic Grattan to the apothecaries—King and Nicholson were their names—who promptly sent their assistant Edward Hanks to our lodgings, whereupon Grattan went on to find Locock, who fortunately was at home. Hurrying to the bedside, Locock found Hanks standing at a loss, and Helen in convulsions and hysterical. "Oh doctor, I am dying," she told him, which was a sad though reasonable truth. Then she continued in her raving, as Handcock later reported: "My mother died in the same way, yes, my poor mother! Oh, my poor mother!" It has often grieved me that this coincidence of suffering should have oppressed Helen in her final hours, and not only because of the rumours it appeared to license, which gave the utmost offence to my own name. At the time, however, none of us was distracted by such thoughts, and Locock fixed his mind instead on delivering a new prescription, and on watching a kind of peace descend. "Oh doctor," then said the dear girl, "I was gone to Heaven, but you have brought me back to earth."

It was not permitted for her to remain where she so desired to stay. When Locock subsequently went on his way rejoicing, Helen's pains returned as if at a signal, and although Hanks was again summoned, neither he nor anyone else to hand could reinforce the shattered bastion of Helen's defences against the most intense and, as it proved, final assault of her affliction. Her lovely frame could no longer control the demon which made it suffer, and her spirit preferred to take up a calmer station, where it might look down in pity and sorrow on all those who mourned her passing, and have ever since kept a vigil for her in their hearts. She died, I believe, with the fingers of one dainty hand fixed so tightly around the wrist of the servant Grattan, it afterwards had to be prised loose with some force. [4]

The shock that Eliza and I felt, on arriving back at the house around four thirty in the afternoon, and finding Locock already there, drawing a sheet over the face of one whom we desired to see more than any other—the shock cannot be measured. In answer to my question "Why?," which was all that I could utter, Locock answered, "Mischief on the brain," which was as good (or as bad) as saying nothing. And for the whole of that evening, *nothing* became the complete subject of my melancholy meditation. A mere ten days previously, my little band had been crammed with schemes for salvation, with our minds fixed on purpose and progress. Now we were full of misery and confusion, unable even to take a light dinner (which I counselled would be restorative) for thinking of her lying in the nether room, whose beauty would never shine on us again.

Would that I had been able to prolong my grief further, or give it the scope that it deserved. But it was not to be. Eliza and I upbraided ourselves, and said we would do so eternally, for our neglect of a final farewell to our sister, and immediately became clamorous for an inquest, which was soon arranged. It was discovered that an accumulation of water had amassed at the base of Helen's brain, and that curious specks had appeared on the coat of her stomach, which were blamed on the shellfish and the bottled beer. There were no other symptoms, and the wretched event of the death was accordingly deemed natural, though it hardly seemed so to those who mourned. Nor, I am compelled to add, did it appear so to my enemies, who immediately began implying motives, and insinuating crimes, that I cannot bring myself to say aloud, even today. Yet I have never considered their accusations worthy of a rational rebuttal; to prove the sincerity of my feelings, I have merely to point out the lasting evidence of my sorrow. [5]

The inquest was not the only business which crowded upon me, denying me the feelings I should properly have entertained at that sombre time. Even in the midst of my sorrow, the jaws of my creditors did not cease from snapping at me, tearing my own vital spirits. On the very evening of Helen's death—with her body yet warm, and her hands only composed upon her breast a moment previously, so that her extinct form might yet have been mistaken for its sleeping but living counterpart—I was compelled to pay a visit to my detested Sharpus. At the time of my arrival he knew nothing of my loss. By the time of my departure, I had acquainted him with the fact that death, which had deprived me of a sister I loved, had in the same stroke provided a means of settling my account with him. [6]

It was my only consolation during this desolate time. Never can a family have sat down to their Christmas feast with so little appetite for merriment, as I did with my brood a matter of days after we had laid Helen in the earth. While the pleasures of London sounded in the streets outside, and the bells sent their message of happiness through the frosty air, we kept within our lodgings. Whenever we looked back to the past, we saw only a futile race to escape the contrivances of a malign fate. If we glanced ahead to the future, we saw prosperity we could not easily enjoy, knowing whence it came. The thought of our new life being planted in the body of our dear sister, and growing from her as if she could still nourish us from beyond the grave, was shocking to me. On the last night of the year, I recollect, I went to my bed long before the hands of the clock had stood to attention at the top of the hour. I could not easily master the feelings which boiled within me. When I closed my eyes and implored sleep to take me in its forgetful arms, the face of Helen appeared before me with a terrible clarity. Her expressionless gaze, and the plain simplicity of her continuing existence in my mind, hurt me more than a thousand threats and remonstrations. I believed that she would haunt me to Eternity, and never find a settled place among the things that have been.

1. It was traditional for householders to pay their local creditors at Christmas; because TGW left Linden House on 12 December, he was able to avoid doing this. As well as Eliza, Helen, Madeleine and his son, he took with him two servants: Sarah Handcock and Harriet Grattan.

2. In the last two days of her healthy life, Helen continued her legal business at a furious pace—presumably because she had arranged with TGW to complete arrangements before the family left for France. On the morning of Monday, 13 December, she went with Eliza and Madeleine to the Palladium and asked for a form for the assignment of policies, only to be told that there were none in the office. At midday she went alone to see TGW's lawyer, Lys, whom she had never met before, and whose rooms were in Took's Court, Chancery Lane. She asked him to draw up a will for her in which she left everything to Madeleine. While two copies were being made, Lys's clerk Francis Slokum heard her say that she was taking such precautions because she was about to go abroad.

Helen removed the copies of her will from Took's Court in the early afternoon, then went with Eliza to see another attorney, James Bird, whom she knew slightly because he had previously done some business for Mrs. Abercrombie. At this meeting, Eliza seems to have taken the lead. Eliza gave Bird a form of assignment (saying it came from the Hope) in which Helen agreed to transfer her policy worth £2000 to TGW for a nominal fee of 19 guineas. Bird duly completed the document, but when he asked for his fee, Eliza said "they would settle the point with her husband" (Curling, p. 238).

The following day, 14 December, Helen went to a third lawyer, Thomas Kirk (whom she had also never met before), and requested a second form of assignment: for her £3000 Palladium policy to be transferred to TGW. (This meant TGW now had assigned policies worth £5000.) On 19 December, TGW brought Helen papers to sign which transferred a policy worth £3000 to John Atkinson, from whom he had been borrowing since the mid-1820s. This meant that he would fall under immediate suspicion if Helen were to die, since he had illegally put himself in the position of a beneficiary, but he appears to have felt that his debts left him with no choice. It would have been comparatively easy for him to raise a loan on one or other of the assigned policies, provided he was not suspected of foul play.

Also on 14 December, Helen completed her last piece of legal business. She went to see TGW's uncle Robert, a lawyer who worked at 7 Furnival's

Court for the firm of Wainewright, Smith and Giraud, and drew up a second will, in which she left her estate divided equally between TGW and Eliza. (Robert Wainewright was a witness to this will, and his involvement suggests that he had remained in touch with TGW since TGW's father's death twenty-five-odd years earlier. No details about their relationship survive.) The practical advantage of this, from TGW's point of view, was that it allowed him to make himself or Madeleine the heir to Helen's £16,000, as he chose. The disadvantage was that it deepened suspicions about his responsibility for Helen's death.

3. A "black draught" was a laxative.

4. Was TGW a murderer? And if so, who were his victims? The questions are as hard to answer today as they were during his lifetime—though this has never stopped people expressing strong views. When TGW was tried in 1837, the judge said that there was "no evidence of other crime than fraud," leaving TGW's detractors free to insinuate that he was guilty of killing his uncle, his mother-in-law, Mrs. Abercromby, and his sister-in-law Helen. The evidence? The say-so of the long-serving Sarah Handcock, who described how all three people died with similar symptoms. The weapon? Strychnine, which had been produced for the first time as recently as 1818, and could not yet be easily detected at autopsy, since the symptoms it produced were very similar to those associated with tetanus. The motive? Greed, in most accounts, basic necessity in others.

Over the years, the case against TGW has remained flimsy, but the chorus of accusing voices has grown steadily louder. He has been branded "a monster egoist" (Thornbury, p. 324) and a "suburban aspirant to aristocracy" who, "having failed to achieve distinction as an artist, a writer, or a dandy . . . was now able to gain some notoriety by playing Satan to a meek audience" (Curling, pp. 310–11). Further charges have been pressed: murders committed during his life in France between 1830 and 1837. Melodramatic details have been added: a Borgia-like poison-filled ring, which he is supposed to have emptied into the goblets of his enemies with a flourish. A callous indifference has been suggested: in many versions of his story, he is supposed to have said in Newgate that he killed Helen "because she had such thick ankles" (in fact this proto-Wildean remark was attributed to him some time after his death). Bogus psychologies have been created: Havelock Ellis described TGW as "a perfect picture of the instinctive criminal in his most highly developed shape" (Ellis, p. 17).

In the witness box, TGW never admitted to anything except forgery. In his life as a writer, however, he sometimes brushed against other kinds of crime. As Van Vinkbooms, he imagined himself imprisoned for theft; as Bonmot he said that he "could not choose but take the devil as his guide"; and as Weathercock he said that he was "soothed" by his art-trances "into that desirable sort of self-satisfaction so necessary to the bodying-out [of] those deliciously voluptuous ideas perfumed with languor which occasionally swim and undulate like gauzy clouds over the brains of the most cold-blooded men."

These and other such remarks are suggestive, but they still prove nothing. So what about the more substantial accusations? First, what about Sarah Handcock's evidence? At this distance it is impossible to say whether she was reporting things as she found them, or getting her own back on TGW for some reason or other—non-payment of wages, for instance. Secondly, what about the weapon? Cornwall remembered "particularly" that TGW's library in Linden House included "two or three old books on poisons" (Procter, p. 194), and it is also possible that TGW owned one new one as well—*An Essay on the Action of Poisons on the Human Body,* the first such work in English, which was published in 1829. Strychnine itself was available from an apothecary.

Lastly, what about his motives? By inheriting Linden House from his uncle, he improved his social position and fulfilled a childhood dream, but at the same time he disastrously increased his debts—as he may or may not have anticipated. By murdering Mrs. Abercromby he possibly disposed of someone he did not like (for all we know), and (more certainly) broke his ties with other members of her family—Eliza's brother, for instance—who might have been making financial demands on him. But his immediate financial gain was negligible. Mrs. Abercromby died worth a mere £100, and following her death her two daughters Helen and Madeleine wrote to the Ordnance, asking for the continuation of payments (worth £10 a year) which had been granted in 1812.

The idea that TGW killed Helen is much more plausible, since in the weeks before her death he had designed the operations in which she played a key role. Yet even here there are confusing elements. Would Helen have gone along with the scam knowing that she would end up dead? It seems improbable—and far more likely that TGW intended to complete the fraud, disappear to France with his entourage, then fake Helen's death and collect the insurance money. At some stage, and for reasons that will never be known, circumstances seem to have changed.

If TGW was indeed guilty of murder, we have to ask: was he acting alone? Various commentators, clearly more appalled by the thought of a female murderer than a male one, have insisted that Eliza Wainewright was "guiltless though misguided" (Norman, p. xi). At TGW's trial, the Attorney-General himself referred to her as "the puppet of the plaintiff." In fact, she seems to have acted throughout with great determination. TGW, in his ticket-of-leave appeal (1845), implied her guilt without actually naming her—since to have done so "would have been infamous, where any human feeling is manifest." Since the ticket-of-leave is economical with the truth in other respects, this veiled accusation must also be considered unreliable. But it is worth remembering that all TGW's crimes were committed when he and Eliza were living under one roof; that twelve of the fifteen visits made to insurance companies to set up the fraud were made by Eliza; and that—as the *Morning Herald* pointed out—it was she who "administered [to Helen on her deathbed] some powder which the doctor did not prescribe." In other words, if TGW did kill Helen, Eliza can "scarcely be acquitted of complicity" (Curling, p. 254).

TGW's more charitable critics have drawn attention to his remarks about having a "giddy, flighty disposition," and suggested that his crimes were committed during recurring fits of "insanity" (Bauer, p. 172). This idea is useful as a way of broadening the context in which we might understand TGW's behaviour. Instead of thinking of him purely and simply as a ferociously frustrated social climber, or an adult in whom childhood damage created terrible imperatives, it allows some connection to be made between his life as an artist and his life as a criminal.

At the centre of both lies TGW's preoccupation with the Self, and with nothing. John Lanchester, in *The Debt to Pleasure* (1996), draws attention to how the artist's "desire to leave a memento of himself" reaches a perverse apotheosis in the murderer's "achieved work": "Where somebody used to be, now nobody is. What more irrefutable proof of one's having lived can there be than to have taken a human life and replaced it with nothingness, with a few fading memories" (p. 225). This idea is part of a thoroughly modern aesthetic, yet it is also a profoundly Romantic one—reminding us that in this sense, as in many others, the Romantic period saw the beginning of distinctly modern life. Not surprisingly, therefore, its echoes reverberate through the work of TGW's contemporaries.

The Romantics generally were very interested in extreme states of mind, and extreme forms of behaviour—and made no secret of their debts to Gothic originals. (One only has to think of Byron's poems, or Coleridge's, or Shelley's.) They realized that their insistence on the significance of the

Self must accept the painful and complex fact that good and evil, violence and tenderness, sense and savagery, are often intertwined.

TGW's own circle was crowded with people who had first-hand experience of violence and crime, and with others who took a keen interest in it. Lamb's mad sister, who murdered their mother, fed his lifelong obsession with transgression, punishment, and what he called "tokens of an unhinged mind." (See, for instance, his "Reflections in the Pillory," and "On the Inconveniences Resulting from Being Hanged.") Cornwall was a poet whose early work (such as his treatment of the Isabella story, which predates Keats's) was fascinated by irrationality, and whose later life—as Bryan Procter—was spent as an Inspector of Lunatic Asylums. Hazlitt kept returning to the idea that "no man ever answered in his own mind . . . to the abstract idea of a *murderer* . . . [but] always takes into account the considerations of time, place and circumstance" (*Selected Writings*, p. 113), and in his *Liber Amoris* he admitted to his own passionate recklessness. De Quincey asked for more understanding of what impelled murderers in his "On the Knocking at the Gate in Macbeth," and expanded his ideas in "On Murder, Considered as One of the Fine Arts." Hood filled his poems with bleakly comic references to gallows, murders, and hulks. Reynolds wrote an enthralled article on the killer John Thurtell. Clare lost his reason. All the *Londoners* remembered the death of their first editor, John Scott, in a duel. Even when Taylor and Hessey had given up their editorship, the magazine kept a column for the reporting of gory crimes, and survived long enough to include the story of Burke's and Hare's body-snatching, and the murder of Maria Marten by William Corder in the Red Barn (1827).

It is impossible to calculate the influence of these things on TGW. But it is safe to say they formed a powerful cocktail which—when mixed with the personal causes of his own "giddiness," and with the influence of Fuseli and Holst—created a climate of sinister possibilities. Ways of behaving that had previously been regarded as taking place in a region beyond all sympathetic comment were becoming the subject of responsible analysis. At the same time, they could not help fascinating those who, like TGW, were already volatile and desperate—perhaps even to the extent of seeming a kind of permission.

5. Locock, who was later knighted, having attended the birth of all Queen Victoria's children, was a lecturer at St. Bartholomew's Hospital, and renowned in London as an "accoucheur." How he met TGW's family is unclear, but he obviously knew them pretty well, since he granted Helen a

certificate of health for one of her insurance policies. The details of his treatment of Helen given in this chapter are all accurate, except for Harriet Grattan's remembering that it was Eliza, and not TGW himself, who administered the powder in jelly to Helen two hours before she died. (Five years later, Locock "did not recollect that he had prescribed [this] powder. The tartar emetic was in solution, the camomile in pills, the senna and salts in draughts, the camphor might have been a powder but he did not think it was.") This evidence, combined with the details of Helen's symptoms, strongly suggest that she had been poisoned by something other than shellfish and beer.

What seems to have happened is this. Having settled their insurance and other legal business, TGW gave Helen a couple of indigestible meals which would throw people off the scent of a crime, particularly since Helen had caught a chill before eating the second of them. He and/or Eliza then tampered with the regular "black draughts" and other potions given to Helen, probably contaminating them with antimony to wear down her system. This would explain her vomiting, shivering, laboured pulse, loss of eyesight and so on. (By giving her tartar emetic, which is the principal salt of antimony, Locock unwittingly accelerated the effect.) Together or separately, TGW and Eliza then put strychnine in the powder two hours before Helen died— disguising its taste with sweetening jelly. About 36 mg of strychnine is the minimum lethal dose, so they would not have needed to use much to kill her.

All things considered, it would be unfair to accuse Locock of negligence. Furthermore, although TGW seems to have altered his plans very hurriedly during December 1830, he cleverly concealed his tracks as a poisoner. If he had used too much antimony at once, Helen would have noticed it and so would the coroners: her sudden death would have been more suspicious than a slower one. As it was, when Locock performed the autopsy on Helen on 22 December, the day after her death, he "mistook the effects of antimony for a gastric chill, aggravated by an indigestible oyster supper; he was then forced to conclude that she had died of a cerebral haemorrhage" (Curling, p. 253).

6. Soon after Helen died, TGW saw Sharpus in the offices of Sharpus's attorney (information from de Chantilly). He told Sharpus that the £610 debt, which was due the following day, would be paid with the proceeds from Helen's life-insurance policies, and also showed him both Helen's wills—the one which left everything to Madeleine, and the other which divided everything between TGW and Eliza. Why did he do this, since their

joint existence could only create difficulties for him? Perhaps Madeleine was leaning on him, saying she would go to the authorities if she did not inherit. Perhaps he was simply not thinking straight. Perhaps he was so proud and/or giddy, he thought he could outwit the law.

There is no evidence to suggest a single safe answer—though it is striking that Madeleine was soon making life difficult for TGW in other ways.

15

I STARVE

*T*he next Act in this play of my Self, though it begins with a single
action, ends in fragments.

I shall waste no time in raising the curtain. Behold! it is the new year 1831,
and what do we find waiting the benefit of our attention? Our hero (myself)
the victim of a trick—a deception worked by powers I had treated as allies,
but that in fact sought nothing but gain for themselves. Who were these
powers? The Insurers, to whom I had paid money, and who now plainly
refused me. How did I reply to their offence? With logic and arguments,
first, then with mightier engines. With help from figures of substance, who
saw the justice of my case, and were prepared to act for me. I stiffened my
sinews, summoned up my blood, and swept forward to challenge these
Insurers in the lists of Chancery. [1]

No sooner had I started on this course, than I realized I must pickle
myself in aspic, if I intended seeing my case brought to trial. No other rem-
edy would allow me to live long enough. And yet, I was fortunate to have
men around me whose confidence in a happy outcome was so complete, they
were able to advance me money—and with this money came a certain ease
in my living, and a revived appetite for pleasure. Although many of the *Londoners* were now lost to me—sunk in the wreckage of that once noble enterprise—other wits, from other parts of my life, continued to entertain me.
Holst, for one, in whose cave of canvases, visors, relics and remainders, etc.,
I would often compose myself for my ordeals.

Nor was this strange, in-between time without new diversions. I am
thinking in particular of a gentleman from Norfolk who lived near by me
in Caroline Place, close to Mecklenburgh Square, with a daughter. This
daughter pleased me, having in her innocence and beauty some of the bless-
ings I had recently lost. It was a comfort for me to play the lover with her
(light-heartedly, I insist). On one occasion, I even went so far as to borrow a
guitar from Holst, and serenade her—only breaking off my serenade when I

noticed an agent of the sheriff's office observing me. The mere sight of him was enough to dry up all the melody in my throat. [2]

No one should confuse such cheerfulness with a cold heart, nor should they suppose that, in my set, I was alone in seeking remedies for our recent loss. My surviving sister Madeleine went so far beyond me in this regard that my own efforts seem paltry in comparison. To the astonishment of all, she announced her engagement to the auctioneer Wheatley, and afterwards married him. Thus it was that a man to whom I owed money, was also the cause of my losing company. [3]

My feelings for Madeleine were moderate, when placed in the scales with those I still cherished for Helen. Yet there was an ingenuity about her, and when she began to signal her departure from our hearth, she altered the shape of everything. Where there had been a crowd of figures, all with overlapping sympathies, now there were empty places. Where there had been elegance, now there was plainness.

Moreover, the agents of Mammon were still tormenting me. I have already explained that, in view of my good prospects, my friend Atkinson had provided me with the means to protect those I loved. Yet as the wheels of Chancery continued their awful grinding, I found my wherewithal dwindling once again. The winter gave way to spring and there was no improvement. The spring blossomed into summer and I became nervous. Summer stalled at its height—stretching its green canopy overhead, sending the birds into the branches for my musical entertainment—and my case became desperate. Therefore, and without any more delay, I revised the plan I had made earlier in the year.

While Helen was still in health, it had been my proposal that she, and I, and all of us, would escape to the Continent where eventually we would rescue our fortunes by redeeming our policies. Now, without Helen as the centre and linchpin of our life away from England, and with the other changes and interruptions I have described, I supposed that the best course of action would be for me to depart alone.

I made no secret of this to Eliza, though it meant forfeiting her love—and my son's. How may a husband and father admit that he is willing to contemplate such seeming heartlessness? Only by asserting that there is another and larger good, which will improve the lot of individual happiness. I will not be mawkish here, and draw out memories of a melancholy conversation. I shall merely say that Eliza understood my argument, and fitted her own mind to it. Before summer was casting its leaves to the ground, she and our boy, accompanied by Handcock (Grattan having gained her freedom), were settled in lodgings in Pimlico. I rested with them for a short while, in the capacity of a swallow on a rooftop, waiting for the inevitable moment when I must disappear.

Yet I could not fly until I had completed such business as was necessary. In the now-nearly-year-long desolation I had endured since quitting Linden House, I had made occasional visits to ensure that all due care was bestowed upon the place—and I am not ashamed to say that, during these sallies, a trust had grown up between me and the bailiff's men, so that I was able to claim a few portables essential to my well-being. For example: the works I had purchased from the Professor, which I now transferred to my wife in Pimlico. My comfort was knowing they existed as a security, if ever such a thing were required. [4]

The relief of this was nothing when weighed against the pain of my separation from Linden House itself. Only Lear on his heath, with his daughters absent or dreadful, his kingdom gone, his friends in disgrace, and the storm reverberating round his ears, could express the passion unleashed in me by the realization that I must effect its sale. Yet I had no choice. I could not execute my plan of escape without such funds as the house represented. [5]

When a man has to face an emergency, the determination that sits in his heart cannot easily be separated from fear. The combination tilts him first one way, and then the other, so that sometimes he seems his familiar self, at other times re-formed and strange. This was the case with me. Looking upon my face and features, and hearing how I would still have hunted after beauty had the means been mine, my former friends on the *London* would certainly have recognized me as Janus. In other respects they would have thought me a changed man—my wings clipped, my plumage dull, my tongue less eager. Accordingly, as I began to make my preparations for departure, I preferred to keep myself in as fixed a state as possible, which meant living almost in secret. I arranged no meetings which could positively be called "final." I wept on no shoulders. I wrung no hand miserably in parting. I gave no last lingering looks behind me. I chose simply to slip out of my former life, letting its talk and business continue, so that as I sank below the surface of things I did not create a ripple.

Would that I had been able to escape my creditors with such easy politeness. For this I blame the lamentable slowness of Chancery. Although I had no reason to doubt my security, so far as my long-term prospects were concerned, I had no means of coping with immediate demands. Therefore, as autumn crept forward, I was advised by certain friends to look lively—even to the extent of bidding my wife and child a premature goodbye, and lodging instead among the curiosities of my friend Holst. My gratitude for his comfort was a little greater than my alarm at the nightmares provoked by his collection. [6]

From Holst's apartments, where I immediately became a creature of half-lights, it was a simple thing for me to escape to Dover, and thence across the water to France. I have said already that this part of my life is a matter of fragments. And where there are fragments there are also absences—guesses, wild surmises, inventions (though it would be better if that word were not taken to mean falsehoods). These things are indeed the best description of my years in France. I knew where I was for the entire duration of my stay, yet in my own best interests I made sure that my somewhere was nowhere. I understood who I was (more accurately: I knew who I had been), yet to keep myself as myself I had to be no one. At some moments I was compelled to step back into my old identity, and deal with matters raised by my lawyers in London, relating to my case. But for the majority of my days, I lived in quiet obscurity, like some species of fish that loves the depths of murky ponds, filtering the gloom for whatever nourishment he must have, changing his position from one weed-clump to another, eyeing the bright suddenness of the fisherman's lure which sometimes dangles in view—and always refusing it, watching the silent world pass overhead, and feeling it is not a thing he need comprehend or even consider. [7]

I would like to remember this as a time of contentment, compared to the tribulations of my more recent history. But I cannot. It was a wandering and low-spirited time. One moment I might be in funds, thanks to some lucky gamble, which allowed me to live with dignity. I recollect in particular some lodgings on the coast, where I moved happily in the company of visiting countrymen, and, in return for a glass of brandy, expatiated on the merits of Bonington, who had already commemorated that shore.

At other times I would be in despair, not believing in the probability of my next meal. I became an aficionado of back alleys, a connoisseur of doorways and ditches, a sentimentalist of starlight coverings. I lived with the spider in the cobweb, with the fox in the roots of the pine, with the thrush in the laurel bush. Mice have stared into my face on the floor of a granary, and vagabonds and prodigals have stumbled against me in the ruins of a villa. High in the cliff overlooking a little beach, I have swallowed a gull's egg without the benefit of cooking. Low down in the cellar of a town house, I have diced for the shirt upon my back. And what did I gain from these deprivations? Only the right to watch my chest continue to rise and fall.

Since I survived these ordeals only to endure further hardships, I may reasonably ask: might it not have been better for me to die? It is only a moment since I found the same question on my lips, referring to an earlier time—and my answer is the same now as then. I am one of those pitiable souls who cannot help but keep a flame of hope alive, as long as I exist. Even the most unspeakable hardship cannot entirely extinguish my brightness, in the same way that no anxiety can altogether darken my mind. This is my salvation and also my curse. I hope that I am capable of deep feeling; I know that I am capable of feeling nothing. I have made of myself what I can.

Grievous as they were, none of my slights was equal to the new blow which now suddenly pounded down on me. During one of my stays in the town of Boulogne, in June of the year 1835, two gentlemen from Bow Street came to visit me. Very good of them, I thought, and said so, and clapped them on the back, though I would more willingly have tipped off their hats. Yes, good of them—except no sooner had they met me than they described how the steps I had taken years before, to lay my hands upon my Trust, had been (I shall use their word) "discovered." As a consequence of this, they informed me, I would immediately become their prisoner, if the leather of my shoe ever again exerted its pressure on English soil.

The preposterousness of this was such that I had no difficulty in smiling at their insolence, then actually laughing as they clambered back aboard their vessel and rolled off across the Channel. Yet when they had vanished, their threats bore on me heavily. I saw that the name of Wainewright, which had been uttered by assorted geniuses, which had drawn admiring sighs from crowds in the Academy, which had meant kindness and entertainment in company, would now suddenly be a prey to rumour, and mean no more than "forger" and "faussaire." This would have been a hard reversal for any man to bear. For such a one as myself, who was alone among strangers, with no friend or wife to lift my drooping spirits, it was cruel. When I recollected that my cousin Foss would bring the suit forward against me, in the event of a trial, I truly felt aghast. For blood to rebel against blood; for a shared childhood to count for nothing; for pity and compassion to dry up at the moment they should flow most abundantly—it may be imagined what darkness closed around me.

As it did so—in the same month that I had my visit from the two gentlemen—I received a second unexpected blow. Thanks to a letter from my friend Acheson, I understood that the engine of the law had rumbled forward to the point at which my case against the Imperial was to be considered.

Thus it was that I endured one of the strangest times in my strange existence. In the warm light of a Continental summer, feeling a mixture of interest and real fear, I read in a common newspaper the report of the case on which my whole life depended—after the drama was over, and with no opportunity to affect its course. Keenly did I ponder the names Michael Bland, Grant Allen and Cornelius Buller (the Directors of the Imperial), gaining from them an impression of grandeur and good cloth. Sharply did I gaze upon the title "Attorney-General," and filled my head with a paraphernalia of black robes. Solemnly did I imagine the panelled chambers of the Court of the Exchequer, and supposed they were an enormous schoolroom. And miserably did I live again through my last December in England, recollecting the tailor Nichols, above whom I had lodged, the severe weather, the oysters and bottled stout, the fair face of Helen as she wasted, the voices of Eliza and Locock, the frantic efforts to restore life, and the more frantic efforts of death to claim his victim. All these jangled together, while I sat meekly at a breakfast table, turning the pages as I read, in the midst of ordinary citizens going about their business—not realizing who was among them.

Yet who was among them? An innocent man, or a villain? At the end of everything, the Jury themselves did not know. They could not decide. They refused to reach a verdict. Nothing! I was neither one thing nor another— not rich or poor, guilty or free—even though Handcock (who had known me since I was but five years old!) insinuated that I was responsible for the most vile crimes, and Locock too—all without evidence. Still the Jury could not decide.

Did this outcome come as a relief to me, since it left me at liberty to continue the life which had become habitual? It might have done, had not such gross slanders been made against me, and had I not despaired of funds to continue a life of any sort. My poverty made me wish for no more than a sleep and a forgetting. My sense of justice, however, filled me with indignation—and seeing how my friend Acheson remained adamant that I would triumph at last, I therefore instructed him to order a retrial, and composed myself as best I could to await the outcome.

This "best" would better be called "worst." Which is to say: I believe there is a nothing beyond mere vacancy, which is in reality an outer chamber of the court of death itself, where we feel our bones ache, and our hearts slow almost to a standstill, while a dreadful monotony fills every hour of every day, and every minute of every hour. In such a state, the pattern of frost upon a windowpane becomes our whole occupation, and the movement of a clock's hands cannot be detected. A butterfly, struggling against a cobweb, grows into a thing of consuming interest. The difference between light and dark is reduced to such insignificance, we might as well drift through both into oblivion.

Thus did my life thicken through that summer and autumn: a stream as sluggish as a flow of wax. And at the end of everything, when the Court at last considered my case a second time, and reached their decision, and the wax at last grew fluid again, and ran—then I wished it to be solid once more. In the deliberations of a morning, in the minds of a dozen strangers, in the bad faith of several I had trusted, my reputation was ripped from me, tossed into the wind, and blown in tatters round about the pendant world. I had expected no less, since I accepted by now that the law was my enemy. But this did not ease the pain of the judgement. Hitherto, even though I had been pushed down among the lowliest creatures of the earth, I had moved among them with a light in my eye, and a spark in my spirit. Now both were extinguished and I became the mere husk; darkness bounded in a nutshell.

In the lives of some men, disaster works like a fire in a forest, burning everything to a barren plain so that new growth may begin. In my own case, there was no such consolation. Accidents made room for larger accidents, that is all, as I found by lingering in France for a further year, sidling among the weeds and wreckage, far from the sun's rays, lost to the world and most things in it. When I exerted myself to enquire after my former life—by making appeals to those who had been my friends, in which I strove to write in my old fantastical way, for their amusement—I received a pittance or silence. If I made an approach to Acheson, it was only to hear of further difficulties strewing my way ahead. [8]

Although I have often insisted that I am not a man who submits easily to the thought of losing his life, I believe that if I had continued much longer in this desultory way, I should soon have reached the day when death might have seemed preferable to the tedium of continuing to draw breath. When I saw this possibility, I knew that I had reached the lowest ebb of my existence. I felt blank as a stone, and thought (in a way impossible for natural stones) that I should crumble into dust and disappear from the face of the earth.

Yet at this very moment, I found my strength suddenly returning. I have noticed this effect in myself before. I mean, that it is only when my fortunes are shattered, and my spirits in despair, that I am able to begin striving again. What is most energetic in me, and what is most degenerate, are kissing cousins. To be particular: I admitted to myself (*sotto voce*) that I would have considered it disgraceful to crumble and vanish. Advising myself more volubly, I recollected the high ideals and brave promises I had celebrated in my youth, when I first set out upon the road to fame. Blowing upon the embers of my own ambition, I fanned into a blaze my wishes to see again the land of my birth, and the faces I loved—even though it might be briefly, and in secret.

How soon and suddenly we may alter our lives! During the whole of my five years in France, I had become more and more stagnant with wretchedness, so that eventually it seemed impossible I would ever stir again. Then, at last, I discovered the energy to attempt some repossession of myself. From the great distance at which I now stand, reviewing these things, I see that it might have been mere recklessness which drove me on. At the time, I believed it was a more sensible sort of power—and truly, it is a marvellous thing, when the planning of a dangerous enterprise makes such demands on a person's skill and cunning, that the danger itself is forgotten. When the evening came on which I went on board ship at Calais, and set my face towards England once more, and felt the salt breeze blowing through my hair and moustaches, I can honestly say that I felt no apprehension, but only excitement. In my foolish calculation, I considered myself forgotten. [9]

1. On 14 January 1831, representatives of the Eagle, Hope, Imperial, Palladium and Pelican Insurance companies met at the offices of the Imperial to discuss the claim that TGW had recently made on each of them. They pooled their knowledge, discovered that Helen and Eliza had lied about several things, said that if they had known the state of TGW's finances they would never have issued policies in the first place, and also agreed that the policies were not sought by Helen for her particular benefit, but by TGW for his own gain, using her name. They therefore decided not to pay up, on the grounds of "misrepresentation." (Suspicions about the cause of Helen's death lay outside their jurisdiction.)

TGW threatened the companies, then took them to court when they told him they would not change their minds, even though this was bound to lead him into deeper trouble. He decided to focus his case on the Imperial, where the policy was still in Helen's name, and where he could bring his suit as her executor on behalf of Madeleine. But he could not begin his action without any money. He therefore went back to John Atkinson, to whom Helen had recently assigned a policy worth £3000, and asked him to advance some funds against this amount. Atkinson agreed to do this, and also put TGW in touch with his friend Robert Acheson, whom W. C. Hazlitt describes as "an intelligent and respectable solicitor." Atkinson was so optimistic about the outcome of the case that he also advanced TGW "a Warranty of Attorney for the penal sum of £2000, a moiety of that amount, or the balance between [TGW's] actual debt to Atkinson and £1000." Atkinson held the Eagle policy as security, as well as Linden House and its contents, and the two other policies Helen had transferred into TGW's name. The agreement was signed on 27 January, whereupon TGW paid off Sharpus, and began preparing his case.

2. Almost nothing is known about this "Norfolk gentleman"—though he and his daughter have been the subjects of some lively speculation. He may have been an army friend of TGW's, who had since fallen on hard times. TGW is rumoured to have indoctrinated him in "the peculiar practices which . . . are afforded by insurance companies" (Curling, p. 274), to have persuaded him to take out a policy of £3000 on his own life with the Pelican, then to have run off with him and his daughter to France—where the inevitable happened. "One evening when coffee was brought in after dinner, [TGW] squeezed poison from one of his numerous rings into the cup of his

friend, who died shortly afterwards in convulsions" (ibid.). According to Wilde, TGW "did not gain any monetary advantage from this. His aim was simply to revenge himself on the first [insurance] office that had refused to pay him the price of his sins." There is no hard evidence for any of these stories, though their persistence suggests that TGW did indeed plan a further insurance fraud, involving this mysterious "gentleman" and his daughter.

3. Madeleine Abercrombie married Wheatley, the auctioneer to whom TGW owed money, and who had valued the books at Linden House, at St. James's Church, Piccadilly, on 19 May 1832. TGW's anxiety that she would tell her husband the secrets of his last few months in England could only have been eased by knowing that if she did so, she would also incriminate herself.

4. These are possibly the drawings Eliza later sold to the granddaughter of Fuseli's friend John Moore. She also sold to Colnaghi a drawing of TGW by Holst which was later bought by Edward Bulwer Lytton, and is described by Colnaghi in a letter of 14 January 1847: "The subject is some Venetian-looking figures apparently at the theatre—and one of them is a very characteristic likeness of the Wainewright whose life you have lately portrayed" (EBL Archive, vol. 3, d/EK, c2, p. 14).

5. TGW was not in a position to use much of the sale value of Linden House for his flight to France, since Atkinson held the house and its contents as security against the loans he had made TGW earlier in the year. When the sale went through in late September, it realized £3,400, of which TGW received £554 16 3d, in cash.

6. In his letter to Edward Bulwer Lytton (14 January 1847) Colnaghi says, "Holst and [TGW] were on the most intimate terms and during the period of his last stay in London while the Police were on his track—he remained hid in Holst's house in Howland Street" (EBL Archives, vol. 3, d/EK, c2, p. 14). The phrasing here raises the possibility that TGW did not remain continuously in France, but sometimes travelled back to London in secret for short visits. By helping his friend, Holst put himself outside the law; there is no evidence that his behaviour was criminal in any other way.

7. On 19 May 1846, Henry Smith, the agent of the Eagle who collected TGW's papers from France, sent them "all" to Edward Bulwer Lytton to help with the background for *Lucretia*, adding in a letter of 26 May that TGW "confessed that he used strychnine and morphine" in his murders. By

the end of the 1840s, almost all these papers had disappeared, though several later commentators have embellished their reputation. Thornbury, for instance, said that they "contained a kind of index to the details of his various crimes, set forth with a voluptuous cruelty and a loathsome exultation worthy of the diseased vanity of such a masterpiece of evil" (Thornbury, p. 336). The facts are: there almost certainly was a diary of some kind, it almost certainly did contain some kind of confession, but the references to it by Smith, Bulwer Lytton and others are so sketchy it is impossible to describe it accurately, or give it much value as evidence. (See Afterword, pp. 256–7.)

8. In December 1836, Helen's sister Madeleine (who was now married to Wheatley the auctioneer) began proceedings against the Eagle, laying claim to the £3000 policy Helen had taken out in March 1830.

9. TGW's time in France is the most obscure part of his adult life. The only known facts are these: He left London in October 1831, and returned in May 1837. At various times in between, he lived in Calais, Boulogne, St. Omer and Paris. In the summer of 1832 he was visited by Acheson's clerk, a man named Young, in St. Omer—Young said that TGW was living "at a lonely country house with a wealthy old Frenchman and that somehow he did not like the look of things." TGW often wrote to friends asking for loans, as Cornwall remembered in his autobiography:

> During his residence in Paris he fell into extreme destitution. At one time I received a letter from him, asking for a very small loan or gift in money, which I of course sent to him. The letter was in his usual fantastic style, referring to some pictures which I then had, particularly to my "dusk Giorgione," as he termed it. But when he had to tell of his wretched state, his tone deepened. "Sir, I starve," he said, adding that he had been obliged to pawn his only shirt, in order to enable him to pay the postage of the letter. His letter exhibited great depression. He spoke of the crowds of gay and careless people—gamblers and prodigals and others—all of whom passed him by—whilst he was without a meal, without a single acquaintance, and not knowing where he could apply with the smallest chance for help. From Paris and Calais he sent over dismal letters to various persons in England for a little help. I pleaded for him to one or two of his acquaintance, without (I am afraid) much effect (Procter, p. 192).

Cornwall ends his account by saying that during his time in Calais TGW "became personally intimate with a married female, whom fear of detection or some other strong motive induced him to poison." This is just one of many unproven assertions which relate to this period. Macready, for instance, says that in Paris TGW "underwent imprisonment for three months on a charge of having poison in his possession for which he could not give a satisfactory account." Talfourd says TGW spent six months in prison. Others have spun out the story of the ill-fated Norfolk gentleman and his daughter. Others again, such as Havelock Ellis, have imagined that "he experienced all the ups and downs of an adventurer's life. One week he would be fashionably dressed and gambling heavily at the public tables. The next, broken in pocket, he would be selling his coat to buy food" (pp. 52–3).

Amidst all this speculation, one thing is clear: although TGW probably earned a little from his painting (Wilde has him going on a painting trip to Boulogne), he was extremely hard up and wretched for most of the five and a half years he was away from England. And especially wretched after January 1835, when the Bank of England (thanks to some prompting by Foss) discovered his forgeries of 1822 and 1823, issued a warrant for his arrest, and sent two City Runners, John and Daniel Forrester, to interview him in Boulogne. They came back to London empty-handed, since there was no extradition treaty between England and France.

Five months later, on 29 June 1835, TGW's action against the Imperial at last got under way. During the trial, TGW's servants Sarah Handcock and Harriet Grattan made serious allegations against him; Locock excited suspicions by saying, "The majority of poison cases leave no trace at all"; and the Attorney-General, Sir John Campbell, insisted that Helen "was the instrument of the plaintiff." The word "murder" was used towards the end of the proceedings, but the jury was asked by Lord Abinger to ignore this possibility, since it was "calculated to excite a prejudice." Instead, they were told to concentrate on three questions: "Was the policy of Miss Abercromby *bona fide*, or was it really the policy of the plaintiff; was it material for the Imperial to know that other policies had been taken out; and was there 'wilful misrepresentation'?" After deliberating for six hours, the jury sent a note saying they were split six against six. A juror was then withdrawn with the consent of both parties, and the defendants thought the case was at an end—which it was, until TGW ordered Acheson to call for a retrial.

The second hearing was held five months later, on 3 December 1835. Talfourd later said that Lord Abinger (whom he knew) was "the most consummate advocate of his time," and was "disposed always to pleasurable associations," but on this occasion he seems to have run out of patience. He said the case was "pregnant with suspicion," but that even so "it was unnec-

essary to consider for a moment whether murder had been committed."
Once again, the jury was directed to concern itself solely with the insurance
matters in hand—and this time they returned "almost immediately," finding
for the Imperial "on the grounds of misrepresentation, and of Miss Abercromby having no real interest in the insurance." It would have been impossible for anyone reading the trial reports not to suspect that TGW had killed
Helen, and possibly other people as well.

16

I AM NOBODY

Show me the man who has not stood in the prow of a ship, straining his eyes for the first glimpse of home, and suspected, when the white of a cliff or the green of a hill first appeared, that he had imagined it. At sea, more than on land, our time is full of uncertainties. A gull hanging in the sunlight might be light itself. A dolphin in the waves might be our own shadow speeding through the waters.

I write this remembering another and much longer voyage that I shall come to presently. But even during my short crossing from France to London in the spring of 1837, I lived betwixt and between. When the coast of Kent at last came into view, touched by the rosy fingers of Aurora (about whom much has already been written, so I shall pass over her effects here), I doubted for several minutes whether it was indeed England before me, or an hallucination. Eventually the scent of vegetation wafted out to me, and decided matters.

Our entrance into the mouth of the River Thames was a trial. Winds, which had blown gently during our crossing, now could not leave us without a challenge, and began slapping our sails in a rage. At the same moment, curious currents worked energetically beneath our hull, as if there were an experiment afoot, to divide salt water from fresh—which required our entire vessel to be lifted into the air occasionally, until the business was completed.

It had always been my intention, when at last I came within reach of London Town, to keep out of public view, below decks. Now, however, seeing that our upping and downing had sickened my fellow passengers, I had no choice other than to brave the open air, where the breathing was sweeter. (Sweeter, but not so dry, I reckoned, that any Runner or Thief-taker would consider it advisable to patrol the banks keeping an eye out for such as myself.) In the shelter of the main mast, with my muffler pulled up around my nose and mouth, I therefore returned to my mother country in a triumphant solitude, my only audience being a host of stinking flats and weed-beds, and shacks staggering out into the stream on spindly legs.

Arrival in Tower Dock required a more lively sort of ingenuity. Having paid my fare when first coming aboard in Calais, and not deeming it necessary to bid my Charon farewell, I stepped down into the hubbub of the quay as soon as my vessel had berthed, declined all offers of porterage, lowered my hat over my eyes, and immediately made off through the early morning towards a part of town where I was a stranger to everyone.

The place I had chosen was Covent Garden, which I knew was a ramshackle area, and therefore likely to confuse my enemies. Now I plunged into its midst as though dust and debris were my natural element, and after an interval of twisting and turning, came at length to a basement where the one window was meshed by a blind, where the door slouched in its frame as if exhausted with the effort of standing, and where a bed straddled the whole floor, squeezing its wretched little washstand so that it seemed, on its thin legs, in a state of great agitation.

Once I had gained this sanctuary, and begun breathing more easily, the thought came to me that what I imagined to be a place of safety was in reality a snare—and I the tethered victim, unable to escape. Everything that had formerly seemed brave in my behaviour now struck me as foolish; everything that had felt necessary was a thing I could do without. The faintest cry in the street rang upon my ears like a blacksmith's hammer. The rattle of a coach was a hangman's cart in my imagination. A dusty sparrow, which alighted on the crossbar of my window, and began pecking at the frame, was the fingernail of a suspicious hand, summoning me out into dangerous broad daylight.

Daylight! The bright shoot of heaven, in which our bodies flourish and our souls prosper. Daylight! The natural element of one made for clear pleasures. Daylight! Which I had learned to shun. Indeed, after my last few years, I was so well practised as a creature of shadows, I entered upon my new life with as much disturbance as a ghost. And within a brief while, I had made a number of small excursions so successfully, I began to suppose I was actually invisible, as I desired to be. This made me bold. So bold that one evening I walked as far as Pimlico, and stood across the street from where Eliza and our son lived, hoping I might see them at a window. I did not. Another time I called on my friend Holst. Did I believe that I could continue like this? I cannot say—and no more could I have said at the time. I was living from moment to moment, and had no thought of what lay beyond the morrow.

It was not long before my freedom was all used up. After a few days of my new, lurking life, a warmer evening than usual brought me to the vicinity of Holst's house at a corner of Fitzroy Square, where I delayed for the sole purpose of greeting a lady I found there, speaking with her ordinarily of this and that. Fool, to think that any degree of ordinariness attached to me! With our banter taking its easy course, and the twilight turning to real darkness about the lamps which had been installed in that district—a darkness crowded with fluttering moths—I suddenly heard the voice of Daniel Forrester in my ear and felt his touch upon my arm.

Forrester was the name of both the gentlemen who had previously interviewed me in Boulogne—the two being brothers. I shall never forget Daniel's actions on this second meeting, since everything that follows depends on them. "Mr. Wainewright," he said, an expression of glee transforming his solemn face, "I have been looking for you for a considerable time." I told him that I did not know what he meant, but it was to no purpose. The lady with whom I had been speaking vanished as if she had never existed; the wood of Holst's door never again knew the rap of my knuckles. The moths in their little universe continued to dance and skim; and I put myself in the hands of my unwelcome companion as surely as if I were his servant and he my master.

It is the task of a gentleman, in such a circumstance as I now found myself, to behave with due dignity. On our journey to the Giltspur-street Compter, I therefore informed my captor that he had no reason to fear my anger, or to suppose that I would make any struggle to escape. In truth, now that the process of my imprisonment had begun, I felt that I stood at a mysterious distance from myself—thanks, I dare say, to my good conscience. My only deception was to pretend that no anxiety was mixed with my innocence, in which I suppose I succeeded, since during my first hours of incarceration, I was treated as though I did indeed have no cause for worry.

The following morning I was removed to the Mansion House, the residence of the Chief Magistrate of the City, the Lord Mayor. It was here that my condition began to alter—not so much owing to the conduct of my interrogator, as to the brutal witness of my cousin Foss. When I first entered the Magistrate's room, and saw my cousin's familiar face (familiar, yet not seen since I had first hidden myself in France) I believed that rescue was at hand. How, I asked myself, could like quarrel with like, blood with blood? Yet his response to my smile was an angry stare, and an impatient flick of his hand, meaning that the proceedings should begin.

They did so, simply enough. When Alderman Sir Peter Laurie asked me "what I was," I was determined not to seem cast down, and wittily declared, "I am nothing," deprecating even the notion that I was an Artist, since I could not be a gentleman if I had a profession. Sir Peter smiled at this, then composed himself when a clerk of the Bank of England came forward and read the list of my supposed misdemeanours. Had I been in my cousin's position, I should certainly at this point have remonstrated that a man cannot reasonably be called a criminal for taking what was already his. But with the plainest words, he did no such thing, and instead scuttled all my hopes. "The signatures of myself and my father are both forgeries," my cousin announced, and immediately sat down out of sight behind me, whereupon the beautiful gardens that we had played in together as children were blasted, the stately rooms we had walked through together broken into dust, and the river of natural sympathy which runs between all creatures of the earth, and in which they gain refreshment, dried up and left its cracked bed naked to the sky. In the desolation of the moment, I could think of nothing except my cousin's face, staring from behind me. I could hear nothing but the word "prisoner" falling like a stone from Sir Peter's lips. Not even the thought that I might soon have a rope placed about my neck—since the penalty for what I had done was death—could find a lodging in my mind. I was entirely consumed by anger, and by shame. (Furthermore, it still did not occur to me that the full extent of the law would be required in my case.) [1]

I will not describe how I submitted myself to the next stage of my life; it is impossible. I am referring to my arrival in that detestable carbuncle, that Bastille of bestiality—Newgate—and I shall effect my journey there exactly as it seemed. In the twinkling of an eye: a twinkling which nevertheless altered my condition entirely. Finding the massive walls looming above me, the blackened statues of Mercy and Justice frowning down at me, the low door creaking open to admit me, the stinking corridors conducting me into the heart of my deprivation, and the mannerless rude rituals of my guards all about me—then indeed did I feel cut off from my true Self.

The days of my incarceration were fewer than a month, but longer than infinity. I shall not pile further humiliations on myself by remembering them again, except to insist that the lives of innocent men are inevitably ruined by those who suppose the mere fact of an arrest to be tantamount to a confession of guilt. Because of this prejudice, eyes which long to gaze upon green leaves and open streets are made to scan dripping walls; faces which deserve to feel the healing softness of a summer breeze are inflamed by the horrible stench of foul humanity and rotting straw; mouths which have tasted the most delightful fruits of God's plenty must eat oatmeal and mouldy bread, and make no difference between breakfast and dinner; intelligences which have heard the most noble music, performed by the finest artists, must listen instead to the dolorous clanging of the handbell swung by the bellman of St. Sepulchre, which means some wretched soul will soon die.

Imagine me, then, if such a thing can be done, with the door on to the street already bolted behind me, my descent underground already accomplished, and the prospect before me nothing more or less than a cage—a cage filled with a hideous tangle of men: the old and the young, the sick and the ruddy, the silent and the talkative, all huddled together as if certainly on their way to the gallows. When my guide unlocked the door on this rabble, for the purpose of thrusting me in, the entire mass heaved like a sulky pool as it made room. Then, with the key still scraping in the lock behind me, the men immediately pressed round me with a frightening moan, demanding that I pay a fee for the privilege of my admittance. It was beyond my strength to object, and when this sacrifice was made, I was allowed a corner of my own. I am relieved to say this had a partial view of a window, and the dim sky beyond—which had never looked more beautiful.

I believe that if I had been compelled to remain in this cage for the whole of my time in Newgate, I should soon have preferred to feel my neck stretched to extinction. The shock of so much wretchedness was intolerable, and the crying at night, especially the weeping of little children, hurt me deeply. My brain, which had been used to ponder questions concerning beauty and taste, had no ideas to contemplate, only the history of broken hearts. My eyes, which had grown sharp with years of gazing at the noblest images, now craved dullness, so they might not absorb the misery that lay around me.

It was my single consolation, in this dreadful circumstance, to know that I had been able to send word to Eliza, and beg her not to visit me; her delicacy would scarcely have survived for an instant in such a place. I am happy to recollect that she never doubted the wisdom of my advice, and stayed away from me entirely.

Be that as it may, mine was not an indefinite suffering—and in due course (I say "course" since it would do Newgate an injustice to measure its time in days, one there being so entirely like another)—in due course some moderating angel remembered me. In a higher realm of the prison, where it was still possible to pursue a rational conversation, the Governor took notice of my situation, and decided that my treatment had been as I always described it to myself: unjust. After who knows what delays and deferrals, I was therefore scooped from the filthy sink in which I had begun to rot, and removed to a smaller ward. In this place, which had the disadvantage of being windowless, but the advantage of space (there being no more than two other souls inhabiting) I at last received some respect, once I had given my companions to understand that I had surrendered my liberty in the wide world for the not inconsiderable matter of £10,000. Their deference to me, and the sweeter air, was so vast an improvement on what I had previously known, I almost became hopeful again—except that no sooner had I begun to re-assemble myself, than I was once more undone.

It happened as follows, in two parts. The first part involved an agent of the Insurers, who came to discuss with me some business relating to my case. Since I had yet to appear before a Judge, and was therefore still clad in my own apparel, I received him as a gentleman ought, graciously, and bade my other companions make space for him. To my amazement, the agent then began railing at me as though he had no apprehension of the difference between us. "Mr. Wainewright," he said, or something very like this, "it would be quite useless to speak to you of humanity, or of tenderness, or of laws human or divine; but does it not occur to you, after all, that—merely regarded as a speculation—your crime is a bad one? See where it ends. I talk to you in a shameful prison, and I talk to a degraded convict."

Who would not be offended by such language? Who, still protesting his innocence as I was, would not wish to retaliate? Yet I did not retaliate. I spoke to him with a dignity which showed his impertinence. "Sir," I said, "you City men enter into your speculations and take the chances of them. Some of your speculations succeed; some fail. Mine happen to have failed; yours happen to have succeeded; that is the difference, Sir, between you and me. But I will tell you one thing in which I have succeeded to the last. I have been determined through life to hold the position of a gentleman. I have always done so. I do so still." (At this point I made a gesture towards my fellows.) "It is the custom of this place that each of the inmates shall take his morning's turn of sweeping it out. My companions here are a bricklayer and a sweep. But, by God, they never offer me the broom."

My interlocutor—this agent, this poltroon—did not deserve and so did not receive the respect I showed to my everyday companions. And when I had done with him, he retired the worse for our encounter. My second visitor—or visitor*s*, I should more properly say—were not so easily parried. As anyone may suppose, I spent long hours in my cell to no special purpose, drifting in a kind of trance as a fish might do across the ocean floor, encountering suddenly the gleam of treasure that has long been lost from the world's sight, or the ruin of a craft which once sailed proudly and was full of hope. In such a mood, with a book open on my knees, but my mind neither quite on the pages nor exactly forgetful of them either, I heard a sudden gasp at my cell door, and on pulling myself back to the present, recognized the face of one I had entertained with other literary men in Great Marlborough Street. It was Macready, that genius of Tragedy, whose Richard had done greater villainy than any I could imagine myself.

"My God!" he burst out at me, "There's Wainewright!"—so that immediately I saw myself as he did: a poor shabby-genteel creature. Whereupon my look of shock turned to one of self-pity, and thence to fierce shame. I held his gaze for a moment longer, while his silence humbled me. Until that moment, I had still on occasion been able to consider myself a king of infinite space. When the instant passed, I was already and entirely myself: a bedraggled dog, an object of damnation. [2]

It therefore came about, on the day of my trial, that I was sunk so low in my esteem, I could scarcely believe I was the defendant in my own case. My wardens conducted me up from my cell through countless winding corridors towards the Court, at such a brutal speed that whatever sensibility I still retained was lost in the process. By the time I came into the light, I had a ringing in my ears, and a dazzle in my eyes, as though I had been dragged through the centre of the earth itself, and landed on the far side of everything I knew.

I am never inclined to give a poor idea of myself, and yet I suppose that I looked about me *stupidly*. I, who on the morning in question, had taken customary pains with my appearance, brushing my coat and smoothing my hair and moustaches, so that all those who looked upon me should know me for what I was (and am). A man in whom stupidity has no place. Yet I felt the greatest difficulty in bringing my attention to bear on the Serjeant, when I heard him utter my name. By now, however, my giddiness had less to do with the manner of my conveyance into court, and the brutalities I had endured in recent days, than with my belief that I did not deserve to answer any of the charges made against me. In addition, I was beginning to take an excessive delight in the panelling and vaulting of the room in which I found myself—the gilded figures of the lion and the unicorn set magnificently above me, and all the signs of pomp—which passed for beauty, to eyes long since deprived of pleasure.

However they distracted me, these sights also acted as an encouragement to my spirits, and meant that when the Serjeant eventually addressed me, I had no difficulty in answering him. I pronounced: Not Guilty, to everything he said. At this show of truth and bravery, I was immediately ushered down into the bowels of the earth once more (so that I was beginning to feel like a cork under a waterfall), and found myself part of an ill-lit conversation about how the best could be made of my situation. The Governor of New-gate himself was there, a red-faced, squashed-nose man, who seemed to have spent his whole existence in a room too small to hold him comfortably; also, the agents of the Bank, who were sleek and pink and well ventilated, as might be expected. I shall not rake over the details of what was said, only emphasize that I was assured that, if I withdrew my plea of innocence on all counts, and changed it to an admission of guilt in two respects, then I should receive a punishment merely nominal—not to mention escaping the noose. This advice issued directly from the Bank Parlour, and I was satisfied of its worth.

Returning to the Court, I felt in a more cheerful humour than I had known for a long while. I seemed able to look beyond the pale of the moment, over the bewigged heads and beyond the solid walls around me, to a time when all my troubles would be a memory, and my place among equals be secure again. My very coat seemed to sit more elegantly upon my shoulders, and my hair to shine with an animal vigour. But Justice did not share in my mood. Justice did not bend her ear to my appeal. Justice came in the form of a black-browed savage, who condemned me to a length of suffering I cannot compress into a lifetime's deliberations.

Transported! The word entered my breast like a knife blade, finding my heart and touching it with a tip of icy steel. Transported! To feel my life shot forward, like an arrow from a bow, towards a destination that was not yet given a name—only AWAY. Transported! I felt my lips opening, ready to remonstrate at the injustice, but strong hands seized me before I could make a sound, and hurried me back to my underground existence. Transported! Everything that was fixed and clear in my brain broke loose at the sound, so that the Court itself broke into fragments, whirling pieces of sky and wooden panelling, and the scarlet of the Judge's robes, and the black wings of the aldermen, and the skewering gilt horn of the unicorn, and the whole rabble of the gallery, together into one mass.

In the midst of this, as I felt myself carried towards the black mouth of the passage which would soon swallow me, one sight detached itself from the others and remained clear. At the low door of the gallery, I saw some gentlemen of the press, and some boys in sloppy hats, with their suits all out at the elbows, who were running off to the offices of their newspapers. They had forgotten me already (I mean they had forgotten me as a fellow crea-ture), and were preparing to build me again as a new form of myself: a mon-ster of cupidity and pride. As if I were caught in a nightmare, and yet at the same time awake to understand the machinery of my dream, I imagined their words flying hither and thither like a flock of black crows, cawing my story to everyone whether they were minded to hear it or not. The horror of it fell down upon me as if it were a real storm of bad weather, saturating my face and hands.

I thought of my cousin Foss at his home, hearing the news—my cousin who had brought me to my fate; I supposed that he would be nodding complacently to himself, and wished him dead on the spot. I thought of Eliza, listening to the black crows winging above Pimlico, and I suffered for her even though she and our child were now strangers to me. I thought of the dear faces which had once crowded my table, full of talk and laughter, and which were now turned away. I thought of Linden House, and the beauty I had collected there. I thought of all these things, and then I imagined the black crows rising in one mighty flock, travelling off elsewhere, borne upon the winds of the world, so that wherever I landed, they would be sure to have arrived there before me, and would certainly have sounded my name in their filthy voices, meaning that I could never hold up my head as I once did, or possess myself again. [3]

1. TGW returned to England in May 1837—an extremely dangerous thing for him to do. A warrant had been issued for his arrest for forgery (then a capital offence), and there was also a risk that he might be tried for murder. He seems to have been driven by impatience (with his life in France), vanity (he thought he could get away with it) and an unconscious wish for punishment. All these things were anticipated in *Egomet Bonmot:*

> *I swore the world which scouted me should see*
> *That I could be reveng'd—and terribly*
> *I kept my promise—what I've done I've done.*
> *It might be death to some, to me 'twas fun.*

It is also possible, as W. C. Hazlitt said, that "there was a lady in question." Cornwall adds weight to this idea in his autobiography, saying that TGW became "personally intimate with a married female" in Calais, "whom some fear of detection or other strong motive induced him to poison" (Procter, p. 191)—whereupon he fled to England pursued by her sister, who also "became attached to him" (ibid.). The story of his arrest was carried in the *Morning Advertiser* on 12 June 1837, and the transcript of his interrogation appeared in the same paper the following day.

2. The actor William Macready had dined with TGW in 1821; the other guests had included Hazlitt, Cary and Cornwall. On 27 June 1837, Macready went to Newgate—with Charles Dickens, John Forster (who would later become Dickens's biographer) and the illustrator Hablot Browne ("Phiz")—and saw TGW, as Macready records in his *Reminiscences* (p. 401).

3. Newgate prison, rebuilt by George Dance the younger between 1770 and 1782, was reckoned "one of the best public buildings in the metropolis" (Curling, p. 143): it was a large-scale Piranesian construction, comprising two huge windowless blocks, both faced with rusticated stone, flanking a central Gaoler's Lodge. Inside, things had been planned for order and segregation, with seven different categories of prisoner each having its own division. But conditions soon became as vile and corrupt as they had always been in the older versions of the building. Cells built to hold eight hundred prisoners were holding over a thousand by 1817.

Cruel systems of governance were evolved by warders as well as the inmates. These were negligible, compared to the greater cruelties of the law itself. As crime levels rose through the eighteenth century, the number of hanging offences climbed from around fifty to two hundred, and executions were performed with the specific intention of shaming the criminal. (Public executions were not outlawed until 1868.) Furthermore, reformers such as John Howard could do little to control the ways in which prisons elaborated the punishments handed down by the courts. In Newgate, what the *London Magazine* called the "very scandalous practice" of the treadmill did not exist—but there were whippings, bullyings, beatings, and solitary confinement. It was to investigate such barbarities that Dickens made his visit to Newgate with Browne, Forster and Macready.

TGW seems not to have been too badly treated during his imprisonment—but he was shocked by his sentence. He was tried during the Midsummer Sessions at the Old Bailey on Wednesday, 5 July 1837, before Serjeant Arabin (the original of Snub in *Pickwick Papers*), Alderman Wood, Mr. Justice Vaughan and Mr. Justice Alderson. The whole process took less than a morning, and he was sentenced soon afterwards. His prosecutors had delayed bringing him to court because they could not decide whether the insurance offices should charge him with attempted fraud, or whether advantage should be taken of his forgery on the Bank of England to procure his transportation for life. The interested parties held a consultation, the Home Secretary was informed of the difficulties, and the opinion of the law officers of the Crown was taken. In the end, it was decided to try him for forgery only, since there was no strong evidence to convict him of murder.

In his trial papers, TGW was accused of "endeavouring to have the sum of £2,250 part of a certificate share and interest to which Robert Wainewright, Edward Smith Foss and Edward Foss were entitled in certificate Stock transferable at the Bank of England transformed assigned and sold by virtue of a forged letter of Attorney 15 May 1823 . . . also a sum of £3,000 17 May 1824." At his first appearance in court, TGW—a "gentlemanly" man, "wearing moustaches"—pleaded not guilty to all these charges. He was then removed, while officials of the Bank of England discussed what to do next. In the end, he struck a deal with them, and with the Governor of the Bank of England, whereby he agreed to plead guilty to two minor charges, neither of which carried the death sentence, on the assumption that his sentence would be lenient. It was not.

No wonder he felt cheated. He had been given to understand the Bank did not want to "shed blood," and was anxious to "deal mercifully with those whom they were compelled by duty to prosecute." (This reflected a widespread feeling that it was unreasonable for forgery to remain a capital offence.) Furthermore, TGW himself persisted in thinking that the money he had obtained by fraudulent means was in fact his by right, and that even if his actions had been criminal, they were mitigated by the passage of time.

In an article on transportation published by the *Monthly Review* in 1812, Joseph Lowe had said, "It appears to be taken for granted that transportation beyond the seas will not long continue a favourite form of punishment," then added more gravely, speaking of the prisoners sent to America between 1666 and 1775, "The majority of the convicts were of a disposition neither to be meliorated by lenity nor terrified by severity; and, hardened in their crimes, they made even the poor and miserable natives the dupes of their knavery" (*Monthly Review*, vol. LXVIII, pp. 1–2) (information from de Chantilly). These remarks were typical of contemporary liberal opinion, which argued that transportation was a barbaric, short-term solution to a complex social problem.

The authorities persisted, despite such doubts. The same crude ideas that had originally fuelled transportation to America also propelled the First Fleet to Botany Bay in 1787. During the 1830s, the courts were especially energetic. Between 1831 and 1840, 43,500 male and 7,700 female convicts were dispatched—more than were sent in the two previous decades together.

17

A DESPERADO

Reviewing the past few pages of this Confession, I see that I have spoken repeatedly of my innocence; or, rather, I see that I have objected to being too severely punished for the actions I once took. It could hardly have been otherwise, since my story has reached a stage of courts and claims, challenges and counter-claims. Henceforth, however, I shall consider my case proven, and desist from urging the value of my own argument. I mean, that I shall consider myself unjustly punished, and prove myself right by giving nothing other than the record of my treatment. It has been of a barbarity that ordinary minds will struggle to comprehend.

I have already explained that I was hurried from Newgate on my way to Portsmouth. What with the various changes necessary, and the poor condition of the roads as I travelled south, our journey which began in darkness also ended in darkness. My companion, who had protected his ankles from the bite of his irons, had shown a wisdom I regretted was not also mine. Even the lurchings of the coach were enough to break my skin, so that when I stepped down from my eyrie at every switch of horses, I found myself more and more painfully prevented from walking. If I had expected sympathy in this, I had deceived myself. I do not think that my companion and I spoke more than a few sentences during the whole of our time together, and the only interest shown in us by our fellow passengers was the same that a farmer shows in a fox: he would shoot it if he could, and failing that would beat it and spit upon it.

A body accustomed to labouring, or other manual work, might have reached our destination in some semblance of itself. My own frame had known nothing like the buffeting and jostling, the drenching and blowing, which it received through that day. Whatever scenery we passed, no matter how tame or how grand, my mind flew about in all directions, seeking to reassure itself that in reality this journey was no more than a route from Chiswick to the Strand; and these hoof-beats were the thunder of Contributor, willing in harness; and my destination was George's, where I would refresh myself before strolling up to Colnaghi's again, taking all the time a gentleman should. When we gained the edge of Portsmouth at last, and the salt sea wafted through my head to revive me from my daydreams, I still could not readily believe that the fate befalling me was indeed my own.

Lights were out in the town, except in the rudest taverns, where I suppose they were never dim, so that we achieved the dockside unobserved. As I jangled down upon the quay, however, with a rattle which made me feel that I was not a human body at all, but a collection of objects, the moon slid from behind its cloud and revealed my destiny: the black hulk, lying a little way from the mud of the shore, like a wicked Noah's Ark. The whole enormous construction, though it was some distance off, nevertheless seemed to rear up above me, ribbed and barred and moulded by massive rusty chains, as if it too were a prisoner, and not merely a kind of floating cellar for wretches who were trussed up in the same way. [1]

A longboat appeared, rowed by fellows of swarthy and villainous appearance. Nevertheless, I spoke to them kindly, and thanked them for their help, though for my pains I received nothing except a hand in my back which sent me sprawling and clanking into the gunwales, where my companion Aram (as I shall continue to call him) hurtled after me.

When we had crossed the narrow water, and come in under the towering shadow of the hulk—like bathers landed at the foot of an immense cliff—a most revolting stench of humanity, and a most melancholy combination of shouts and groans, rolled over us. It is a curious thing, that when a man finds himself in adverse circumstances, he will generally discover a palliating interest in its being new. While this lasts, it is the only consolation he may expect. In my case, however, there was no such relief. The view of the ship, the sense of its animal existence, and my pitiable difficulty in scaling the chains which hung down on all sides, in order to gain the deck, were so precisely the enactment of a nightmare, that I had no feeling of newness at all. Everything had a horrid familiarity, which hung about my heart like drops of lead.

My concentration on my own safety throughout this operation was such that I did not notice how many others there were, fetched from points along the harbour, and brought on board at the same moment. With the moon now standing clear in the summer sky, sending its light across the surface of the water, and shining with a misty glow in the rigging of vessels which lay off from us, we were ordered into a ragged line and made to wait. For what reason, I know not. Some of us, I noticed, were still clad in our daily apparel, and when our waiting was eventually done, these fellows were ordered to change into coarse suits such as the rest of us already wore. The guards, who were evidently the lowest class of humanity, and devoid of all feeling, took a great pleasure in seeing these men shed their rags of home, and stand naked in the moonlight before they received their new coverings.

There then followed another strange interval of waiting—meaningless except to give our guards an opportunity to prove their power over us. Each of them carried a large and ponderous stick, and when one of our number enquired whether we were to be kept standing all night, two or three of these sticks felled the poor unfortunate to the deck, and kept on repeating their blows long after he had become insensible. I could not look at this, although the guards enjoined us to pay attention to them, and "learn a lesson." They were apparently convinced that we had done so, since when the beating was over, we were immediately led below decks.

It was, as I have said, a summer night, and from the warmth that rose up to me from the hold—so thick with odour that I almost choke at the memory of it—anyone would believe that the moon burned down upon us with the heat of the sun in a desert. It was a heavy, enveloping heat. A heat ripe to rottenness. A heat which worked its way busily through our skins and then lay on the insides of them, next to our hearts and other organs. Within its complete and glistening world, my dread increased a hundredfold. By the time I had been ordered to my place—which was a hammock bed strung between the ship's wall and a bar running down the centre, in line with a hundred or more other hammocks, each like the cocoon of a butterfly which would never awake—by the time I had found my place, I had vowed never again to breathe through my nostrils, and had become a kind of hanging mouth. So were the others around me also hanging mouths. They were all gaping and shining like fools, and many had their hands clasped over their ears as well, so that they could not hear the miserable cries and curses which filled the air.

There are some who, when blighted by cares and oppressed by their passage through the world, find their wakefulness increases in proportion to their misery. I am one of those whom Morpheus favours. When misery begins to threaten me, I defeat him by the simple expedient of closing my eyes and embracing slumber. It is my days that trouble me; not my nights. No sooner had I gained my hammock, therefore, than I fell asleep in it— though I had never encountered such a thing as a hammock before. And no sooner had I fallen asleep, than I was woken up. This was my routine for the next few days, and all of it was performed with the double-irons still upon me, as they were upon my companions. Other routines followed: as first light broke, we were taken on deck, where the pleasures of breathing fresh air were first tainted by our being presented with a bowl of thin gruel, then altogether destroyed by the effort of scrubbing decks. This performance lasted an hour or so, with our guards diligently goading and striking as they chose, before we were required to fold up our hammocks and proceed to further labour.

The inconvenience of this new work was felt acutely by our guards. Each of us was first checked to ensure that our irons were fast, then searched to ensure that we had nothing improper concealed about us, then helped into rowboats to ensure that we did not fall, then rowed across the water to ensure that we did not make off independently, then divided into groups on the dockside and delivered into the charge of taskmasters to ensure that we would not be idle, then set under the care of a First and Second Mate to ensure that we did not escape. At noon we were fetched back on to our hulk for food (which in reality nourished us no more than it would have done a mouse, and as far as the flavour was concerned, may even have contained that creature). When this was swallowed, we were shipped to shore again for more portering, and almost at six were back on board once more, when we were prepared for "school," as they termed it, before being ordered to rehang our hammocks and then to crawl into them exhausted.

I have suffered such severity since that time that I cannot now regard my labours as especially harsh. And yet I know that because I was so unfamiliar with exertion of any kind, my limbs cried out bitterly against the use made of them. What with the bleeding around my wrists and ankles, and the occasional hits that I received from the guards, I am surprised my energy did not drain out of me entirely.

It is the "school" I recollect most easily. It was a time intended for the primitive education of those amongst us who were generally unlettered and untutored, of which there were a good number. Having no need of such instruction, I was left alone—and on one occasion even gained permission to write a letter to the Courts. Because I was still at an early stage in my punishment, I had no real expectation that my confinement would suddenly end. What irked me, however, and has been wormwood during the long time since then, is the knowledge that I was considered to be a desperado. Me! the companion of poets, philosophers, artists and musicians—a desperado! Anyone would smile at this—no, I think anyone would feel for the man, educated and reared as a gentleman, who was now the mate of vulgar ruffians and country bumpkins.

I dispatched my letter full of hopelessness, and submitted myself to my continuing routines, since to object to them would have been to increase my misery. And what came next in our little treadmill of events? Divine Worship, of course. This evening hour of prayer, etc., was a comfort to some, while others found consolation elsewhere. (It was not a difficult thing to bring drink on board if a fitting toll was paid, nor even for there to be a woman smuggled up.) For me, however, neither a contemplation of the life beyond, nor a dalliance among the pleasures of this life on earth, gave an adequate entertainment. In truth, as I have tried to explain, my circumstances had removed me so far from myself I did not know how to find consolation. I was merely a body enclosing an emptiness, and with each passing day this emptiness was filled with new and desperate experiences, which I feared in due course would make a whole man: me.

The longer I pondered this development—with such parts of my brain as survived the shivering blows of my portering on the dockside, and my suffocating at night in my hammock—the more strongly I resolved not to let it become complete. No matter that everyone considered me a desperado: I should not behave as one. No matter that I received blows I did not deserve: they would not knock me out of shape. No matter if my blessed Art flew off and perched in the highest tree imaginable, beyond my reach: I would not betray her. Whatever Self I had pulled together from the pieces of my past life: I would keep faith with it in secret. I would not, like the poor creature in *Frankenstein,* become the thing my circumstances strove to create.

It is the fate of all unfortunates that they should be prevented from directing the course of their own lives, and must, instead, follow a course set by others. No prisoner on that foul hulk knew the duration of his stay, and as I made the vows of resilience I have mentioned above, I did so believing that I should languish in Portsmouth for weeks or longer. On the evening of no more than my fourth day, however, when I was expecting my hands would soon become accustomed to the frottage of labour, and my ankles mend eventually, I was marched on deck with certain others, and informed that on the following morning I would be moved on to the *Susan,* which had anchored near by, and set sail for Van Diemen's Land. [2]

This news was given so bluntly, and with such evident relish at my having no right of reply, I think it might fairly have knocked the breath from my body—except that I was immediately made busy with preparations. Van Diemen's Land! As my guards set about reclaiming the clothes in which I had travelled down from London, and issuing the regulation jacket and waistcoat made of blue kersey, the duck trousers, the yarn stockings and woollen caps in which we would clad ourselves for our journey, I felt the name trickle into my veins like poison. I knew nothing of the place beyond its reputation, which was enough. A dreadful song that we all knew on the hulks, and elsewhere, raced round my memory—in fragments but coming at me every way I turned: "The very day we landed upon the Fatal Shore, the planters stood around us, full twenty score and more, they ranked us up like horses, de dum de dum de dum, they chained us up to pull the plough upon Van Diemen's Land."

It was a simple ditty, but a true one. I supposed the place to be one enormous torture chamber, where those set to keep order spent their days devising more and more cruel punishments, and those ordained to be my companions were so depraved by pain, they would all become mortal enemies. I imagined men hooded and chained, men with their backs flayed for the least offence, men preferring to bring on their own deaths rather than stretch out their mental suffering. Yes, in a matter of seconds I saw all this and more—women running from me, shivering in rags, horribly degraded; young boys looking up at me with piteous tear-stained glances; bestial guards, driving me before them through a hideous landscape of burned earth. I saw all this, and felt it squeezing my heart, at the same time as a quite different fear overcame me: the fear of being so far off from everything I knew. I thought that I could already imagine myself upon the fatal shore of the island, calling back to my present Self in England from some moment in the future, but sealed behind a tremendous thickness of glass, which nothing could penetrate.

As I say, these visions seemed to come instantly, like bolts of lightning; yet considering what followed, they must in fact have occupied me for several moments. Long enough, anyway, for one of my warders to set about reshaping my skull with his cudgel—whereupon the visions altered, and I saw myself as a lone traveller on a deserted road, my head sunk down and my shoulders weary, dragging my feet through sand while the sun hung directly overhead. When I went below decks for the last time, to sleep, this vision also changed, and I dreamed of myself as an infant laid in a doorway, whose broken-hearted mother had swaddled him in a light cloth, but could do no more for him, and had herself departed into the mist and starlight.

On the morrow, there was no opportunity for such poetic reflections: everything was bustle and haste. Indeed, in the course of our being transferred from our hulk to the *Susan,* during our clambering up and down, around and about, forwards and back, and then of arriving below decks in our new accommodation, I almost had the illusion of a little freedom. My guards could not have made me undertake these actions without my agreeing to them, and perversely I found this a comfort.

In the days before being informed of my destination, I had seen the *Susan* lying close by, and had admired her size. The brave bare masts against the sky, and the noble design of her hull, had seemed no part of my suffering. But when I now clambered below her decks, and strung up my hammock among the rest, and felt the dark pressure of her wooden walls around me, and smelled the oppressive air, and heard the cries of my companions echoing, then I understood that the beauty of the vessel could avail me nothing. This made me reflect on other occasions when Art had brought no relief—notwithstanding the adoration I had shown it, expecting its loveliness to heal my hurts. Contemplating such a failure, when the hopes of its opposite had kept my mind afloat through many years, produced in me now the sure expectation of shipwreck and disaster. [3]

1. Prison hulks were large, decommissioned warships, and from the 1770s until the 1850s were widely used as overflows from crowded prisons on the mainland. Initially, conditions on board were chaotic and revolting; then John Capper, who was in charge of hulks between 1813 and 1847, made some improvements, including a cellular structure of incarceration. However, he did nothing to improve standards of sanitation and ventilation, which were appalling.

2. TGW was held in Portsmouth Harbor from 23 to 29 July 1837 (information from de Chantilly).

3. Tasmania (Van Diemen's Land) had first been named by Abel Tasman in 1642, in honour of Anthony Van Diemen, the Governor General of the Dutch East India Company, for whom he was leading an expedition "to map the remaining unknown parts of the terrestrial globe." For years after that, it remained relatively untouched—though it was visited by Cook in 1777, and by the *Bounty* in 1788 and 1792.

The first 279 convicts reached Van Diemen's Land in 1804, the same year that its capital, Hobart Town, was founded; in 1830, two thousand prisoners were arriving every year. By this time, its name had become synonymous with cruelty. Reports of its penal colonies at Maria Island, Norfolk Island, Macquarie Harbour and Port Arthur were especially horrible. Some spoke of the "unnecessary severity" of the regimes themselves; others of prisoners hanging one another, of convicts escaping and living as cannibals, of large-scale opium addiction, and in one case of "an unfortunate individual [who] was thrown down into a cavern . . . and there deliberately killed by a lame wretch with a crutch" (Lemprière, p. 31). Several of these murders were suicide pacts, devised by prisoners who could no longer endure their conditions. It was not unknown for three convicts to form themselves into a gang, in which Convict A agreed to kill Convict B, for which he would then be executed, and for Convict C—who had acted as a witness to the crime—then to win the reward of becoming eligible for murder himself in a newly formed gang.

Much of the blame for these conditions lies with Sir George Arthur (1784–1854), "the archetype of the pious colonial strongman, [who was] charged [in 1824] by the British government with the task of rendering all transportation a perfect terror to the criminal classes" (Hughes, p. 380). When he was replaced by Sir John Franklin (1786–1843) in 1836—the year before TGW arrived—it was expected that a milder regime would begin. But there was not sufficient government support for this, so Franklin's own instincts, his wife's cultural sympathies, and the liberalism of his Private Secretary, Alexander Maconochie, had only a limited effect. Eventually, however, Parliament began to pay attention to the advice of reformists, and to feel the shifting weight of public opinion. In 1843 a sixty-year-old "battered old beau," Sir John Eardley-Wilmot (1783–1847), was appointed Governor, in the hope that he would succeed as a reformer where Franklin had failed. Difficulties on the ground, and tensions between London and Hobart, made this impossible.

Eardley-Wilmot was sacked by Gladstone in April 1846, six years before the end of transportation to Van Diemen's Land, and a little over a year before TGW died. In other words, the cruelties which were designed before TGW arrived on the island were never thoroughly revised during his time as a convict. This meant that he spent the last part of his life in the grip of the most barbarous penal system that England has ever devised, in "the worst spot in the English-speaking world" (Hughes, p. 371).

18

A - A - A - A H !   Q U E E !

J shall be hard pressed to do justice to my journey, since its horrors could be described only by a pen dipped in fire, and for the more ordinary reason that I passed much of it in darkness. This began as follows. While the *Susan* slipped the embrace of Portsmouth harbour, and entered the rolling waters of the English Channel, I was confined below decks with the other passengers. Groups of men, in all imaginable attitudes, lay, stood or sat in a foul phantasmagoria of half-lit limbs and faces. Callot might have drawn it. Dante might have described it. There were old men, young men, boys, stalwart burglars and highway robbers, all packed side by side with wizened pickpockets and cunning-featured area-sneaks. I discovered a forger swinging in a hammock beside a body-snatcher. I heard a man of education learning strange secrets of the house-breaking craft. I studied the expressions of a ruffian of St. Giles, taking lessons in self-control from the keener intellect of a professional swindler.

Meanwhile, the wide world of the sea continued its remorseless but invisible life, and as the noises of the harbour fell away, and with them the white façade of the town, and the green hills behind, my only reality was the one I have described. Many of my comrades wept such copious tears I believe the victims of their villainies would have been astonished, and forgiven them immediately. Others set up a low roaring, which seemed meaningless. Others again cursed the home where they had been born, and which had made them suffer, and shouted, "Come on you devil!" and such like things—meaning, I suppose, the lives which lay ahead of them. I could understand this, but it shocked me none the less, since I wanted nothing so much as the life which lay behind me, and safety. [1]

Indeed, at that despairing moment, and during many of the days following, I endured such extraordinarily clear visions of home and friends I might as well have been drowning in the sea and not floating upon it. I saw the brilliant windows of Linden House, rising above me so that I seemed a child again, treading the springy bed of cedar needles as I came up through the garden after amusing myself with some solitary game. I saw Mr. P. and the dusty eyes of his portraits examining me from the walls of his Painting Room. I saw the swirling fogs of Fermanagh and the brightness of the Strand. I saw devils and heroes rushing from the pencil point of the Professor, and sporting on colossal acreages of paper as if the whole sky were their theatre. I saw Lamb and Hazlitt, Clare and Procter, all crowding round my table in candlelight, and eager to be entertained. I saw my wife and son—but put them out of my mind instantly. Also my cousin Foss. Also my dear Helen, calling to me as she lay in torment. Also my judges. Also my own face, with my hair shaved and my eyes sore with weeping. All these things jigged up and down in a terrible dance, helpless in the rhythm of the waves:

> *Rush! splash! gush! dash, whick-whack!*
> *Wack! whack! u-g-h!—u-g-h!—rush, whack!*
> *Gust, whick! dash, whack! splash; whack!*
> *A-a-a-ah! quee!*

and then those other noises of the stern pump:

> *Bang! bang!*
> *Hippo-tick!—yappee!—tick!*
> *etc., etc.*

My visions of the past, as I have said, seemed to torment me for several days together—but now that I am looking back at them, I see they must in fact have entertained me for a mere twenty-four hours. No sooner had the coast of England sunk from sight than our guards set about rousing us from our reverie (or from our plotting and infamy, as they undoubtedly supposed) and required us to come up on deck for exercise. These guards, who were in fact soldiers bound for duty in Van Diemen's Land, under the command of Major Bunbury, took a particular pleasure in reminding themselves of their responsibilities by punishing us, their charges, for our least offence, and sometimes for no offence at all. During this journey I saw incidents at the mast-head—floggings with the cat and suchlike—which led me to suppose that if there is indeed a God in Heaven, He should certainly have reached His Almighty Hand down through the clouds and administered mercy before we reached our landfall.

Dreadful as they sometimes were, our excursions above deck (which were carried out in small groups or gangs shackled together, in rotation) were most eagerly desired after a period of confinement in darkness. As the longer pull of the open sea began to exert itself, and stronger winds blew at us, many of my companions fell ill, which made the air we breathed in our dormitories no better than might be found in a stable. (Some thought had been given to this, I grant. At the two hatchways into our quarters—one fore, the other aft—our guards set up miniature sails, which were meant to catch a portion of the wind and direct it on to us. This was never adequate for a proper ventilation, however, nor did it afford us the freshness we longed for. Moreover, in times of tropical heat and stillness, such as we found when we drew close to the equator, the sight of this limp device added to our misery, reminding us of all we did not have.)

Being a "W"—for "Weathercock," and not a "B" for "Bonmot," which would have done as well—I generally made my appearance on deck late in the afternoon, when the rest of the alphabet had completed its course of breathing, and departed. Recollecting certain great works that I had perused, and priming the delicate but rusty machinery of my imagination, I prepared myself on my first excursion for a prospect of some splendour. And it is true that the instant my head broke free into the real air, while I was still standing half in and half out of the ship, I could not deny a gust of pleasure. I looked about me, feeling uncommonly like a rabbit emerging from its burrow, and took in the wide wilderness of waters—the crumbling peaks and glistening arêtes, and the evening light flickering over every contour, so that a thousand little sunsets were made and marred in each instant.

Then I was forced wholly into the open by an impatient fellow behind me, and my prospect altered. I confronted a strong barricade, loop-holed and furnished with doors, which ran across the decks from bulwark to bulwark at the foot of the foremast. Inside this device, which was no more elaborate than a cattlepen, were some sixty men and boys, dressed in the same kersey as myself, who I supposed were the worst sorts of villain. Outside the pen, with his weapon held smartly to attention, stood a sentry.

Coming as it were face to face with this warrior (who was in truth no more than a boy, with but a sprinkling of fair stubble on his chin), I could not help fixing him with my eye, and noticing that he returned my look. I suppose that *his* intention was to prove the extent of his power over me—which in any case I did not doubt. *My* intention was to give an acceptable demonstration of character—which is why I did not merely meet his glance, but smiled upon him. There was no chance of a response (which in any case might not have been so sympathetic as I wished), since I was rapidly propelled forward, or rather clanked forward, to begin my health-giving journey around the deck. But when I had completed my circuit—feeling all the while how the brave *Susan* rolled beneath me, allowing certain waves the liberty of washing across her, before withering away through narrow draining-holes—when I had gazed my fill on the collapsing waters; when I had heard enough of the wind singing its mournful ditties in the rigging; when I had watched unto somnolence the slap and strain of the sails—when I had reached the end of all this, then I could begin my pursuit of sleep, knowing that I was not without a friend in the world. I had seen, in the expression of that soldier, a look which showed me I still had the capacity to seem amiable.

Everything I have so far said of my journey belongs to its first few days, when each experience had the shock of strangeness. Now: I will not say that as we continued south I became more accustomed to my situation, and therefore less watchful. (What man could ever grow accustomed to the condition of living as a beast?) But I will admit that as the days slipped past, our life on board developed into a tedium so profound there was a difficulty in separating one hour from the next. The steady blow of the Channel changed to the more furious winds of the Atlantic. The sun grew warmer, and baked us more efficiently in our oven. My kind companions seemed even more remarkable in their kindness, and my barbarous ones more barbarous. But my own mood—which on leaving London had been an agony of deprivation and injustice—slumped into wretchedness. I could not squeeze sufficient interest from the sights around me, however surprising they had been only a matter of days before.

Accordingly, I lived on tenterhooks for anything which promised a departure from our great monotony, rather than for whatever comforts of familiarity lay within it. I am thinking here of our first severe storm (after which we became almost sentimental about such things, vaunting our invincibility), in which the planks of our hull groaned like witches round a cauldron, and such a lunacy of cursing and mopping and bailing and shouting broke out that I almost believed we had arrived in Hell without the inconvenience of having died.

I am thinking also of the day we reached the Cape of Good Hope, and anchored in Simons Town, where we took on fresh supplies, and the whole mass of us was brought up on deck to help with the lading. Although the smaller boats buzzed around us, abusing us and making us ashamed, there was a sublime pleasure in the warm sun and the smell of oranges drifting over the harbour. We were near enough to shore to read the names over the shop doors, and the town which lay beyond them looked very neat and orderly, with the barren mountains rising above, and the ragged peaks at the summit which appeared ready to fall at any moment, and crush all the humanity which lay scattered below. At first light, I thought this anxiety might indeed become a reality, when a man-o'-war in the harbour close to us would fire a gun, and the echo of the explosion struck hard against the mountains before returning to us with a force barely diminished by the distance it had travelled.

I am remembering also, and in this case differently, with no feelings of pleasure, how a quarrel broke out shortly after we had left Simons Town. The argument was between two of my fellows over a portion of plum pudding (which we were allowed in our rations once a week, along with a slice of beef and a bowl of pea soup, rather than the portion of biscuit which was our usual repast). There was a charge of theft made by one against the other; a blow; more blows; a knife was seen; and the soldiers came down like thunder. The consequence was immediate, and the punishment more terrible than any I had yet seen. Our Captain (who generally kept aloof from us, as remote as the man in the moon) ordered every one of his charges on deck, and arranged us to witness the flogging of those two unfortunates, the instigators of the argument. When this was finished, I could not say whether the things taken down from the whipping post were alive or dead—and if alive, how they would mend and become human once more. This was done as a lesson to us all, to make us submissive. I needed no such sort of instruction, so all I learned from the spectacle was how those charged with the duty of executing justice are no better than those they judge. Which I also knew already.

Besides these things, and all other interruptions to our routines, which I have since forgotten, there was one further surprise that I must mention. I shall describe it now as the epitome of everything else on our journey, which otherwise would require a more thorough investigation of dullness than any I am capable of undertaking. When we had passed from the Atlantic into the Indian Ocean, and were bowling along towards our destination at a good speed, it happened that we had bad weather for many days together, with the result that our hours of exercise were curtailed. Those of a mind to do so would sometimes huddle under the hatches (which were kept shut to prevent the waves from washing down over us), and listen to the groaning of the masts as they strove to withstand the force of wind which hurtled against them. Others would stretch at their appointed places upon the floor, or in their hammocks, and turn their thoughts from the oaths and sickness of one another towards the pure and flying noise of the water as it rushed beside our heads.

By this stage in our journey, knowing that each minute brought our destination closer, some of our number had begun to suffer more dreadful apprehensions of our fate than any we had yet entertained. Scenes of great cruelty—of repugnant beatings, and the most degraded and extended labour—passed unbidden through my imagination. Worse even than these were the troughs of loneliness into which I would sometimes stumble— lying not so much in the darkness of the ship, as in the blackness of my own mind, where no light ever came, and no promise of relief was ever held out to a beseeching hand. In such a low state, the arrival of this relentless weather seemed a strange kind of comfort. When I considered it, I felt that its mad ragings were the perfect picture of my own thoughts. When I imagined that the storms might become worse yet, and send us all to the seabed never to rise again, I could almost persuade myself that such an end might be preferable to the one which awaited us.

It was, therefore, with some reluctance that I lent my voice, after several whole days pent in our netherworld, to those others clamouring for a visit on deck—unless, we said, we were to suffocate on our own stable-stench. Our request was not immediately granted, which was only to be expected, but when the winds next drew in their breath, and our Captain was convinced that he would not see his human cargo swept away by Neptune's tremendous blasts, a few of us were allowed up above in little shivering groups.

Thanks to this generosity, I soon found myself in the mid-decks, shackled to other brave souls who were willing to risk their lives for a lungful of salt water—and witnessed the most terrible and melancholy incident of our entire voyage. We were sailing rapidly, as I have said, and waves were dragging eagerly over the prow and rails of the *Susan* like mighty claws. What with the confusion, and the low sky pressing down upon our heads, I felt that I was travelling below the surface of the water, not upon it. Everything was rage and cataract; nothing was steady and in one place. The very breath in my body seemed not to want to belong to me, but to come and go in frantic gasps.

To my amazement (since I had done nothing to provoke this in myself, except glance off to the stern sometimes, and marvel at the enormous towers of water there), I began to reflect on our proximity to the Southern Pole. It is, I admit, a thought to smile at, since in truth we were very far off from that region. Yet while I might make myself blush at the oddity of the fancy, I cannot but admit to it, since it led to a further thought which has remained with me ever since. No sooner had the idea of the Pole entered my mind, than I also began to reflect on its peculiar and fascinating productions—icebergs. I half believe that I saw some examples, drifting on my right hand, clear enough for me to make out their luminous blue slopes and blinding white crests, though in truth they were a kind of hallucination or invention. In such a situation as I was then, any man may suppose that impossibilities are facts—that is not in the least remarkable. What is more striking is this: I understood, as I pondered the vast and icy creations, that I was conceiving of my own brain as a kind of Antarctica, from which large pieces were breaking loose, and floating off hither and thither across the ocean, each taking a precious load of knowledge and memory, then gradually dwindling and diminishing as they travelled north into warmer waters, where soon they were squalid relics, not mighty cathedrals of ice, and finally nothing at all, just a slosh, a slap, a breaking wave which is a shape for a moment, and then no shape at all.

I was snatched from this vision by a most urgent commotion behind me—which carried through the roaring of the winds only because so many voices were joined together. When I looked to discover the reason, I found a knot of soldiers standing close to the helm, all pointing off the stern and acting most excitably. Of course I then turned myself, to share in the object of their interest—which was indeed astonishing. Moving at a height above the waves which brought it almost on a level with my head, and a few yards only beyond the rail of the *Susan,* was a shape that I believed for an instant must be an angel come to fetch me to Heaven—but which I soon knew was an albatross. If the wind blowing about me had not already squeezed copious tears from my eyes, I would certainly have shed them then. The bird was a thing of remarkable beauty, making no visible effort to keep pace with us, never beating its enormous wings, but rather setting its whole body at an angle to the air which supported it, and speeding forward in that fashion. [2]

I immediately thought of Samuel Coleridge, having on several occasions had the honour of meeting that great and prodigious genius. Yet while I insist this was a natural connection for me to make, I have since wondered whether it did not in some way beget the unfortunate consequence that followed.

Be that as it may: while we continued sailing alongside the bird, I started to recite to myself some appropriate lines from my friend's poem of the Ancient Mariner, and before I had made my way through half a dozen or so, I noticed one of the soldiers raise his musket to his shoulder and take aim at the bird. I do not know whether I began to utter a protest at this desecration, since I would certainly have known such a thing to be useless, and likely to result in an injury to myself—but whether I did or not, the wind kept everything to itself. While the bird still hung there, seeming motionless as it breasted the blast, its white bosom quivered as it suddenly received the musketball, and immediately blushed crimson—whereupon the bird, rather than falling headlong into the waves, tipped its wings until they brought it over the deck of the *Susan,* then meekly folded them in the attitude of a suppliant. The crash as it fell was silent, yet appeared to run through the whole length and breadth of our world, and even to stun the soldier who had brought about the downfall of God's creature; he stood dazed for a full half-minute. When he at last came to himself, it was to begin a kind of frenzy, in which he set about the poor creature with the stock of his musket, and eventually drew his bayonet from its sheath at his belt, and cut off the head. His fellows, who watched this exceptional performance without a word, being perhaps of a more superstitious nature than their colleague, then roused themselves and pulled him back from his work, declaring that they would now assist him in carrying the body below to the galley, and discussing how they would eat it, and generally congratulating one another.

Such guards as remained—and there were a few of them only, but sufficient for the purpose—immediately turned their attention to us, and decided that our exercise was finished. With that, we were marched back to our quarters, which for the first and final time on my journey I was not sad to regain. The cruel death of the albatross seemed to portend a tragedy, and I was glad of an opportunity to contemplate its approach. Accordingly, I lay awake in my hammock for a large number of sea miles, reflecting on the ways in which beauty is given to us for our delight, but is always condemned to vanish.

I have heard it said that when a man has been at sea for many days together, and absent from everything that is familiar and precious to him, he will long for a sight of land with the same tenderness that he feels for his dearest love. Yet I have also heard that on being vouchsafed this sight he longs for, his passion will immediately fade, and bitter disappointment arrive in its place, because nothing in our experience matches our expectations.

In my own case, I both dreaded and desired the end of our journey—but when the day came for us all to be called up on deck, and for our Captain to point out the green mountains of Van Diemen's Land on the horizon, the balance between these two feelings slipped, and I understood that I had reached the blackest day in my whole calendar of darkness. The reality of my situation entered the very foundations of my Self and consumed me utterly. All my long time in London I had been on friendly terms with hope. During my time of making-do in France, I had at least breathed the pure air of liberty. On board the *Susan* I had entertained the precarious notion of living between two worlds and belonging to neither. Now my future became my present, and within its dismal and humiliating boundaries the whole course of my life struggled to find its shape.

Between our first sighting of the Island, and our arrival, our guards kept us at tiresome tasks of cleaning and tidying, so that when evening drew on, and hills which had once resembled clouds were hills indeed, our floating home was in a better condition than it had been at any time since leaving port. A visitor on board might have believed we took pride in it, or even pleasure. When our duties were done, and still with every appearance of willingness, we formed ourselves on deck in a ragged kind of battalion, and were encouraged to pay attention to the new world that we were entering.

It is a fact, and one often noticed by our philosophers, that a man cannot easily believe a thing to be true until he feels it as a sensation. No matter how dreadful the intelligence I had formerly received, and no matter how often my blood had frozen at rumours, I could not suppose Van Diemen's Land to be a real and palpable place before I had seen it with my own eyes. As the *Susan* left the Tasman Peninsula on the south-western horizon, and a pilot boat darted out from the mist of Adventure Bay to guide us; as the wide reaches of Storm Bay spread out around us; as the curling headlands began to encircle us; as the shaggy slopes of Mount Wellington reared up before us; as the sea birds began making their harsh cries across the steadying water—as all these things occurred, I felt a genuine amazement at the sight of men working in the open here and there, and of smoke rising from fires and chimneys, as if such things were possible only at home, in the world I knew, and not here.

The shock of this discovery, however, was soon assimilated, only to be replaced by another and differently disturbing notion. This island, this Sodom of misery and epitome of vice, this satellite of humanity, where inhumanity flourished: it was beautiful! As we drew towards the harbour, where the estuary narrowed somewhat and the river (named the Derwent, which inflamed me with cruel memories of Wordsworth) wound off between verdant hills towards the centre of the country, a view of bare hills swelled up in our stern, which seemed to glow silver in the last light of day.

(I later learned that these hills had been home to the original settlers of the place—whalers, who had cleared them for their habitation. For most of the year, while their owners are away at sea, they have a ruined and forlorn air, and sheep may be seen wandering there, grazing in and out of doorways.) Nor were these hills the only forms of nature which pleased me. The bald summit of Mount Wellington, which in winter I would see mantled in soft snow, was scored and fretted so that it resembled a gigantic church organ, and seemed in its immensity to mock the settlement of Hobart Town, which crept across the more lowly slopes around the harbour. [3]

As I examined these things, and enjoyed the wealth of fresh impressions, which fairly dazzled me after the monotony of our long time at sea, it was impossible for me to prevent some excitement from mingling with my apprehension. There was a fascination in seeing the semaphore messages, signalling our arrival, running between Mount Nelson and the Mulgrave Battery. There was a poetry in the casks being trundled across Salamanca Place. There was a beguiling story in the sight of red-coated soldiers keeping company with a New Bedford whaling Captain. Yet I did not have to resolve this complication in my feelings immediately. When the *Susan* had found a berth amidst the immense mass of shipping which filled Sullivan's Cove, and we had begun to grow accustomed to the stillness which now lay beneath our feet, we were informed that we would not be set on land until the following morning, there being certain formalities to prepare. Such was our Captain's confidence in the security of the place he allowed those of us who preferred to sleep on deck to remain there throughout the night— which option was taken by the majority.

So it was that I began my life as a transported convict, receiving the impression that the world about me, which was in reality a complete prison house, was no less than its old free self: a spectacle of moving waters and fixed stars, of pastoral farms in wooded hills, and of the many and varied noises (reaching us from shore) which constitute the sound of humanity going about its business. I believe that I did not once close my eyes that night, but stared continually up at the sky, in such close company with my associates, who were themselves all suddenly silent and wondering, that as we were silvered in the moonlight we might have been herrings in a shoal. At one moment I heard the laughter of a party returning from their journey upon Mount Wellington, complimenting one another on their very interesting excursion. At another I heard two men discussing how a boy they knew had been drowned, his legs entangled in the kelp. As a background to all this was the occasional music of a band, playing for some sort of festivity. (The effect of these happy notes was wonderfully melancholy as they tinkled through the ships around us, and fell into our ears.)

There then followed a diminuendo, of men and women going home to their families, and an undertow of big warehouse doors being drawn shut, of lighter domestic doors closing more softly, and (which of course I could not hear, only imagine) of wicks purring as they were turned down in lamps, while silence inherited the world. Or not silence, precisely, but the different sounds of night—life's other kingdom. The murmur of sea winds through the enormous woods which grew around the Town; the occasional sharp cry of a creature (strange to me) echoing on the vales and slopes; the slap of a fish as it rose and fell back through the black surface of the harbour. Above and beneath all this came the sound of the water itself—a gently rolling, restless thing, like the sigh of a man as he breathes out his grief over and over, never satisfied that his sorrow can be done with and cancelled.

1. The *Susan* was a massive vessel of 572 tonnes, launched in Calcutta in 1813, and used regularly to carry convicts from England to Van Diemen's Land. The voyage usually took a little more than a hundred days; the *Susan*'s record time (achieved in 1842) was 92 days. She left Portsmouth with TGW and around 300 other prisoners on 29 July 1837, and reached Hobart on 21 November. Six prisoners, one guard, and the First Mate died during the voyage.

The Master of the *Susan* was Henry Neathy and her surgeon was Edward Hilditch—a lazy man who passed all his duties to one of the prisoners, Peter Barrow, who later worked at the notoriously harsh Boys' Reformatory at Puer Point. The *Susan* also carried 30 soldiers, four women, seven children, and some kind of religious adviser—though what kind precisely is not known. Many convict ships were tyrannized by evangelists who seized on their captive audience and deluged them with sermons and solemn advice. TGW is described as having "declined" this kind of instruction, though his convict record gives his conduct on board as "good." The fact that his name is bracketed on the lading list with "Eugene Aram" suggests that he associated with this man during the voyage.

2. In his account of being transported to Australia in 1831, Joseph Mason refers to

> Albitrosses which are a very large bird some of them Grey some white & some brown [B]oth sorts with several others are flying day & night with only short intervals of rest on the water and they never go near the land except to lay their eggs and hatch their young The soldiers and sailors in our ship caught many albitrosses by throwing a strong hook baited with a piece of beef or pork into the sea and let it drag at the stern of the vessel They come round the ship most and are easiest caught in rough stormy weather (p. 34).

3. Hobart Town was founded in 1803; when TGW arrived there thirty-four years later, it had a population of approximately fourteen thousand. Charles Darwin, who visited in the *Beagle* in January 1836, described it as follows:

> The streets are fine and broad; but the houses rather scattered: the shops appeared good. The town stands at the base of Mount Wellington, a mountain 3,100 feet high, but of very little picturesque beauty: from this source, however, it receives a good supply of water. Round the cove there are some

fine warehouses, and on one side a small fort ... Comparing the town to Sydney, I was chiefly struck with the comparative fewness of the large houses, either built or building. This circumstance must indicate that fewer people are gaining large fortunes. The growth, however, of small houses has been most abundant; and the vast number of little red brick dwellings, scattered on the hill behind the town, sadly destroys its picturesque appearance.

19

NUMBER 2325

lthough I say my eyes did not close during that long night on deck, I must in fact have swallowed a part of Morpheus' delightful draft, since suddenly I found that I was soaked through with dew, and cold, and would certainly have noticed the change from my former comfortable state, had I not slumbered. At any rate: with my fellow star-gazers, I was on my feet in an instant (and in a cacophony of clanking), clasping my arms about me and shivering. The morning was red, with a thin mist shrouding the surface of the harbour, and a much more dense veil drawn across the face of the Mountain. I was gazing at this, listening to the grumblings of my companions, when for the last time I heard my guards call their "Rouse out there! Turn out! Turn out! Huzza! Huzza!"—and then add the words which were new: "Going ashore! Huzza for the shore!"

In the event, our disembarkation did not take place until we had lined our stomachs with bread and soup, and this delay allowed me to examine my surroundings more carefully. On our starboard side, the Black Rocks and cliffs of Bruny Island appeared most forbidding: strange catastrophes of stone, tumbling and twisting in the battering waves. But as the sun lifted clear of its misty appurtenances, the whole landscape also brightened, and the heavens became blue, somewhat darker than the ocean skies we had become accustomed to, and colder to look at, with a touch of ice in their high dome.

This beauty helped to steady me when I at last stepped on to *terra firma*—which, I might say, seemed not in the least firm, but rather to move as though I had trodden upon a whale; the sensation remained with me for several days. I found myself immediately in a column of twelve or fourteen men, all of us still in chains, led by a crisp-looking guard, to the Prisoners' Barracks in Campbell Street. Our journey, which lasted a matter of moments, took us along the dockside past the same large warehouses I had lately heard rattling their doors, and beyond them I glimpsed neat streets of diminutive redbrick houses, none of them with any pretension to elegance, crowding over the hills which lie between Mount Wellington and the Derwent.

I resented the ugliness of these dwellings, but not even my disappointment, nor the various dreads that hovered about me, were enough to quash my pleasure at leaving the *Susan*. I looked upon her (I do not mean that I went so far as to turn my head) as a place of intolerable torment, and if I had any further thoughts about her, then or later, it was merely to wish that she would sink to the bottom of the sea and rot, at a time when none of her suffering cargo was on board. Even now, I happily bid her farewell once more—that floating den of vice. Farewell! May she founder in lonely grief, in some remote and freezing ocean, while the spirits of all those she carried jeer and rejoice at her passing. Farewell, I say, and again—farewell!

If there is any gusto in what I have just written, I regret it. I regret it because the descriptions I am coming to next, if they are to seem true, must be approached with the sternest words in the lexicon. I have said elsewhere that at various times in my existence I had been brought to the lowest point of despair. Compared to what now lay in store for me, these sloughs were as nothing—mere gentle dips and declivities in my fortune.

I shall say what I mean bluntly, as it deserves. When my column reached the Prisoners' Barracks—a ramshackle affair of dormitories, cook-houses, etc., built of rough timber from the forest near by, and arranged round a dusty yard—I was first interviewed for my particulars. The fellow who did this, seated at a coarse desk above which hung his even coarser face, blotched by the heat and wind of the island, was an insolent fool, who asked me: What was my offence? When I told him "Forging a power of Attorney," he entered this information with a suspicious leer. I was then examined by Dr. Edward Bedford, and "mugged" as they say here—or described. When I saw the rude hand of my examiner blundering across the ledger, reducing me to a set of one-word definitions, I knew the lies about my nature, which had begun at my trial, and deepened ever since, had reached a new profundity. [1]

Yet I could do nothing, save hope to avoid any extreme punishments. And one thing more, which I shall now mention. On that first evening ashore, 22 November 1837, hanging in my hammock like a lump of cheese in a muslin sock (and having no more space—about eighteen inches—than on the *Susan*), I resolved that I would quietly and inoffensively pursue any chance to prove the loyalties which had shaped my former existence. I would not forget my blessed Art, nor her inspiring dictates.

If I had known how far off these things would be during the next bitter while, I might not have been so bold. As it was, everything that befell me strengthened my resolve. I could not live as one-in-many, as I had done before, and I could not find it in me to seem facetious and light-hearted. But I could honour the same true gods of my worship, and so raise myself above the common mass.

This "next bitter while" began soon enough. I passed a week or less waiting to discover my future, performing hours of temporary labour on the wharves, and learning the strange differences of my new life. In due course, I was fetched before the Appropriation Authorities, as the Regulations demanded, and given to understand the terms of my punishment. My Judges in London had already requested that I be employed on the Public Works, but I well knew how the labour of prisoners depended in some measure on their skills, and I therefore expected to wield a pen and not a shovel. To this end, I approached the officer who was to decide my fate, feeling a strong desire to assist him with the sensible decision I believed that he must take. When he enquired my trade, I told him "Clerk," and followed this with some information concerning my ability with languages, my reputation as an Author, and my interests as an Artist. Naturally, I looked for sympathy with these things. But my words produced nothing except a spluttering guffaw, whereupon my officer—my fate, my god of the moment—waved me away from him like a fly. The judgment that I must work on the roads came rolling after me like a heavy stone.

I felt so nearly crushed flat by this intelligence, I was incapable of complaint or remonstration, and once I was out of my tormentor's presence, there was no opportunity for either. Never in my most dismal fantasies had I supposed that I should suffer such torture. Never did I conjecture that a body bred for comfort, and all the opportunities of ease, should be so damnably degraded. Never did I imagine that a mind cultivated for wit and intelligence, and for a speaking companionship with beauty, would find itself in such a wilderness of stupidity. When I regained my place in the Barracks, and gathered myself again, I honestly believed that I would prove incapable of the tasks which lay ahead, and that therefore they must soon be the agents of my destruction.

There is a spirit of devilment in the cruellest taskmasters, which prevents them from allowing their charges the satisfaction of any such release. The following morning, when I began my new career, I would not have believed my guards willing to show such restraint. Their scorn was so severe, and their eye for punishment so sharp, it seemed probable that none of us would live beyond nightfall. Yet it was the special skill of these supervisors to keep us in the middle way of suffering—exhausted by our toil but not broken, most wretched in our hearts but not entirely without spirits. At the close of every day following, I discovered a mite of energy remained in me, so that I could promise myself I would survive on the morrow.

I have said before, when opening the history of my life on board the *Susan,* that I felt flummoxed by the difficulties of telling one day from another. This new period of my existence, in which I spent almost a full year at work upon the roads, presents a similar difficulty. Here, indeed, the routine, the terms and conditions, the silence, the beastly facts of fetching and carrying, were all so nearly identical, I did not feel that I was living similar days in succession, but the same day over and over—as though time had been forbidden to pass, and I was condemned for eternity to tramp upon a treadmill, which gave me the sense of moving forward, but in fact kept me in one place.

Since it will represent them accurately, I shall therefore compress the story of my labours into a single day. My companions and I were woken from our slumbers before sunrise, usually around 5:30 a.m., and within a half-hour we found ourselves marched out through the wooden gates of the Barracks. I say marched, but no army ever proceeded as we did. Clad in the vile uniform of the canary, and some of us with the word FELON stamped upon our backs, we were kept in groups of fifty or so, with guards to each group. In one of our hands we carried a napping hammer, which rested upon our shoulders; with our other hand we held up, by means of a piece of rough twine, the heavy chains that bound our ankles. So we went, shuffling at an agonizing pace, and with the eyes of any early risers in the Town looking at us with contempt, until we reached our destination.

Throughout this journey, and through the long hours that followed, our overseers would patrol freely up and down the line, swinging the stout canes with which they pointed out to any straggler the sin of his weakness (with a good few heavy blows upon the back). If there was a more heinous crime committed, such as the uttering of a single word, then the cat-o'-nine-tails would appear, its whistling claws immediately splitting the skin, after the uniform of the offender had been pulled up in readiness.

At what we called "breakfast" there was an allocation of short rations and water, which we ate wherever we happened to be situated. At "dinner" there was an hour for our self-recovery, and at dusk we returned to our Barracks, where we would be locked up once more, after another mouthful of refreshment. (On rare occasions, if we had travelled very far into the country, we spent our nights in large wooden rooms—which we ourselves had dragged on iron wheels to our workplace. Having no windows, they in fact resembled boxes more than rooms.)

It is the intention of all such regimes to prevent any individual from expressing his Self in any way whatsoever. I am not speaking here of Personality (which was a luxury we had all abandoned), but of something more commonplace—such as sickness, or any ordinary frailty. At first appearance, any such weakness would not be investigated, to see whether it was real—but the offender would be paraded in the Lumber Yard, stripped to the waist, and treated to a dose at the flogging post, while the rest of us stayed in the darkness of our dormitories and set up a loud wailing, so that we could drown the dreadful whistle and crack of the tails. [2]

The more frequently I served as the unwilling auditor of these punishments, the more my sympathy grew for every offending wretch. Because some bad characters feigned illness to be relieved of work, and invalids were presumed to be shirking their duties until they were proved otherwise, I saw men whose genuine feebleness meant they were close to breathing their last taken out and flogged towards death's embrace like unwilling nags at a steeplechase. I have also seen some confined with lunatics, and all sorts of other indignities. And I have recollected, as I pondered these things (and kept the recollection to myself) Rembrandt's depiction of Christ upon the Cross, the ghastly, broken-stretched body nearly torn asunder by His own weight, fainting with loss of blood, which now runs in narrower rivulets from his slit veins, his temples and breast drowned in sweat, and his black tongue parched with the fiery death-fever.

Considering myself, in the general way of things, to have led a most unfortunate existence, and been denied the lucky bias of fortune, I expected every day that I should be singled out for punishment such as I have described. Yet in this respect at least I was blessed. I never suffered more than some light blows from my overseers now and again, which leniency I regarded as nothing less than a form of justice, since I always performed my duties on the gang with an equable steadiness, and was judged to be a person of good character, so that I was often spared the heaviest tasks.

I see that in my determination to describe my conditions, I have neglected to say what these tasks entailed. In a word, they were nothing (though everything). One time I would be in a gang which felled trees and cleared scrub. Another, I would be levelling ground. Another, I was breaking stones for the surface of the road. Another, I would be hewing blocks for the curb. There. Nothing and yet everything, as I have said. It is enough.

What I would dwell on more willingly, and shall therefore make my last word on this melancholy subject of the gangs, is the country our work took us into. Van Diemen's Land is an island where the landscape quickly grows impatient with its latest beauty, and changes from wooded hills, to barren flats, to estuaries, with remarkable swiftness. Everywhere there are eucalyptus trees which, as botanists know, shed their barks, not their leaves, and so seem always in a state of shabby undress. Other varieties include the Woody Pear and the Bunya Tree (of which I have tasted the milky seeds with some pleasure). These and their leafy companions often grow together in astonishing density, and sometimes I have felt, gazing upon them, that I stood at the beginning of Time itself, before humanity had come into the world. I might even have relished this sensation, had I not recognized it as a part of my task to destroy innocence—as certainly as the innocence of the island's original inhabitants had already been destroyed. (I recollect seeing with shame, but no surprise, the treatment handed out by the settlers on the island to those whose families they denied a just inheritance.) [3]

The creatures which hunted in these mighty thickets were a part of the whole picture of destruction, and although this renders them a supplementary source of grief, I cannot but smile in naming them. The kangaroo is a remarkable animal, and I dare say noble-minded in its way. (I not infrequently found a specimen had bounded into my dinner pot, with salt, pepper, onions, and two or three strips of pork.) But "skippy," as I have heard it called, is predominantly a curiosity, seeming to be an assemblage of different forms, and not one entire unto itself. So is its smaller cousin, the Potoroo. So in a different sense is the Devil, having a head too large for its body, and jaws too large for its head. (The small and striped Tiger I never saw, but have heard it is a better-balanced thing.) With all this oddity on the ground of the island, and the strange brightness of the air above it (the shocking green and reds, etc., of the parrots and lorikeets, which fly everywhere like fragments of a dinner service)—with all this oddity it was impossible, for at least a few of the minutes which constituted my day, not to be diverted. Each pleasant sighting gave me to think that, beneath the level of humanity, lay a stratum of creatures with whom I could happily converse (if I shared their language) on matters such as the importance of dressing well, and of drinking at the fountains of sensual delight.

When I had endured the rigours of the gangs for almost a year, my overseers took pity on me. Noticing that I had never once complained (in their hearing), they decided in their wisdom that I had suffered the shame of a yellow uniform for long enough, and so removed it from me; and also, in the same mood of enlightened benevolence, unclasped the chains from my ankles, at which release my delight was so immense I truly felt weightless, and believed that I might float upwards from the surface of the earth.

I was soon reacquainted with the usual consequences of my actual mass and volume, when these same overseers described the different tasks they had devised for me: I was to become an orderly in the Hospital. [4] Yet while I had no stomach for illness, even this news came as a relief. Not to be so weary in my body; not to have such heaviness in my head, but rather to have work with dignity—even, it was indicated, to have the opportunity to practise my drawing again, if I so desired . . . If I so desired! In the space of an instant, I almost came back into possession of my Self.

But what sort of Self remained, for me to call it my own? I have admitted that I was spared the worst kinds of punishment on the gangs yet, in spite of this, the effect of so much demanding labour upon a constitution which was not built to withstand it had done me real and lasting harm. It is strange to say, but I felt this more keenly when I left the gangs than ever I did when I worked with them. I expected that, after the sheer weight of labour had dropped from me, I would spring upwards again like a tree which has been bent down and suddenly released. I did not. I more closely resembled a tree which has been espaliered into a new and unnatural shape, which it can never relinquish. A stoop that had grown habitual did not correct itself. The skin of my fingers and face could not regain their white softness. My hair and moustaches, which had once glowed, had no lustre. For all these reasons I became a stranger to my own image. [5]

Before I describe my duties in the Hospital, I must pursue one further idea. During the time of my greatest suffering—when my oppressors found the most loathsome labour for their humble servant to perform—I had little inclination to examine the connection between my circumstances and the crime for which I had been condemned. There was, I mean to say, no energy for extraneous thought, only for the arduous matters in hand. Besides which, I suspected that if I allowed my mind to run in this direction at all, it would never stop, and would drag me headlong into a still deeper misery.

When I turned my back on the roads, however, and had a greater opportunity for reflection, my sense of the injustice done to me began to rise, and, having risen, quickly overwhelmed me. The callous cruelty of my cousin Foss; the knavish tricks of the Governor of Newgate; the stone hearts of my Judges: all these haunted my imagination. In the night, especially, the repeated thought that I had done no more than take what was already mine—this gnawed at me so that I felt less and less like a poor prisoner, and more and more like Prometheus upon his crag, where the eagle tears endlessly at his liver.

Now, to the Hospital. Spending my days among clyster-pipes and gallipots, leeching cups and blood porringers, I had a sufficient acquaintance with death to last any man for a lifetime. Indeed I would sometimes smile to myself (though generally the muscles governing this performance had wasted to uselessness), considering how in my earlier existence I had dallied with fancies of horror, and now found them a reality. I shall prove what I mean by giving another epitome, pressing together the experience of months into a single day. Thus, and without delay.

Huzza! Huzza! It is not yet light, but a cold and luminous glow illuminates the sky, as the last moon- and starlight reflects off the Derwent into my dormitory, and our impatient guards rouse us from our slumbers, shaking our hammocks as a parent might shake a sleeping child before setting off upon a journey, only with more force, and we are tipped out into the chilly air to perform our appointed tasks.

A mouthful of grog—and then a soldier appears, my own and particular to me, who is my companion downhill from the Barracks to the Hospital. Because I am no longer encumbered by shackles, but trusted to stay close like an obedient puppy, I take the most extravagant long strides, relishing the freedom of each step, as the fingers of Aurora grip the summit of the hills to the east, and that ever-new Goddess appears blushing with the delicious effort of her elevation. Her crimsons fall into the strong current of the Derwent, flashing a million fires. The kookaburras and lorikeets begin their clamour. The fish in the streams lift an eye to the heavens, and sink down into a place of greater safety. And myself, your prisoner? I fill my lungs with the sweetness of nature, unable to suppress my pleasure in all things sensual, and knowing that in a few more strides I shall arrive at the gatehouse occupied by that old dullard Samuel Hopkins, whom I shall greet warmly in spite of my disdain for his ignorance of everything beautiful, because it is in his gift to make or mar my time entirely.

And now indeed I come to it: the Hospital, which is a simple yellow-brick edifice, with assorted outhouses, and the gatehouse with a door like a sentry post, and in the door Mr. Hopkins. Good morning, my pudding-faced, pond-witted friend! What may we do for each other today? For my part, I can promise a sketch of your sow and piglets if you so desire, and in return, you may speak kindly to me, as I continue (taking a last few lungfuls of free weather) on to the office of the Superintendent, where my guard is dismissed and I am ordered to wait. Perchance now for a while I shall twiddle my thumbs, and wish that I had eaten a heartier breakfast. Perchance there will be some beguiling labour to perform, such as the mopping of a floor. Perchance again, and in recognition of my genius (which, as I say, has now been acknowledged as existing, since I am no longer confined among the lowest of the low), some once vital organ or other has been left for me to draw and commemorate. Let me whisk the covering off this dish on the table here, for example. As I suspected: a liver so raw-looking and mottled with brown spots it might be the face of a flabby country gentleman who has ridden for miles through English rain, and come home richly attired in mud but without a fox to reward him for his trouble. [6]

But hush! Who is this, that now disturbs me from my reverie? It is our esteemed Surgeon (Assistant) Edward Bedford, offspring of Holy Willie, exactly on time, as I am. [7] What has he for me today? Not one thing but many, as is his wont. While the clocks across Hobart Town stand a little short of nine o'clock, I follow at his heels into the first ward, where we are greeted by the unconscious groans of some poor souls who are past caring what may befall them, and the sensible gasps of others who see the approach of their fate, and run their eyes over one of their own arms or legs, fearing that soon they may never call them their own again. I carry in my two hands a tray of instruments, which are used either to further or to allay these anxieties, watching the Doctor turn back the heavy cuffs of his frock coat, and softly palpate a pink parcel of anatomy here, or a bruised and horrid ditto there.

During my earliest days in this trade, I required the utmost restraint, not to cry out for the pain of those I attended. Now I have learned to harden that well-tuned and sentimental organ, my heart, and feel nothing except my own relief at suffering no pain more severe than a toothache. Moreover, I have seen Dr. B. show as much skill with a blade as ever I saw Mr. P. show with a brush, and as a result give life itself, and not merely a likeness. Let me demonstrate this by offering an instance of one patient, who might stand (I should say "lie") for any number. Imagine him carried into the surgical room, ordained as our first job of the day. He has already drunk brandy in large quantities, and drams of tincture of opium, so that he is stupefied, and as we survey him, we observe that one leg has the perfect form and ivory whiteness of a carven Classical hero's, while the other is fly-blown, and has a strap tourniquet tied around the upper part, to control haemorrhage.

From the Doctor's vest pocket, a watch chimes one, two, three, four, five, six, seven, eight, nine. His capable hands then take up the large amputating knife (our patient now being held firmly by me and others, about the shoulders and arms) and makes a wide, semi-circular sweep of the blade, from the inside of the thigh, beginning beneath and cutting up and around to meet the point of the commencement. "Pressure," Dr. B. then calls out, his voice drowning the now continuous but muted complaints of the patient, whereupon I apply a finger to the artery, while the doctor severs the muscles and their sheaths in the leg. Another assistant then slips a crimsoning tray beneath the patient, before drawing away from the incision, by means of an ingeniously placed cloth, the hindering and weeping mass of flesh. In this way, the bone is exposed for the saw, which the Doctor immediately uses with a will. It is three minutes past nine when he drops the limb into a bucket placed near by for the purpose.

Such memories are not an unusual thing with me. At some times in the Hospital, I have seen a woman delivered of such a monstrous child, and in such agonies herself, that the breath has been driven straight out of her body—and I have quietly taken away the remains. Or I have watched a child have the bone of its arm broken, so that it might be fixed more perfectly— and I have calmed the piteous cries. Or I have smelled the stench of illness rising from a mess of bandages (which swaddled at their centre a human form)—and I have poured ammonia and vinegar over them, to sweeten and savour the atmosphere. I have done all these things, and so well, they have made me appear insensible to suffering (which would most certainly set tongues wagging against me)—and I have congratulated myself upon the firmness of my purpose.

At other times, my duties demanded less of the murderer's art. One moment in the wards I was a fetcher and carrier of linen, which must be frequently steeped in water and then thoroughly dried and exposed. Another moment, I was a benevolent nurse, administering medicines and comforts. Another moment, I was preparing gruel, or shaving a stubbled chin, or combing the lank locks of a poor faded beauty. Another moment, my fingers were tongs for all sorts of nuisance (such as bones and rags and other articles), or claws for removing provisions illegally stored beneath a bed, or pincers for holding my own nose when I climbed down to clear the rivulet which ran alongside our building, and which readily became a most distressing channel of filth.

It would, no doubt, appear strange to those acquainted with my former existence to know that the compliments I had once been paid for my blessed Art ranked in my mind not much higher than the praises I now received for my work in the Hospital. From the first, I had nothing but kindly encouragement from Dr. Bedford. At the knee of his father, that distinguished and powerful instrument of the Almighty, he had learned the need for charity towards his fellow creatures; and in return for my assistance at his operations, etc., he gave me the benefit of his good opinion. In different circumstances, I believe we might have become equal friends. The same would have been true of his young colleague Frederick Brodribb—and for my disappointment in this respect, I must blame blind fortune as well as circumstance. [8] This veritable Apollo (as Brodribb appears in my sketch of him) was a person of great promise and a most admirable disposition; zealous and indefatigable in his attentions to the poor people under his care, and a son of whom any parent might be proud. Alas, that virtue is not rewarded. Alas, that simple goodness is not an armour against all that threatens it. When the fever raged in our Town (at a time I shall shortly mention), and the rooms of the Hospital overflowed with the dead and dying, an arrangement was made to appropriate the synagogue at the junction of Argyle and Liverpool Street, where poor Brodribb was appointed the senior man. A boy, with a man's troubles! Within a few days, his diligence had worn down his ability to resist infection, and he too was conveyed to a place where none wakes, unless it be for everlasting refreshment. Until that time, I suppose, his spirit will still walk the wards, asking gentle questions and receiving grateful replies, and looking always to your humble servant, as a very present help.

I cannot neglect to mention a third person now, and so collect my sponsors into a Holy Trinity. When Dr. Clarke was appointed Surgeon in 1840-whatever, and all manner of reforms were put in train at our Hospital, he brought with him a brother-in-law, Dr. Nuttall, who became my daily companion for almost four years. [9] Indeed, in all my time at work on the wards, Nuttall was the only man I met who bore himself like a complete gentleman, and did no discredit to his breeding. He had about him a spirit of elevation which even Dr. B. (on account of his extreme busyness) and Brodribb (on account of his youth) could not match. No one should be surprised, therefore, if I say that this fine man kindled in me the desire to lay claim once more to my freedom and my good name—by persuading me that I should do more than merely execute a drawing here and there, but actually take up brushes again, and set to work as a Painter. Nuttall was the Pole Star on my journey to this ideal, and its most heartening companion. His encouragements and indulgences were essential to my well-being. [10]

As I have indicated, I cannot recall these men without attaching them to the more severe test we faced together—namely, the Great Epidemic of 1839. This catastrophe began when our summer was at its most intense, and a sudden infection ran through the entire Town at a great rate. Very soon our wards became more crowded than Piccadilly on a holiday afternoon. Almost an entire road gang, for example, which in total numbered one hundred and twenty men, fell sick at the same instant and arrived at our gatehouse in a crowd. They considered themselves most unfortunate to be so afflicted, I need hardly say—but in truth they were not so unlucky as another gang, which fell ill just as suddenly, and lost a half of its complement before it had even reached the same gates.

Within a single month, almost a tenth of the Town was stricken, the disease proving no respecter of position as it flew between cottages and mansions. Dr. B. himself was ill for a duration, so that I was compelled to go about my duties without a guide. Brodribb, as I have said, was entrusted with the ward in Solomon's Temple, and promptly fell a lamented martyr to his cause. There were others, too, whose names have since faded from the roll, who performed innumerable acts of kindness for their fellows, and took no reward for their trouble, only death. [11]

It was a wonder to me that I was spared this great and universal slaughter, and moved among its victims inhaling the same air as they, with impunity. Before the tide of sickness had receded, I even began to suspect (and others confirmed) that I was possessed of a charmed life. I did not, however, always experience this as the blessing that may be supposed. As I contemplated what little anxiety some patients showed, concerning their own recovery, I almost envied them their lack of resolution.

With which thought, I now mean to draw breath, lest I be pulled once more into a melancholy I cannot easily master. Suffice it to say: each day I worked in the Hospital, I went about my duties thinking that the passage of the hours was like a tide which swept out one load of humanity to meet its Maker, and then brought in another to take its place for a few hours, until I thought that I had once again become like the Mariner in the poem by my friend Coleridge, who walked the parched decks of his vessel among the bodies of his dearest fellows (and of his own brother's son), while the sultry main beneath him burned a still and awful red.

In my imagination, I saw myself wandering for all Eternity through those whitened sickrooms, while imploring hands stretched out towards me from every side. Knowing that I was unable either to help or to heal, I might equally well have been a man walking in the rough landscape hereabouts, who feels the snatch of thorns against his legs as he goes, but will not be troubled by such small annoys, and continues on his way regardless. [12]

1. TGW appeared before the convict authorities on the morning of 22 November 1837, in the Barracks in Campbell Street, Hobart, where he was given a number and had his particulars taken:

2325 Wainewright Griffiths Thos.
>   Central Criminal Court (Old Bailey) 3rd July 1837
>   Transported on ship *Susan* 21 Nov. 1837. Life.
>   Transported for Forgery, Gaol report not known, Hulk report
> Good, Married 1 Child, Stated this offence, Forging a power of Attorney in order that the money which was left to my Wife might come to me. Married one child. Wife Eliza. I have been separated from her for some years.

After giving this account of himself, TGW was "mugged":

Trade: Painter; Height 5/5½; Age: 43; Complexion: Pale; Head: Oval; Hair: Brown; Whiskers: Brown; Visage: Oval; Forehead: High; Eyebrows: Brown; Eyes: Grey; Nose: Long; Mouth: Large; Chin: Long; Remarks: None.

He was then examined by the Colonial Assistant-Sergeant, E. S. P. Bedford, found to be fit, and dispatched to another part of the Barracks (which was known as the "Tench"—short for Penitentiary), where he was put in a cell.

Four days later, he appeared before the Appropriation authorities, and the details of his punishment were confirmed. It had already been ordered by the Secretary of State in London that he would be "employed in the Public Works" (Record Book of Colonial Offences, vol. 48, p. 28, Tasmanian State Archives). For many years, it was believed that he was sent to the Rocky Hills Probation Station, outside Hobart—but as Crossland pointed out in 1954, Probation Stations did not exist until 1841. In fact, as Crossland also says, TGW was housed in the Barracks in Campbell Street until the end of 1838, and put to work for a year in a chain gang on the roads near by.

The details of this miserable existence are given in Van Diemen's Land's *Convict Regulations*. Each gang was made up of 30–50 men, with one supervisor per 20 prisoners, and the *Regulations* demanded a "degrading" and "a very formidable punishment at the commencement, gradually relaxing in severity, each successive mitigation being expedited by good behaviour, or retarded by ill-behaviour."

TGW's punishment was surprisingly harsh. Generally speaking, the authorities tried to make a connection between the past and present occupations of prisoners—as is proved by the assignment of convicts from the *Susan* itself. No more than 23 of its convict cargo of 193 were put to work on the roads, and TGW was the only one who had not previously done some kind of manual labour.

Why was he singled out in this way? His assignment form gives a clue. Next to the trade description "Clerk," the guard transcribing TGW's details added "understands Greek & Latin, has been accustomed to Write for the Journals—first Rate Painter in drawings and writing [*sic*]." These words, which spill impatiently out of their little form box, conjure up a picture of TGW trying to impress his interviewer, and irritating him instead. (Elsewhere on the same form, we get another glimpse of the interviewer, who seems to have begun writing "Chiswick" as TGW's "Native Place," then found himself unable to spell it, and settled for 'Richmond' instead.)

There is another possibility, besides vindictiveness. Although TGW had never been tried for murder, only for forgery, rumours of his killings travelled with him to Hobart. Maybe the Assignment Officer put him on the chain gang to punish him for these suspected but unproved crimes.

2. Marcus Clarke, who emigrated to Australia in 1863, says in his novel *For the Term of His Natural Life* (1874) that when individual beatings were carried out on convict ships, "the rest of us would set up a sort of bestial boohoo, in which all other sounds were confounded" (p. 38).

3. The Aboriginal population of Van Diemen's Land had been reduced from several thousand in 1804 to 97 by 1837.

4. The site of the Colonial Hospital, where TGW worked, is now covered by the Royal Hobart Hospital, opposite the Theatre Royal (the Royal Victoria in his day), and close to the Barracks on Campbell Street. It had been completed in 1820, and was a plain symmetrical block built of yellow sandstone. On the ground floor and first floor were two wards, 18 feet by 28 feet, and behind them ran a skillion which held two smaller wards, 13 feet by 20 feet. There was a separate morgue, kitchen, and lock-up, etc. The allocated space per patient was 3 feet, which meant there was room for 56 beds in all—which were attended by two surgeons, two apothecaries, three free settlers, and a dozen assigned convicts such as TGW.

The building was extremely basic, and often horribly overcrowded. In 1835, when death rates at the Hospital reached alarming heights, Governor George Arthur at last proposed a new hospital—but his efforts caused widespread resentment, and it was left to his successor, Sir John Franklin (who arrived in January 1837), to calm things down. This involved more reorganization (moving female patients to an annexe in the main building) than it did reconstruction: conditions remained primitive at the best of times, and woefully inadequate at the worst.

The typhoid epidemic of 1839 finally forced the hand of the authorities. When Frederick John Clarke took over as surgeon in 1840, he hired and fired staff vigorously, and planned a new building on vacant ground adjacent to the existing site. It was opened in May 1843, with room for 123 beds, and was praised for its "handsome style of construction": it was a plain two-storey affair, with wards opening off central passageways, and behind it various annexes soon grew up to cater for the demands of the growing population.

TGW had experience of the old Colonial hospital, the new building, and the self-supporting infirmary for free settlers, which was built in Davey Street in 1840. His work in the Colonial building began in December 1838 or January 1839, when he was assigned there for the second stage of his punishment as "an invalid wardsman without pay." In practice, this meant that he received "a full diet and such medical attention as his conduct indicated," but later he became eligible to receive 6d a day on top of this. His duties were always demanding and often depressing—in those pre-anaesthetic days—but judging by the evidence of colleagues he was conscientious and uncomplaining. One of the hospital surgeons later suggested that he might have curried favour with the authorities by acting as a kind of spy in the Barracks and the Hospital, saying that "he rendered me on many occasions important service by giving me such early information of malpractice in progress or in contemplation as enabled me to interfere with advantage." Others refer more simply to his "unexceptionable conduct," his "unvarying propriety of demeanour" and his "unvaryingly good conduct."

5. The physical descriptions of TGW in Van Diemen's Land are generally unreliable, since they tend to combine facts about his appearance with highly prejudiced views about his moral character. In one, for instance, he is described as having "a snake-like expression, which was both repulsive and fascinating. His conversation and manner were winning in the extreme. He was not intemperate, but grossly sensual; with the intellect of a Pericles and the passions of a satyr" (quoted in Crossland, p. 11). However, the similarities between TGW's undated self-portrait inscribed "Head of a Convict" and the earlier portrait by Holst are striking. He seems to have been a

slightly built man with a too-large head, who kept his dark hair and moustaches long, and whose expression mingled disdain with self-doubt.

6. Prisoners with artistic skills were often employed in hospitals, where they could do anatomical drawings as well as menial tasks. (TGW's contemporary in Hobart, the painter Thomas Bock, left behind some brilliantly detailed paintings of diseased internal organs.) If TGW did produce any such drawings, they have disappeared—though his small, recently discovered study of some bird's feathers shows his aptitude for this kind of work.

7. Edward Samuel Picard Bedford was the younger son of the Revd William Bedford (see p. 236). He was born in Van Diemen's Land, studied in England, and returned to his birthplace in 1823, aged twenty. He worked as Assistant Surgeon in the Colonial hospital, then moved to St. Mary's Hospital in the early 1840s.

8. Frederick Brodribb was the fifth child of William Adams Brodribb, who went to Van Diemen's Land in 1817 and became the colony's first solicitor; he also held important posts in local government. The family lived in the Old Verandah House on Elizabeth Street. Brodribb first met TGW when he was "walking the wards" as part of his training to become a doctor; he died of fever on 31 March 1840, and was buried on the site of what is now St. David's Park.

9. Dr. Frederick John Clarke was fifty-seven when he arrived from Co. Wicklow, Ireland, as Colonial Surgeon in April 1840; his brother-in-law Dr. Robert Kennedy Nuttall, then aged twenty-four, was immediately appointed Assistant Surgeon. Nuttall was a cultured, intelligent and historically minded young man. He encouraged TGW to return to painting, championed him when he made his ticket-of-leave appeal, and generally spoke well of him, noting in his memorandum book: "It may be as well to record that I saw [TGW] daily for four years while he was a prisoner in Van Diemen's Land." The Nuttall family ended up with "the most representative collection of [TGW's] pictures in existence."

10. Like many convicts, TGW relied on opium (which he had previously taken with Holst and others in London) to dull the pain of his sentence. One witness remembers that his teeth were brown from chewing opium sticks, and another said that he "used to take a dram of opium a day; and it was to procure this indulgence that he practised painting." This sounds like an exaggeration, but it is certainly possible that as well as buying opium when

he began earning money for his labour and his paintings, TGW also stole it during his time in hospital.

11. See the *Hobart Town Courier*, December 1838–March 1839, which calculated that altogether a tenth of the population of Hobart was stricken with the disease, which it described as being "of a low typhoid type," originating in "atmospheric causes" and "the unfavourable and peculiar circumstances under which [the convict] class of the community is placed."

12. Crossland (p. 342) and others suggest that TGW may not always have been as "amiable" as his supervisors believed. "Whilst [TGW was] a patient in the hospital," an unnamed and possibly unreliable contemporary remembered,

> [another] convict was brought in, evidently dying. At a glance [TGW] detected the fatal premonitory indications in the man's face—and gliding to his bedside with catlike steps, he hissed into the dying man's ear, "You are a dead man. In four and twenty hours your soul will be in hell, and my arm will be buried up to that (touching his elbow) in your body dissecting it."

20

LOW CUNNING AND REVENGE

I must now describe a part of my life which I never experienced as a continuous time, but as a confusion of small moments all heaped together. I am speaking of the opportunities given to me, when the first and hardest blows of my punishment were replaced by lighter and less frequent strokes: I mean, when I was allowed to return in earnest to my blessed Art. [1]

The very notion will no doubt seem an impossibility, or a ridiculous joke, when it is repeated along the Strand, or in Colnaghi's—entwined with canary song! Indeed, on first arriving in Van Diemen's Land, I myself expected to find a desert where no painting brush had ever touched a canvas, and no eye had ever looked upon a companion's face, intending to re-create it with sublime dexterity. I soon discovered, however, that the Muse knows no boundaries, and has even made a home on this desolate shore. The admirable portraitist Thomas Bock, who would later undertake valuable services for me, had done more than most to encourage Feeling and Form— and had sufficiently flattered the self-regard of a few wealthy settlers, he was already receiving regular commissions for his efforts. There were others, too, who had taken themselves off in a search for panoramas, and returned with sketches of estuaries and suchlike, which they had then worked into acceptable landscapes.

There was, needless to say, no sign of my own Poetical School—because there was no requirement for it. Merely that kind of landscape which is entirely occupied by the tame delineation of a given spot: an enumeration of hill and dale, clumps of trees, shrubs, water, meadows, cottages and houses; what is called a *view,* and is little more than topography, a kind of pictorial mapwork. [2] Even among those who cared for all things marvellous (I am thinking here of my friend Nuttall), I could detect no enthusiasm to explore the mysterious labyrinths and side alleys of the brain. There was only an appetite for gazing outwards and organizing. Perhaps this was the result of timidity in the inhabitants. Perhaps (and more forgivably) it was because the world in which they found themselves was so full of natural wonders: giant monarchs of the forest, which reached into the dome of Heaven; creatures, such as those I have already mentioned, which even the most active imagination could not easily construct; vistas, which brought together an infinite variety in a little room.

At any rate, when my work at the Hospital became somewhat more relaxed, which was the case after about 1840, and I was allocated time to earn a few pounds, and to begin establishing myself in society—I saw that I must learn to moderate my ambitions as an Artist, if I intended to make any headway. Where I had once plunged eagerly into strange visions and strong desires, I now addressed myself to those who wished for nothing more sensational than exterior portraits. To this end, I buried thoughts of my Professor, Fuseli, at the dark backward of my mind, where he could practise mystery in secret, and brought forward into his place the handsome and reliable Mr. P.—in order to satisfy the demands made upon me.

I will say nothing to compromise these pictures of mine. But I will immediately embellish what I have hitherto only implied. In so far as my works pleased others, they pleased me. In so far as they did not reflect the whole of my genius, they disappointed me, and I resolved always to keep myself at a distance from what I had made.

In spite of this, no one ever accused me of slighting my gifts, or of dishonouring the responsibilities which my commissions brought me. In the eyes and minds of all who knew me, I was the eccentric (I dare say) but devoted servant of my Muse, traversing the low hills and hugger-mugger streets, with my materials—pencil and watercolour, never oils—strapped in a box upon my back so that I resembled an honest journeyman.

Follow me, therefore, as I begin my efforts—which, for the sake of convenience, I shall once again compress into a single day, as I have done with other parts of my story, though in reality they were spread through a whole length of years.

I have left the Barracks early—a trusted fellow, but not so trusted that I am allowed to venture abroad alone. Therefore I have at my side, where a free man has his shadow, my guard—a sleepy-eyed, surly young dog, who has as much interest in my work as I have in his, which at least means we can both enjoy the luxury of silence and mutual indifference. We proceed along Campbell Street, where a view of the harbour and its ships in the refreshed light wakes in me a kind of melancholy wonder, then along the dockside, past the latest shipment of wretches, and eventually turn inland beyond the Government Buildings until we arrive—knock, knock—at the door of Sir

Alfred Stephen (still so early I fear he may yet have the crumbs of his break-fast around his distinguished chops). [3]

Sir Alfred is the first of my important beneficiaries, and a lawyer of dis-tinction. So much distinction, that I am instructed by my guard not even to speak while I am working (as if he, my guard, had as much knowledge of etiquette in his entire head as I have in my little finger). But I am a compliant creature, and therefore agree that his advice is sound, and follow Sir Alfred (once he has indicated that he will be pleased to endure the ordeal of my attentions on his veranda), and smile at him when he sits partly in sunlight, partly in shade, with the plain wall of his house behind his head, so that I have nothing to distract me, and smile again as I alternately peer closely into his face, then conceal myself behind my easel, then peep out again with my pencil raised to skewer his high black cravat, his dandy curl, the cupid's bow of his mouth—which in reality is blunter and more severe than I render it.

All this while, my guard withdraws to the far end of the veranda, behind me, where I hear him light a cigar, then have the stink of it wafting across me as I continue my quiet bobbing and bouncing at the easel. I wonder whether Sir Alfred will break his granite solemnity (I am not worthy to be considered a companion in conversation) to tell the insolent young chimney to extin-guish himself. But even this is beneath his contempt, so the smoke continues to float across us, and the pencil to make its scratching, and the heat of the day to increase, until the guard flings the bitter end of his weed to the ground, obliterates it with his boot, and comes towards me and growls in my ear. I understand him without listening, and tell him (in a whisper) that I shall be done before the sun has climbed above those gum trees which pro-tect the garden from the road, and throw their silver-edged reflections on to my paper.

One moment—a blank sheet! The next—a miracle of personality! I step back from my easel, gazing with critical pleasure at my own creation—but I am not allowed to stay in this attitude for longer than a minute. My guard is at my shoulder again, breathing smokily, and Sir Alfred is out of his chair, bending to inspect his image. There is a moment of general immobility, when I think my subject will deign to speak to me, perhaps to congratulate me on my efforts—but no, he is too proud to say that he is grateful. All he will do is to drop a little money into my hands, letting the coins fall thickly through his fingers, giving me to understand that my role now is to acknowl-edge his patience with a mumble and a bowed head, before I am shown the door.

This final courtesy is performed by my patron's wife, my patron himself having paced off to a back room where more important business awaits him. She is a jaunty body and will not stand upon ceremony, but fits herself in between me and my guard (which he does not like) to ask after my health, and my continuing work at the Hospital, and to wonder why I am beginning to stoop—am I weary? I admit that this is true, I *am* weary, but I do not add that those others who suffered on the roads with me are weary too, some of them so weary they will soon sleep everlastingly. I am still keeping my counsel, thanking her for her kindness and wishing for more, when my foot suddenly touches the road outside her door, the door closes, the sunlight beats down upon me and my shadow, and I experience a brief fit of giddiness. It is a moment in which I glimpse, in my mind's eye, the portrait I have left behind, and imagine it starting its life without me—like a child which in due course will turn into a man, if fortune smiles on it.

Then I am once more at my artist's march through the dusty morning, arriving without any delay at my next appointment. This is not so demanding as the recent encounter with Sir Alfred, because more familiar. My subjects are Fred Brodribb and his sister (Miss Frances), of whom I have spoken already, and whom I would consider friends if my circumstances allowed it. They, too, usher me out to their veranda, but with such a to-do of "How are ye?," and "Where shall we sit?," and "What assistance do you need?," that I feel I might have arrived on the moon—which my guard also thinks, and dislikes, and of which he informs all and sundry by a series of harrumphs and glowerings, whereupon they dismiss him back to the Barracks. Poor fellow, he is so respectful of his work, and at the same time so wonderfully bored by the play of my pencil, that he stands for a while in a complete quandary, and finally runs off like a guilty boy, calling over his shoulder that I had better watch my step, or else.

But I pay him scant attention, having already left the world he inhabits, and slipped instead across the gilded boundary of a better, where I may see the good and youthful faces of Master Fred and his sister more clearly— exalted by a transmogrifying eagerness. With my easel standing once more on its dainty legs, and with my sweet-natured pair of subjects seated on two plain joint stools, so that I can show them in their innocence and simplicity, I stare until I feel their personalities rise out of them like spirits; whereupon I continue pensive, unconsciously placing my pencil in my mouth several whole minutes, when at length its bitter taste runs through me and I withdraw it in disgust.

Withdraw it, and immediately set to work, capturing the vision I have conjured up, which gives pleasure where none previously existed. But alas, the illusions of Art! Alas, that what survives by my sleight of hand cannot survive in fact! Within a few weeks of this alchemy, Fred's handsome face, the same face that smiled at me, and to which I gave a look that will endure the returning gaze of generations, will be dead and buried in the ground. Dead, for no reason but his kindness.

I shall dwell no longer upon this sad scene, but take my next commission. Farewell! sweet pair of angels; farewell! There is no time to waste, even for you. The sun has completed half its journey to the zenith, and my guard has appeared once more, marching me onwards quickly, with my journeyman's box and easel banging against my backbone, so that I soon reach the house of another friend—Dr. Nuttall. As I unpack the tools of my trade, he takes his chair in a corner, away from the sun, and arranges himself for me in a severe twist. He seems to be shaking hands with himself, and this, like his attire, makes him formal and dignified. Yet his hair, which I have often seen disordered as he walks the wards of the Hospital in a long rapture of sympathy and self-forgetting, looks almost *on end*, it is so loosely brushed from his brow. Noble face! (Noble whiskers and moustaches!) Discriminating Soul! I would have clasped you in the arms of friendship wherever I had found you. To have had your admiration and trust in this desperate place has been a comfort indeed.

I cannot repeat the process of my creations—it is a mystery even to me myself. Suffice it to say, therefore, that after another spell of reflecting, of staring upon the flesh and speculating upon the spirit, I persuaded the good Doctor to slip out of his mortal frame and take up residence on my paper (which has yet to acquire a frame). Whereupon, being friends, and knowing that we shall soon see each other in the Hospital under a different dispensation, I bid him a brisk goodbye, and set out on my way. My guard, who pops up again at my shoulder, the moment I have left the shelter of this latest roof, seems suddenly to take an interest in my work. But no, it is not an interest in me. It is an interest, rather, in himself. He councils haste (in a gruff voice more likely to produce fear) because I have many more commissions to discharge before I am permitted to lay down my instruments. And until that time he is bound to me—and to a career of tramping, waiting and cigar-smoking, as though I were his gaoler and not he mine.

Therefore, at an almost ridiculous speed, I am ushered into the presence of Robert Power, who is no less than Surveyor-General, and whose handsome face I dissect with a flourish. [4] He is a good old man, with a taste for luxuries that cannot easily be obtained here, and is eager to cast his mind far afield. As I work, I am rewarded with a few choice stories from London, which he has heard from his sister who lives there. The excitement of these is so intense, and the scenes he describes so vivid, I can scarcely keep my hand steady as I tease out his essence and lay it bare. And then, unwittingly, he piles punishment upon my pleasure! Rambling here and there, up and down the Strand, in and out of coffee shops, over parks and through teeming thoroughfares, he mentions that prolific genius and friend of the people, Charles Dickens, with whom his sister is acquainted. To any heart but mine, the name would bring delight. In me, however, it creates such a storm of opposing feelings, I am compelled to step back from my paper for a moment and bite my lip—and cannot, when questioned, divulge the manner in which I have encountered this distinguished Author.

When I have composed myself, and completed my task, I am mercifully whisked off again. Goodbye, kind-meaning Mr. Power—goodbye before my brushstokes have dried upon the paper, and your face is set as it will look for ever. Goodbye and good cheer, as a return for your faith in my skills.

Next (after a short tramp through the noonday heat) it is the turn of William Crooke, my House Surgeon at the Hospital, to whom I have already rendered important services on other occasions, and now offer the gift of immortality in a silent but speaking likeness. No sooner is it done than I am hurried away once more, since the sun is already beginning her descent, though still beaming with enough enthusiasm to light up for me the familiar features of James Fitzgerald and his wife. They are the Superintendent and Matron at our Hospital, and both immediately benefit from my generosity as a bestower of beauty; in due course, they will repay me by giving their good opinion of my character to the Governor of the island.

What, am I suddenly now your superior in speed, Mr. Guard? Do you not know that Art makes demands as well as the Military? Look: the sun-chariot is now positively racing down its slope, so that shadows begin to darken our little world. There is so much yet to do! A double curiosity, first: the Cutmere twins at their house in Barrack Street. It is their father (our gatekeeper) who often supplies me with my materials, and I thank him now by presenting him with his Jane and Lucy, even more perfect (I believe) than they appear in life: [5] Jane, with a slight bend in her figure, as if she were looking *round* the solid object of her sister's gaze; Lucy, with a delightful curl of hair, and an even more delicately elegant neck. It is not honourable for a man to praise his own achievements, but I must permit myself to suggest that in these two creations, anyone may see that I have captured the future in the present—the woman lurking in the child. Supposing this to be true, it also allows me to say that, in executing this work, I recollected more painfully than for many months the gentle faces of Helen and Madeleine, who were the earliest companions of my woe. Helen! And now dear Jane Cutmere, with her inquisitive stare. She too discovered the world to be unforgiving, and went before her time to the embrace of her Heavenly Father, leaving her own father disconsolate for ever.

How they gambol round me while I pack my equipment back into its box, these tender-hearted girls, and follow me out through their door, whirling and twisting around my legs like kittens. I would stop longer, and pet them and play, but the light glancing ever more deeply across the trees now sends an accusing look into my eyes—whereupon I show great resolution and jerk the door shut behind me, and take myself off to quieter regions.

Suddenly and for the first time in this day of days, I find myself out of sorts. Why, I wonder? Most likely it is due to the whimsical nervousness of Mrs. Downing, the next on my list. As I am setting up my equipment, in the cool and echoing sitting room where she receives me, I drop from my paint-box on to the floor a small nothing which she graciously stoops to retrieve for me. But when I advise her that such refined fingers as hers should not trifle with anything of mine, she starts back, abruptly recollecting that I am not the thing I seem to be—an Artist—but a convict, and that therefore the nothing I may happen to have dropped is in all probability a suspicious something.

I have no reason to consider this remarkable, and yet it increases the irritation which has begun to grow in me. Therefore, when I am finishing my work with this doubtful lady, I feel that I must add to her confusion by making an ostentatious show of swallowing the piece of bread I have been using to mop my paper. This is clearly considered alarming—which pleases me so much I immediately increase the effect of what I have done by swallowing my paint water in one draft. Disgusting expedient! Delicious effect! To see this anxious matron totter and stare is all the payment I require for the labour of producing her portrait, though not all that I receive. Mrs. Downing is the wife of a wealthy store-owner (a man of the future), who is digging deeply in his pockets for my emolument—so deeply, that I have flattered his dearest love out of all recognition, turning her red hair into a masterpiece of fashionable ringlets, and her costume into the sort of extraordinary confection one might see in Vauxhall. [6]

Yet I have not done the bidding of my commissioner entirely. I have not been able to give beauty where none exists, only sentiment. This will not be exactly as you desired, dear fainting Madam, to whom I now also say farewell. But recollect that I am the master of sentimentalities, and your face will therefore outlive you, with all your timorous excitements stilled.

And now, immediately, I arrive at Hawthornden, the charming residence of Holy Willie. [7] My portrait here, which is done while my guard removes himself to the kitchen, where he can quench his hot boredom in a pot of cool cordial, is a form of contrition. Contrition, Janus? Yes, contrition. I have lived all my life outside the pale of religion, and in this latest picture, I endeavour to prove its authority. I mean: no sooner has my subject arranged himself in his favourite chair (a fine old green leather article, though I pay no attention to this in my drawing)—no sooner is he settled, hands folded meekly in his lap, than I set about giving him an aspect which is at once familiar and lofty. This is what I understand by contrition: it is a picture which shows respect for what I cannot share. There are many, godly and ungodly, who have quailed under the Holy Willie's gaze in life; now it will look across the whole plain of history, and meet the eyes of thousands it never knew, silently commanding them to doff their hats, for here they are in the presence of strength and quiet power.

It is the habit of such august personages as the Reverend Bedford to take whatever is given as their just deserts—which he does. While he stoops over my sheet, examining himself, and drying the paintwork of his face with his own breath, there comes a complacent sigh. He considers himself well pleased. He will continue to include me in his prayers. He is grateful for this taste of immortality. But he will admit none of these things aloud. Instead, he will take me to his door and usher me into the street once more, indicating by a slight bow of his head that he will encounter me again before long. I smile, to see him so satisfied, but I feel a mischievous pleasure, as well as a real one. Namely, this: thinking that if he knew my next port of call, he would not seem so smooth with me. He would summon me back instantly, and perhaps even delay me with some of the grog which my faithful guard (stumbling out of doors to fix himself at my side once more) is now wiping from his lips. For what reason? Because my next subject is none other than his son Edward's enemy, and our Inspector of Hospitals, Dr. Clarke—on whose account Edward removed himself from a position he had long held, and went off to St. Mary's breathing fire against his usurper.

This knowledge quickens my step; yet when I arrive at the house of Dr. Clarke, I find myself casting back fondly to the scenes I have just departed. [8] Clarke is, in truth, a fierce and staring fellow. Unpacking my paints and brushes while he shrugs himself into a high-collared coat, adjusts his dark cravat, straightens his pale waistcoat, and prepares to meet my gaze, I soliloquize in silence: Sir, I feel a sincere admiration for you, and an equally sincere respect for your position, but I cannot persuade my admiration to thicken into liking—and therefore my hand is powerless to present you to posterity with affectionate curves and gentle graces. Your passions are fine in their way, but can gain you only respect, not friendship. Yet, to speak sensibly, I understand how you need to be tight and fiery, in order for the poor invalids of this Town to receive the attention they deserve.

For this tenacity, Sir, I salute you, as soon as our sitting is over, with a sort of hurried bow—hurried, it must be said, because my honour for you is less than the relief I feel at leaving the cold comfort of your home. And with that done, and the door clicking shut in its frame, and the tools of my trade once more banging against my backbone, I have an instant in which to hear the wheels of the sun-chariot actually brush the tree tops along the road, ruffling them with the breeze of its flight, and rousing the birds there into a last fit of calling before the long night's sleep. Let me hesitate here in the dust for another instant, and enjoy their murmurings. Let me reflect that I have only two further commissions to complete before my day's work is done. Let me breathe easily and be slow. But such indolence is not allowed. My guard places his hand upon my shoulder, and half pushes, half drags me onwards, telling me the light will soon be gone (as though he himself were Rembrandt, and understood such things), and I must not slacken now.

I would resist him, pointing out the lateness of the hour, and the delicacy of my constitution, were it not that my next subject is my favourite of all: Julia Sorrell. [9] Julia Sorrell, of such wit and elegance, she seems a meteor in this dull place. Julia Sorrell, who is slandered by envious tongues, for her beauty and amity. See, here she is now, opening her front door herself, as though she had no need of servants to protect her from the world, but wishes to engage with it freely, chatting and smiling while she shows me through her hall and into the parlour where she has prepared the site of our interview. There is no sign that she thinks me anything less than a gentleman; and I, accordingly, return to her all the easiness that she bestows—on my paper. Delightful, I tell myself, bending once more to my work—delightful, and because she is delightful, deprecated. Beautiful, and because of her beauty, maligned. In the waning light, I examine the lovely face, framed by its simple jewellery, tilted a little on the flawless neck. In a daze of admiration, I search her shining eyes and see the trace of difficulties she has endured, which remind me that I too have laboured under the burden of a false reputation. That I too have endeavoured to cover my existence with a fine finish, only to have it scumbled by fools. She, at least, has her life before her, and the freedom to embrace it. I have ———. I have the skill to show a woman at a delicate moment in her existence, breathed on by scandal but capable of resisting it. When I stand back from my easel at last, I see the grace of her true nature illuminating everything I have done, and gleaming from the page. It is a lovely reciprocity.

A reciprocity which ends when the courtesy of her indulgence ends. As gracefully as she met me a moment ago, Miss Sorrell now leads me to the door again—my brushes dried, my pencil put away, my box locked shut, my coat pulled on. Goodbye, sweet lady, goodbye. I am once more the journey-man, setting out upon the deep-shadowed roads. To pass so rapidly from warmth and gaiety into this dreary silence and vacancy; to have the sparkle of elegant company replaced by the dog-chatter of my guard: it is a trans-formation which cannot but suggest the larger changes I have suffered. I stand at a loss for a moment, watching the sun slip behind the Mountain, and hearing a gust of wind rattle across the iron roofs of the poor houses, not caring whether my guard allows this or no. To my astonishment (for I almost expect a blow across my back) he lets this pause lengthen, almost as if he shared my own thoughts; then announces that his day is done, since mine is done also—and with that takes himself off back to the Barracks, saying he will see me again eventually.

It is the greatest freedom that remains to me—this occasional neglect—but I know it is a freedom which soon leads to melancholy. I am not speaking here as plainly as I would like. I mean to say this: my freedom in this place may be defined as an hour, now and again, of my own company and mine alone; these hours fill me with sorrowful reflections; these reflections, though sad, are (I insist) far superior to the labours I am compelled to under-take as my punishment; *therefore:* my melancholy is the expression of my freedom.

Which thoughts, as I say, detain me in the road for a good few minutes. When they are done with, I feel my spirits settle again, take a glance at the early moon and stars, and calculate that before I am wanted at the Barracks, I have a chance to step into the Wheatsheaf, where I may down a tumbler of brandy to fortify myself for the remainder of my journey. It is not my first visit there, nor will it be my last, since among the fellows it entertains are some who value me for my day's work, and may even fill my glass for me, in return for some firelight sketch or other. Tonight, for example, I shall exe-cute myself (in a manner of speaking): the Head of a Convict, very charac-teristic of low cunning and revenge, with my hair all flattened about my head, and my jaw set—a thing dashed off, which Nuttall (who would never frequent such a den as this) has often requested, and shall now have, to prove that these eyes (my own) which burrow into the souls of others, may also be turned upon myself. [10]

Is it a determined face? Or is it a defeated one? Is it a man wretchedly out of place, or perfectly in place? Is that a smile playing about the lips, or the beginning of a sneer? Is that gaze fixed in anger, or dismay, or some other emotion entirely? Does it show a virtuous man or an evil one? Fools! even to suppose such questions might be worth putting. It is a picture of Janus, whose business it is to avoid a plain answer. It is the face of Mr. Neither-one-thing-nor-the-other. Mr. Look-two-ways. Mr. Here-and-there. Cunning and revenge, indeed. Also simplicity and passion, longing and dread, hope and despair. Drink to me, now that I am done with here, and stepping out once more upon my journey. Drink to me twice, or twenty-two times, as you may think fit. But do not drink to me once, to a single thing.

1. During the last part of his life in Van Diemen's Land, TGW was involved with a distinct community of like-minded painters. It was a community for which people in Hobart generally felt considerable respect. Regular shows of new work were held in the framing shop run by Robin Hood in Elizabeth Street, and in the early 1840s, Lady Franklin, the culture-loving wife of the Governor, even went so far as to build a Temple of Athene under the brow of Mount Wellington.

The best of them, Thomas Bock (?1790–1855), was an engraver who was transported in 1824 for helping to arrange the abortion of his lover's child; soon after arriving in Hobart, he became a trusted citizen (he designed the four-dollar bill for the Bank of Van Diemen's Land) and a popular portraitist—the first, in fact, to work professionally in the colony. Other prominent figures included William Gould, William Charles Piguenit, Benjamin Duterreau, Bock's pupil Robert Dowling, Charles Costantini, and James Scott.

TGW produced his earliest convict works while he was still housed in the Barracks and spending much of each day working in the hospital. (The first that can be accurately dated is *Edward Lord,* which he painted in April 1839.) Eventually, when he was given his ticket-of-leave, he relied on his painting for the whole of his income. It has sometimes been falsely suggested that he was "denied the patronage of the best people when the full story of his crimes reached Van Diemen's Land" (Crossland, p. 126). In fact he was "peculiarly fitted to speak for the noblesse of Hobart Town in the 1840s; of a good family himself, well educated, a man of great gifts and social graces, he stood for an order of society inextricably bound up with the hopes and aspirations of the time" (ibid., p. 41). This—and the closely knit nature of Hobart society—is borne out by the fact that of his fifty-three known sitters, thirty-three are related to each other, and all are well-to-do.

For at least one hundred years after his death, TGW's reputation as a painter, like the reputation of his fellow convict artists, declined steeply. As Curling pointed out in the mid-1930s, many important details about his work were forgotten or hushed up. Occasionally there were public exhibitions—such as a show of ten pictures organized in Hobart City Hall in 1931. From time to time one would appear in a sale room. Yet even today, when examples of his work hang in many major Australian galleries, there is no complete and reliable catalogue of his works (though Crossland gives a helpful interim account of some sixty-odd works), and a large number remain hidden away "in the hands of a few private collectors, or as family totems handed down from generation to generation" (ibid., p. 140).

The fact that none of TGW's paintings is signed (with a single possible exception, see note 10 below) makes the business of saving his reputation especially difficult. When he lived in London, he did not sign his work because he felt that it would be beneath his dignity as a gentleman. In Hobart, other pressures pushed him into anonymity: pressures that connect with his interest in the Self generally. His effacement, like his pseudonymity, is a powerful compound of pride, self-dislike, disappointment and modesty.

All the same, there is now enough work by TGW in Australian galleries to prove that he was one of the best Australian portrait painters of his day— one of the most skilled, and one of the few who describe a whole, clear section of contemporary society. The majority of the works are small, and use a charcoal pencil or watercolour on paper stretched over a fine-grained canvas. There is often a touch of pure white to add highlights. This manner of working is similar to Bock's, but it is widely agreed that TGW's style is more delicate, and his effects more subtle. (TGW also did a certain amount of non-portrait work in Van Diemen's Land, but very little survives. A scrapbook owned by Henrietta Garratt in the 1840s, for instance, contains five drawings which may relate to a performance given at the Royal Victorian Theatre in Hobart.)

Admittedly, the quality of the portraits is inconsistent. TGW tended, when he finished working on the faces of his sitters, to paint their bodies and their hands in the most cursory way; he complied all too readily with the colonists' wishes to preserve their wives and children as "happy in smiling childhood, radiant with joy" (as the *Colonial Times* of 26 June 1846 said of his portrait of the McClean daughters); and he often painted his male subjects as effortless dandies—which seems implausible, and a way of concealing character rather than revealing it.

In other words, there is a disappointing fluctuation in TGW's work between sentimentalism and conservatism. But there is something else about his figures that generally makes them memorable and distinguished. In London, his debts to Fuseli, Holst and Blake prevented him from finding an original vision; in Hobart he was less fussy, and able to make some striking psychological insights. His portrait of *Edward Lord* (1840), for instance, inscribed "who in 1804 erected the first house where now stands the city of Hobart Town," shows its wealthy, dynamic subject sitting in a high-backed chair, slightly slumped, meeting the viewer's gaze with a half-hypnotized, half-concentrated stare. The tousled hair indicates a busy, open-air man who cannot stay long—an impression that restrains the dandified element suggested by the high collar. It is at once purposeful and relaxed, like all his best late works, for instance *Julia Sorrell, Dr. Frederick John Clarke, Robert Kennedy Nuttall, The Rev. William Bedford,* and *Frederick Brodribb.*

2. This passage, which comes from TGW's *Essays* (pp. 115–16), is a good example of his debt to Fuseli. It is lifted almost word for word from Fuseli's *Lectures on Painting* (p. 27)—as Horst Schroeder pointed out in "Wilde, Wainewright and Fuseli," *Notes and Queries*, vol. 241, no. 4 (December 1996), p. 434.

3. Sir Alfred Stephen (1802–1894) arrived in Hobart in 1825, where he worked as Solicitor-General. He was also a lawyer with a successful private practice, and after working as Attorney-General from 1832 to 1837, became Chief Justice of New South Wales in 1842.

4. Robert Power reached Van Diemen's Land in 1840, and the following year became Surveyor-General of the Administration of Lands Department. He died in 1869, having bought several pictures by TGW, and held office in the Parliament as a Sergeant-at-Arms. His aunt was Lady Blessington, who knew Dickens.

5. Jane Cutmere died in 1845, aged twelve. Her twin sister Lucy died in 1854, aged twenty-one.

6. There are several other stories of TGW alarming his subjects, many of them unreliable. On one occasion he apparently made a sitter scream aloud by sharpening his pencil "fiercely"; on another, he was exasperated by a Miss Chalmers, a friend of the Misses Butler, and finished her portrait by showing devils emerging from her mouth and nose. The portrait was later destroyed.

7. William Bedford (?1781–1852), father of TGW's surgeon friend Edward, and known as "Holy Willie," was born in London, and became Assistant Military Chaplain to Van Diemen's Land in 1821. According to the Australian *Dictionary of National Biography*, he was "chiefly responsible for creating all the Anglican congregations in the colony," and first met TGW in the Barracks, where he held a weekly service. He was appointed Superintendent of Schools in 1830, but the following year was passed over as Rural Dean, and mounted a campaign of protest which lost him the confidence of the Governor. He subsequently quarrelled with his new Bishop, Nixon, who was appointed in 1842, and spent the last years of his life bitter and unrepentant.

8. Dr. Frederick John Clarke was Deputy Inspector-General of Hospitals in Hobart, where he arrived on 24 April 1840. He immediately set about restructuring the organization that he had inherited. Edward Bedford was replaced by Dr. Robert Officer as the man in charge of the Colonial Hospital—and soon resigned and went off to build his own hospital, St. Mary's, which catered for free settlers rather than convicts.

9. Julia Sorrell was the daughter of William Sorrell, the registrar of the Supreme Court. She had an "undisciplined and tempestuous nature," according to the Australian *DNB,* and before marrying Thomas Arnold—the brother of Matthew the poet—in 1850, she had twice been engaged. She was also alleged to have seduced Lieutenant-Governor Eardley-Wilmot, and although this was probably a false rumour, it precipitated his recall to England. She was a famous beauty, but her teeth rotted and fell out when she was still young—which one would never know from TGW's affectionate and admiring portrait. Among the children she had with Thomas Arnold, one grew up to become the novelist Mrs. Humphry Ward, and another married Leonard Huxley.

10. TGW's self-portrait, inscribed "The Head of a Convict, very characteristic of low cunning & revenge," is undated, and was originally owned by Dr. Nuttall. Its present whereabouts are unknown. John White owns a painting by TGW, which he believes to be another self-portrait and which is signed. It is possible that this signature may have been added, or at least intensified (according to the evidence of photographs taken over several years) at a later date.

21

MISERABLE PETITIONER

*I*n my last chapter, which should properly be called penultimate, since I am now almost arrived at the present in which I am actually living (flurry of coach wheels rolling to a halt! Coachmen shouting "Woah! Woah!" Passengers jostling!)—in my last instalment, as I say, I hurried the work of several years into an account of a single day. My intention was to give an impression of the great busyness I felt in the service of my Art, and of the eager call there was upon my services. In the course of this grand collapse, or conflation, I had necessarily to omit certain details concerning my own history. I shall now conclude my story by making good this deficiency. Though my final words are brief, they touch upon matters of the utmost importance.

The first relates to an intimate fact. I have said already that my months on the roads made no concession to my previous existence, or to my age and condition—and I would have been a very Hercules if my ordeals had not inflicted indelible marks on me. Yet in spite of these, when I was released from my torment, I performed my work in the Hospital with a willing hand and a determined spirit. Not even the worst of our epidemics caught me in its embrace. Not even continual care for others could infect me with their mortality. I was reckoned, as I have already said, to be a charmed man— which I regarded as proof of my moral worth, and of my innocence.

It is a sad truth, that even as the most redoubtable monuments must fall, and great Troy itself crumble into a level plain, so that scorpions and snakes crawl in the footsteps of kings and princes, so must a healthy constitution crumble. As my duties in the hospital began to ease, a feebleness afflicted me as if it were taking advantage of the change. In a short while, my whole system became nervous and irritable—not so severe that it kept me from my painting (although this often required a particular effort), but enough to persuade me that I had been brushed by an angel's wing.

For a time, I was a patient and bed-bound: a horizontal form in the place where I had long worked as a vertical one. My doctors, who were of course my superiors, and would willingly have cured me in order to re-engage my services, exerted themselves on my behalf for this reason. (And, I am sure, out of pure affection.) But there was little to be done. I consumed a daily dose of *vin opii;* I was occasionally bled and purged; I was fed and watered. Otherwise, I was left to my favourite company—myself—and grew, by the simple expedient of staring, an aficionado of cobwebs and ceiling cracks, a scientist of sunlight upon walls, the Magellan of their damp patches, and the Cortez of a single pictureless nail. [1]

Once in every several days, some visiting apothecary, or doctor friend such as Nuttall, would remember that I had eyes in my head and a mind behind them, and bring books for my diversion. I consumed these with the eagerness of Crusoe falling upon a beefsteak after his ordeal of wild pig and what-have-you—and revisited with pleasure some glorious scenes of the imagination (such as the home of Crusoe himself, and also of Uncle Toby). But my appetite for pages being voracious, these books were quickly exhausted, and my hours of blankness renewed again, at which I became attentive once more to the calibrations of old Sol, and the geography of the Country of Damp. The nail, I thought, I would willingly hang myself from, if I did not soon suspend something else upon its point.

It is the tendency of men, when thus left to their own devices, to develop thoughts and ideas which engross them utterly. So it was with me. Ever since my first moment in Hobart Town, I had brooded on the loss of my freedom and my good name. Yet while I had been at work on the roads, and for much of my time on the wards, the burden of my employment had prevented me from dwelling on my lot with much (what shall I say?) *consistency.* Now that time and tiredness weighed upon me, and my mind was at liberty to roam wherever it chose, I had all the opportunities I desired to ponder my situation and how to end it.

I reflected that I had so far survived my ordeal by clinging in secret to some notion of my Self, and to imagining what this Self might become, given pleasant circumstances. But I was not so puffed up or trusting that I expected to be rewarded for this by the authorities. Indeed, it had often seemed to me that I was deliberately punished for my past achievements. This being so, I well understood that if I meant to apply for a ticket-of-leave—which would grant me the freedom to live and work within the boundaries of the colony, if not actually to begin thinking of home again—I should allow a respectable number of years to elapse before making my Petition. This was common practice, among such as myself.

There were, however, others about me whose kindliness made them impatient in my cause. Nuttall was especially insistent that I be given my ticket immediately, since he and his brother-in-law Clarke, our Inspector and also a supporter of mine, were due to complete their term of office on the island shortly, and remove themselves and their good consciences to India, which would mean an end to their connection with your humble servant.

Nuttall spared me the details of his coaxings and cajolings on my behalf—so that he might also spare me the pain of frustration—while I continued at my slow patient's pace along the narrow road of boredom and recovery. The sun changed its course across the sky. The shadow of the nail grew to a different length, depending on whether it was dawn or dusk, summer or autumn. Faces came and went in the beds around me—some back to good health in the world, others to darkness, where they now lie waiting for the last trump to rouse them for their final exertion.

As this time crept by, I gradually waxed stronger in my body, and was able to quit my bed, and thereafter to make expeditions with my painting box strapped upon my back, as I have described. The Hospital accordingly became a sort of lodging house for me, which I was always pleased to depart, and always grateful to find expecting me when I returned. Not so grateful, however, that when Nuttall at length called on me, and explained that my ticket now had all necessary support, I did not hesitate to press my advantage. Within a matter of moments I had devised the words for my statement; within a few moments more I had arranged for my acquaintance Thomas Brock (whose skills as a calligrapher were famous) to transcribe it for me. I sent it on its way with the blessing of my own signature:

To His Excellency Sir John Eardley-Wilmot, Bart., Lieutenant-Governor of Van Diemen's Land, etc, etc, etc:
    The Humble Petition of T. Griffiths Wainewright praying the Indulgence of a Ticket of Leave.
    To palliate the boldness of this application he offers the statement ensueing. That *seven* years past he [w]as arrested on a charge of Forging & acting on, a power of Attorney to sell stock *13 years previous*. Of which (tho' looking for little credence) he avers his entire Innocence. He admits a knowledge, of the actual committer, gained tho', some years after the fact. Such however were their relative positions that to have disclosed it would have made him infamous where any human feeling is manifest. Nevertheless, by his Counsel's direction, he entered the plea <u>*not*</u> *Guilty,* to allow him to adduce the

"*circonstance attenuante* " viz. That the money (£5200) appropriated was, without quibble, his *own,* derived from his parents.

An hour before his appearing to plead he was trepanned (thro' the just, but deluded Govr. of Newgate) into withdrawing his plea, by a promise, in such case, of a punishment merely nominal. The same *purporting* to issue from ye. *Bank Parlour,* but, in fact from the agents of certain *Insurance Compies.,* interested to a heavy amount (£16,000) in compassing his legal *non*-existence. He pleaded Guilty and was forthwith hurried, stunned with such ruthless perfidy, to the Hulks at Portsmouth, and thence, in 5 days, aboard the "Susan," sentenced to Life in a land (to him) a moral sepulchre.

As a ground for your mercy he submits with great diffidence his foregone condition of Life during 43 years of freedom.

A *Descent,* deduced, thro' Family Tradition & Edmonstone's Heraldry, from a Stock not the least honoured in Cambria. Nurtured with all appliances of ease and comfort. School'd by his relative the well-known Philologer and Bibliomaniac Chas. Burney D.D. brother to Mdme D'Arblay and the companion of COOK. Lastly such a modest competence as afforded the *mental* necessaries of Literature, Archaeology, Music and the Plastic Arts; while his pen and brush introduced him to the notice and friendship of Men whose fame is European. The Catalogues of Somerset House Exhibns, the Literary Pocket Book, indicate his earlier pursuits, and the Ms left behind in Paris, attest at least his industry. Their titles imply the objects to which he has, *to this date,* directed all his energies. "A Philosophical Theory of Design, as concerned with the *Loftier* Emotions, showing its deep action on Society, drawn from the Phidean-Greek and early Florentine Schools," (the result of 17 years study) illustrated with numerous plates executed with conscientious accuracy, in one vol. Atlas folio. "An Aesthetic and Psychological Treatise on the *Beautiful,* or the Analogies of Imagination and Fancy, as existed in *Poesy, Verse, Painting, Sculpture, Music* or *Architecture,*" to form four Vols folio; with a profusion of Engravings by the best Artists of Paris, Munich, Berlin and Wien. "An Art Novel" in 3 vols. and a collection of Fantasie, Critical Sketches &c. selected partly from *Blackwood, the Foreign Review* & the *London Magazine.* All these were nearly ready for, *one* actually at press. Deign, Your Excellency! to figure to yourself my actual condition during 7 years; without *friends, good-name* (the breath of life) or Art—(the fuel to it with *me*). Tormented at once by Memory & Ideas struggling for outward form & realization, barred up from increase of knowledge, & deprived of the exercise of profitable or even of *decorous* speech. Take pity Your Excellency! and grant me the power to shelter my eyes from Vice in her most revolting and sordid phase, and my ears from a jargon of filth & blasphemy that would outrage the cynicism of Parny himself. Perhaps this clinging to the lees of a vapid life may seem as *base, unmanly,* arguing rather a plebeian than a liberal & gentle descent. But your Excellency! the wretched Exile has a child! and *Vanity* (sprung from the praise of Flaxman, *Coleridge, Charles Lamb,* Stothard, Rd. Westall, *Delaroche, Cornelius, Lawrence* and the God of his worship, *Fuseli*) whispers that the *follower of the Ideal* might even yet achieve another reputation than that of a *Faussaire.* Seven years of steady demeanour may in some degree promise that no indulgence shall ever be abused by Your Excellency's miserable Petitioner

T. G. WAINEWRIGHT

The signature to this is my own, as I say, and came with a flourish. Yet I cannot write it here again without drawing attention to the way I have treated Eliza in my deposition. I shall simply say that as she had been my support in everything, while we were man and wife together, so in this instance I called upon her to help me when we were man and wife apart. For the rest, I have nothing to say which would enrich what I have already written.

Each of us, when we have set ourselves impossible goals, knowing in our hearts that we shall never gain them, guard a little flame of hope that we shelter against the strong winds of certainty. As I lay upon my bed in the ward, or did such work as I could about the Town, I heard the gigantic wheels of Government slowly turning, and saw my Petition moving towards their mashing teeth, in the sure knowledge that it would emerge in the end merely as so much minced paper. Yet for all this expectation, when the news of the failure did indeed reach me, it fell on me like lead, crushing from me every ounce of vitality. I had dared to dream of a life beyond my white walls, and the sunlight, and my pictureless nail. Now these things became once again my entire and futile universe.

But I shall not dwell on my disappointment for long, although I felt it bitterly, because I was not compelled to endure it for long. In the same week that I bade my sad farewell to Nuttall (who left our island with many specimens of my work in his luggage), and felt that without this friend to help me, I might as well tumble forthwith into the grave, and beg for the earth to be heaped upon me, I received the information that I was to be given a Probation Pass—of a good quality—which would shortly be announced in the *Gazette*.

I rejoiced in this Pass for its own sake, and because I saw that it must be a kind of preliminary to my ticket, which did indeed follow within a year. [2] During this interval, my health recovered sufficiently for me to complete several of the portraits I have mentioned, and others besides, and also to inform such acquaintances as I had in society that I would soon be moving among them as a free man—almost. This was a vital time for me, as anyone may imagine, and each day mingled caution with calm, safety with severity, enervation with excitement. I was always seeking to distract myself with employment, yet always drawn aside from it into thinking about my ticket. I lived in what I did; yet *that for which I lived* lay beyond it.

Although the period of which I now write was only a matter of months ago, it seems to me like a separate existence. It would please me to say that this is because the conditions of my present life are so improved I look upon all my earlier times on the island as belonging to someone other than myself. The truth is otherwise. The months I spent waiting for my ticket seem remote to me today because they were a time of hope: hope that the ticket would bring my longed-for happiness, and the restoration of my original spirits. And when the news of my deliverance eventually arrived, I did indeed feel at first like a sinner who had found salvation, and rejoiced accordingly. I scissored its hard black and white from the *Gazette* and carried it into the Hospital in triumph. I purchased from an ancient sailor his blue coat, and white peaked cap, so that I might remind myself of how an Artist looked in the old days. I rented a room to call my home, near to the Hospital in Campbell Street. I did all these things, and looked about me hoping that my happiness would now increase steadily—only to find, as day succeeded day in my new life, that disappointment soon grew to dominate and corrode my pleasure.

Had I supposed that Hobart would suddenly be changed into London, and all my old ways and ideals would be restored? Not precisely. Yet I did expect some more vigorous experience of freedom, and a more powerful connection with everything that had seemed possible in my youth. I do not mean that my past was lost to me—nor that I did not dream continually of a return to England. I mean that because I knew the link with my former existence was broken, and could never be entirely mended, my old self and my new self were strangers to one another. Accordingly, I made deliberate efforts to control my desires, and resolved to live modestly (as I am endeavouring to write modestly now, discussing these things)—believing that any strenuous form of hopefulness would only increase my misery.

As I say, I took rooms in Campbell Street, and acquired a cat which still keeps me company there. [3] Throughout my previous life, as even my enemies will admit, I have shown a love for animals which should (if such a thing needed to be assessed) indicate a general warmth in me for all God's creations—human and otherwise. And it is true that the daily sight of this animal (which is a pretty confusion of white, black and gold, with exceptionally soft and deep fur)—the daily sight of this animal is a deep and vivid delight. She has an independence I admire, and a fastidious dislike for foolish sentiment, which helps me to understand the mechanics of my own self-preservation. Yet neither can she entirely hide her eagerness for my attention, and often when I have been separated from her for several hours together, she will hurtle towards me, and entwine herself around my legs, giving most excited mews and suchlike.

At the same time as I enjoy her company, however, her attentions provoke a kind of melancholy. I mean: the sight of her tiptoeing down the hallway towards me, or stretching on a windowsill in sunlight, silently asking for my hand upon her, stirs me to imagine the friends and loved ones—my Eliza!—who will never again salute me with a greeting. The sensation of my loss is so profound it scarcely occurs to me as anything like a thought. It more nearly resembles a series of blows to the stomach, so that often for hours on end I suffer fits of nausea, for which the only cure is sleep.

No, not the only cure; my work is also a comfort. Yet even here, while I am busy seeking out new commissions, I am reminded of everything I have lost. I hear the squeak of the sign above my door—"T. G. Wainewright: Artist"—and catch a lament for my days with Fuseli and Holst, Blake and Linnell. I sit down with some acquaintance or other who knows of my passion for the great authors, and his enthusiasm for an example of homegrown verse in the *Courier* fills me with contempt—exciting my appetite for the punning of Elia, or the crackle of Hazlitt, or the green reflections of John Clare. I work in comfortable houses, kneeling before my subjects to gaze carefully upon their features, and then stand back to view them among the best furniture—and long with a woman's longing for the delights of my bower: Squabbed silk and damask! Chandeliers and firelight! The breath of *Attargul*! [4]

It is for such reasons (although I see what I have given here are facts, not reasons) that the time of my deliverance has become the time of my greatest sadness. I do not mean a mood resembling the giddiness I knew in my youth, or the extremes of despair I underwent during my trial, or when I was on the Continent, etc. I mean the sadness which comes from a steady look at circumstances that are unhappy, and cannot change. I mean knowing that the Self I fed on honey-dew, and brought up to be full of beauty, must for ever pursue its ideal without the hope of an appropriate reward. I mean the loneliness of understanding that home exists, but cannot be reached. I mean the certainty that I shall never again meet a soul who will show me my own soul in its mirror.

And having such certainty, I must also admit that—however the terms of my existence on this island may alter—I no longer expect to arrive at a point where I may lay down my burden and say, "Here Endeth"—unless it be at the point we all come to in due course. By various means, the Self I have made has become more entirely the creature of my body than I ever supposed would be possible. In the spice islands of my youth, and amidst the delights of my glory days, it went adventuring abroad, travelling through the fine minds of friends, and sharing their ambitions. It was a power whose nutriment was love, and whose offspring were Art, music, divine song, and still holier philosophy. In the middle part of my life, it grew less bold, and dreamed merely of survival. Now, in the present, this poor Self, this ambassador of me, knows that if it strays from my breast, and enquires after a place in the world, it will be thwarted. It is a Self which has become a body, and must obey the laws that a body is compelled to obey.

Consider it now. I am seated at my table, the same honest affair that I described at the start of this Confession, watching the breeze lift the heads of bush shrubs as it blows across the land beyond my window. My Self enjoys this prospect—indeed, it seizes upon such trifling things as the only means by which it may move through the world at all, away from society, and with no expectation of pleasures beyond those which derive from nature. At the very notion, therefore, while I am writing these words, a part of me is springing forth, shooting over the green herbs and down to the silver Derwent. Glancing inland, to the left, it sees the tall gum trees crowding to the margin of the river, massing like clouds, tier above tier. Looking to the right, it finds the broadening reaches of the estuary, the flat bald hills, then the turbulent grey of the Bay of Storms, where the day is sinking. Can it see further still? Yes, Janus, my Self can see further still, venturing out into the Southern Ocean, above the hideous waves and the emptiness, where it finds now and again, as though they were swirled in the currents, white hands lifting upwards, and white eyes which cannot see, and white fragments of innumerable wrecks, all glittering among the moon- and starlight. And can it see further still, all the way along the curve of the earth until home itself is visible? No, it can not. Beyond that, there is nothing—which means that my Self must now begin to come back to me once more, winging through the emptiness, over the wild waters of the ocean, into the Bay of Storms, until it arrives at the Derwent, and comes uphill from the river's bank, across the dusty scrubland, and returns into my body, where it sits down patiently, recovering its breath, waiting for my hand to stop scratching across the page at last, so that we all may sleep.

1. TGW was admitted as a patient in the Colonial Hospital on 12 January 1842, though it is not clear exactly what was wrong with him. James Mair, the senior medical officer, told Frederick Clarke, the Inspector, that TGW was "labouring under a diversity of symptoms all indicating an enfeebled state of the system generally," and no one who examined him after this was able to be more precise. A century or so later, Crossland gave a plausible explanation:

> *Encephalitis lethargica* has been suggested; but it seems more likely ... to have been disseminated sclerosis, a disease of the central nervous system in which the areas of the sclerosis are dispersed throughout the spinal cord and brain. Certainly this accords with all the symptoms known to have been exhibited by [TGW]: the enfeebled nervous condition; the slight infirmity of speech; the partial paralysis; the eventual manner of his death; even (what many noted but misrepresented as the attribute of a "shifty" character) the final inability to look upward, to "look you in the face" (p. 376).

When TGW applied for his ticket-of-leave in April 1844, he was described as having been a patient for "nearly two years." This, combined with the growing respect for his work as a part-time painter, meant that when his condition improved he never again had to suffer the worst rigours of the transportation system.

2. A ticket-of-leave was an indulgence, liable to be revoked at any time, which allowed the holder to live "at large" within the colonial boundaries, and to set up any legitimate trade provided that he or she reported to the local police office every six months, and gave in advance any details of plans to travel round the island. It was eligible only to those who had already served a substantial part of their sentence, which means that TGW had little chance of gaining his freedom when he first applied for it.

The fact that TGW was granted a ticket soon after making his application tells us something about the precarious state of his health, and a good deal about his reputation as a "well-conducted man." The sponsors of his Petition were distinguished and conspicuous, and they put their reputations on the line by supporting him.

Nuttall seems to have been the prime mover. Early in 1843 he brought TGW's case to the attention of the Inspector, Clarke, who was his brother-in-law. Clarke then contacted the Staff Surgeon at the hospital, Mair, making a formal request for further information. Mair replied on 20 June, saying, "I have had reason to be satisfied with his general conduct while under my charge. I consider him a man of superior attainments, and I should feel happy if an indulgence could be granted him."

Nothing more encouraging than silence followed this exchange—a silence that lasted for ten months. Perhaps Clarke felt equivocal about TGW. Perhaps he lost sight of the case among other responsibilities. More likely, he felt that TGW would be wasting his time if he tried to petition too soon. In early April 1844, however, and no doubt because he was about to leave for India with Nuttall, Clarke abruptly galvanized himself, and began soliciting testimonials. The House Surgeon, Dr. William Crook (who was later supposed to have referred to TGW's "ingrained and ineradicable malignity") said, "I feel happy to have it in my power to testify to his unexceptionable good conduct during [his time with me]—in addition to an unvarying propriety of demeanour . . . I hereby recommend most strongly the prayer of this petition to the favourable consideration of his Excellency." James Fitzgerald, the Deputy Surveyor of Hospitals, added, "I have always noticed the steady and respectful manner in which he has behaved himself." And William Seccombe, the Surgeon-in-Charge, said, "[TGW] is one for whom I readily add my testimonial in his favour."

Once Clarke had collected these references, and been encouraged by the respect that other influential figures had for TGW, he made a digest of them on 9 April and sent it to Eardley-Wilmot:

> I have much pleasure in recommending the Petitioner to the favourable consideration of His Excellency; I believe if this indulgence which he asks were granted, it would tend much to the Improvement of his health, and that he would be able from his superior talents as an artist to provide for his own wants, and cease to be a burden on the Government. His conduct has been universally good during the long period I have known him and I feel assured that any indulgence or mitigation awarded by His Excellency will not be unworthily received.

TGW made his own formal Petition nine days later, on 18 April; he seems to have composed it himself, and to have enlisted the help of Thomas Bock in transcribing it—since fragmentary drafts survive in Bock's hand. It is an extraordinary document, and it is not difficult to see why some of his critics have called it "hysterical" and "wild," and have said that it "clearly displays the unbalanced, if not insane" state of his mind (Curling, p. 384).

There is—not surprisingly—no mention of his reputation as a poisoner, but there is a rigid insistence on his "entire Innocence" as a forger, and a thinly veiled accusation of his wife. These things, combined with other fibs about his work in London, are proof of his continuing economy with the truth. A similar kind of deceitfulness shows in his boasting about family, connections and ideals. Yet for all this, the Petition is far from being simply despicable. It is written by someone who is clearly desperate to bring his suffering to an end, who is incapable of admitting his guilt, and who can still convey something of his original flowery charm. It has a sublime cheek about it.

The Petition "came briefly to the notice of His Excellency" (Crossland, p. 390), then was immediately sent to the Police Office for "Police Character and the usual Report." A summary was prepared, and this was put before Eardley-Wilmot on 16 May:

> Thomas Griffiths Wainewright per *Susan* petitions for some Indulgence, declaring his innocence of the offence for which he is now suffering—he has been six and a half years in the colony under a Life Sentence and produces very good testimonials—he has been for nearly two years and a half a patient in the Colonial Hospital and Dr. Clarke expresses an opinion that it would ameliorate his bodily ailments if his mind could be relieved by the extension to him of some Indulgence—he has never been charged with misconduct in the Colony.

When Eardley-Wilmot had read this report, he immediately rejected the Petition, "on the grounds that, considering the shortness of the period actually served in relationship to the severity of the sentence imposed, the granting of a ticket-of-leave would be contrary to the Act." But a week later, and without any warning or explanation, TGW received a 3rd Class (the highest class) Probation Pass; this was registered in the Hobart Town *Gazette* on 31 May 1844. It is hard to see why it should have followed so hard on the heels of the earlier disappointment. Clarke and Nuttall had already left for India—perhaps their co-sponsors kept up the pressure? Maybe Eardley-Wilmot, who was by this time an unpopular figure, decided to curry favour by showing sympathy? In any event, the Probation Pass cleared the way for other interventions. On Tuesday 17 November 1844 the *Gazette* announced Eardley-Wilmot's "intention to recommend 15 prisoners," including TGW, "to Her Majesty the Queen for Conditional Pardons." A little over a year later, on 18 December 1845, the Comptroller-General of convicts, Dr. John Hampton, finally received and forwarded TGW's ticket-of-leave.

3. TGW goes out of his way to mention animals in his writing: "the mastiff Blucher" who lives in a pub in Hampshire; the terrier at Colnaghi's the print-seller, which greets him "with a wriggle of recognition"; the "crooked-tailed cat" owned by Thomas Payne the book-seller; his own horse "Contributor"; his cat; and his Newfoundland dog "Neptune," which "in size and colour [was] very like a white bear." He also lingers over animals in paintings. Discussing T. Ward's *The Painful Bite,* for instance, he says, "The expression of the curly puppy licking his bleeding foot, divided between pain and a liquorish itch again to adventure the rat (I *believe* it is), is well caught." Various contemporaries, remembering his time in Van Diemen's Land, mentioned that, towards the end of his life, "his sole living companion was a cat for which he evinced an extraordinary affection" (Curling, p. 238). This tenderness towards a creature is usually mentioned in the same breath as his heartlessness towards humans.

4. Shortly after being granted his ticket-of-leave, TGW found lodgings in 8 Campbell Street, a house owned by one James McDonald, which stood one block away from the Hospital. It was the part of town TGW had always known best. He hung a sign outside the door which said "Artist" and charged four shillings a day for his commissioned work, with a variable fee sometimes added.

Once TGW leaves the convict records, he more or less disappears from the face of the earth. The only subsequent public reference to him occurs in the *Colonial Times* of 15 December 1846: "NOTICE. If Mr. TGW does not fetch away his books and goods left in my house, the same will be sold by me on account of money due to me for his lodging and other matters. James McDonald." By this time, however, TGW was back in hospital, and dying.

AFTERWORD

*O*n 14 November 1846, a little under a year after Wainewright had been given his ticket-of-leave, the Acting Administrator of Van Diemen's Land, C. J. La Trobe, recommended him for a Conditional Pardon, which Curling reconstructed by substituting TGW's name for another:

> A recommendation for a Conditional Pardon having been forwarded to the Queen for Thomas Griffiths Wainewright tried at the Central Criminal Court in the year 1837 it is the Colonial Administrator's pleasure to permit him to employ himself in any lawful occupation for his own benefit within the limits of the Australian Colonies and New Zealand; and that the said Thomas Griffiths Wainewright should have and enjoy all the rights, privileges and advantages which are given and granted to persons holding Conditional Pardons by the Act passed in the Sixth Year of the Reign of Her Majesty IN-TITULED An Act to amend the Law affecting Convicts with respect to Pardons and Tickets of Leave, during good behaviour, or until the Administrator's further pleasure be made known.
>
> The holder of this Pass is hereby cautioned, that this indulgence will be forfeited should any misconduct deserving of such punishment be proved to the satisfaction of the Administrator.

In the same month that Wainewright received this Pardon, he suffered a stroke, and lost the use of his left hand. He was immediately taken into St. Mary's Hospital, where he died nine months later, on 17 August 1847. According to the hospital report, the cause was a "cerebral aneurism." The *Britannia and Trade Advocate* mentioned his death on 26 August, referring to him as "Mr. Thomas Wainewright, Artist," but giving no information about where or even whether he had been buried. It is possible that his body was seized by the hospital for dissection.

In the past, people have tended to judge Wainewright's last few months harshly, agreeing that he was "obsessed with a hatred for humanity" (Curling, p. 26). There is no evidence to justify such censure, though it is clear that in some parts of Hobart society Wainewright never escaped the stigma of his convict history. Eight days after his death, Agnes Power, the wife of the Surveyor General Robert Power, whom Wainewright had painted, wrote to one of her daughters in London (when she was visiting her aunt, Lady Blessington):

> By the by, the unfortunate Wainewright is dead—he died this day week of apoplexy. He had been for a long time very ill, had lost the use of his hand, and was altogether in a miserable state of poverty as well as illness and had gone to the Hospital. Two days before he died, he felt so well that he asked to go from the Hospital and died quite suddenly. He certainly was a wonderful man, full of talent and fuller still of wickedness. The last time I ever saw him he said all he wished to live for was to go home and murder the person who had transported him [i.e. his cousin, Edward Foss]—of course I affected to think he was jesting, but I am quite sure he was in earnest.

Jesting and deceiving, pathetic yet vengeful, "talented" but "wicked": Wainewright was as perplexing in Hobart as he had been in London. Yet at the start of his posthumous existence, his crimes (though officially pardoned) continued to overshadow his achievements, and to cause all sorts of difficulties. No one, for instance, thought to tell his widow, Eliza, that he was dead. On 8 February 1849, having tried to get news from the Foreign Office and the Convict Department, she wrote from 24 Palace New Road, Lambeth, directly to Earl Grey, the Secretary of State for the Colonies:

> My Lord,
> I have to request your Lordship's pardon for the trouble which peculiar circumstances oblige me to cause you.
> In the year 1837 Thomas Griffiths Wainewright was transported for Life, for forgery and left England in August 1837 in the Ship Susan for Van Diemen's Land.
> The forgery was on the Bank of England, by which he obtained permission of the Fund placed under trust of my Marriage Settlement. The Trustees required the sum to be replaced by the Bank, agreeing not to receive any dividend arising therefrom during the life of the said T. G. Wainewright, but that at his death my interest in

the income of course would commence, with remainder to my Son. Two years since, in consequence of being unable to obtain any information respecting him from the Convict Office, and having never received any answer to numerous Letters sent thro' the Post Office, I was advised (it being a matter of importance) to write to the Colonial Secretary at Hobart Town requesting an early reply: up to this period no notice has been taken of the application.

I have received from a private source undoubted information that he died Eighteen Months since;—but in order to receive the income, to which at his death I become entitled, I must produce for the Bank Authorities a Certificate to that effect, from the Government Authorities. I have applied in consequence at the Convict Department, and find that in 1846 he was reported living; and that the List of Deaths did not include him, as far as regards the Quarterly Returns up to 1848. But Mr. Everest suggests that, having a Ticket of Leave he might not at the time of sending the List have been on the spot, and therefore would only be known in the general muster.

My Lord, I beseech you to shorten the suffering I have so long endured, and condescend to expedite the receipt of the necessary Document; for the fact of the decease having been communicated thro' the family of R. Power Esq., the Surveyor General of Hobart Town, who knew him well, of course the official communication can be obtained by your command. I have still further to petition your Lordship to permit the Certificate, when obtained, to be forwarded to Mrs. E. F. Wainewright, care of H. Foss Esq., 81 Pall Mall.

A death certificate was eventually forwarded to Eliza on 1 September 1849; two years later she emigrated to America with her son Griffiths, who gave up a career in the Navy to join her—and disappeared. Her finances were in better shape than they had been for many years. On 27 October 1836, the Governor had authorized the purchase of £5,250 New ½ per cent Stock in the names of Robert Wainewright, Edward Smith Foss and Edward Foss, on condition that all dividends be held for her in trust during Wainewright's life. In 1839, the Bank had agreed to pay Eliza an annuity of £50 out of the dividends. After her husband's death, she could have expected £200 a year. The stock had eventually been transferred into her own name on 31 May 1850.

No one seems to have suspected Eliza of helping Wainewright commit his crimes; she even remained on reasonable terms with the administrators of his former Trust. Wainewright's own reputation, on the other hand, continued to suffer. Nine days after his death, the Colonial Secretary (a "jovial" fellow who looked like "a stalled ox" according to the Hobart diarist G. T. W. Boyes) went through the studio at 8 Campbell Street "to inspect and purchase . . . some sketches . . . at his own price." For the next several decades, it was much more usual to insult or neglect Wainewright than to appreciate him.

This is not to say Wainewright sank entirely from sight during the middle and late nineteenth century. As far as the Victorians were concerned, the abiding interest of his story was that he had been trained for the life of a cultured gentleman, then betrayed his inheritance. How could his two lives be combined in the same story? Only, apparently, by blackening his name, and insisting that his work was terribly infected with his malignancy. One article in particular, which appeared in *Notes & Queries* (3rd series) on 6 October 1866, shows the process at work. It had begun life as a sympathetic testimonial written in 1844 by the Superintendent of the Convict Establishment in Hobart, in support of Wainewright's Petition for a ticket-of-leave. On 14 July 1866, however, it appeared in a furiously mangled form in the Melbourne *Spectator,* with many unsubstantiated slanders added, then was twisted some more before appearing four months later in *Notes & Queries.* In other words, the process of rumour-denigration that had started during the last part of Wainewright's life accelerated rapidly after his death. Instead of being described as a "good character," he became a "marked man—dreaded, disliked and shunned by everybody." Or as *The Spectator* had it:

> If commissioned to execute the portrait of a lady, he would always endeavour to give an erotic direction to the conversation; so that whatever admiration was felt for his genius was neutralized by the fear and antipathy excited by his lewdness . . . He endeavoured to poison two people in Hobart Town who had become obnoxious to him; and no compunctious visitings of conscience ever interfered with the execution of any fell purpose upon which he had resolved.

Such inventions, passed off as facts, were repeated by almost everyone who took an interest in Wainewright's story in the middle and late Victorian period. Assimilating the earlier opinions offered by Talfourd and others, they confirmed the impression of Wainewright as "a man of the lowest stamp"—and were duly reinforced by Walter Thornbury in *Old Stories Re-*

told (1870) and Havelock Ellis in *The Criminal* (1890). In the twentieth century, the current of prejudice against Wainewright has continued to flow strongly. Thomas Seccombe's *Twelve Bad Men* (1894) and Ladbroke Black's *The Prince of Poisoners* (1932) both peddle suppositions as facts, and damn the work by reference to the life. Even the first decent attempt to produce a full-length biography, Jonathan Curling's *Janus Weathercock* (1938), presents Wainewright as predominantly cold, vain, silly, venal and heartless. It is an image that Robert Crossland challenged in *Wainewright in Tasmania* (1954), but which has persisted in such recent works as Edward Dyson's *In the Roaring Fifties* (1960), and the Australian Hal Porter's novel *The Tilted Cross* (1961), and the same author's radio play *The Forger* (1983), where Wainewright appears as Judas Griffith Vaneleigh.

Wittingly or not, these versions of Wainewright depend heavily on the idea of his personality which was first broadcast by Talfourd, *The Spectator* and *Notes & Queries*. But they also have other and larger debts. Ten months before Wainewright died, Edward Bulwer Lytton published *Lucretia: or, The Children of the Night* (first edition, November 1846; second edition, December 1847). It was the first of three Victorian texts that did more than anything to define Wainewright's posthumous reputation.

Edward Bulwer Lytton (1805–1873) is almost entirely unread today, but in his time was well known. He was raised on the enormous estate of Knebworth in Hertfordshire, reckoned to be exceptionally clever, educated at Trinity Hall, Cambridge—where he "pretended to be a Radical, [but] . . . was always a thorough Tory at heart" (Cooper)—and after a brief spell in Europe, got married and decided to "abandon himself to study and contemplation" (ibid.). The result was comparative poverty and a series of novels, including the autobiographical *Pelham* (1828), the political satire *Paul Clifford* (1831) and *Eugene Aram* (1832). While continuing to write prolifically after this energetic start, he suffered bad marriage-trouble, and went into Parliament, eventually becoming Secretary of State for the Colonies, and was raised to the peerage in 1866. In spite of his achievements, his reputation was never secure. *The Times* in its obituary said, "Lord Lytton was a clever and graceful amateur."

Although Bulwer Lytton never met Wainewright, he knew Theodore von Holst well (and commissioned a portrait from him in 1844), and during the 1830s had a reputation as a dandy that would have appealed to both of the other men. In much of his early writing, his flamboyance is coupled with a genuine interest in "the ironical comparison between those whom society makes its idols and those whom it outlaws from its pale" (Cooper)—as *Paul*

Clifford and *Eugene Aram* make clear. *Paul Clifford*, indeed, distinguished itself by becoming known as the first "Newgate novel," thanks to its concentration on issues of crime and morality.

Other "Newgate novels" included William Harrison Ainsworth's *Rookwood* (1834) and *Jack Sheppard* (1839/40)—as well as *Lucretia* itself. They began life as "a form of protest against the criminal law and against the structure of class privilege which that law represented"; they were all preoccupied with "the state of the legal system," and with "the relationship between the criminal and his/her social environment"; and they all built a bridge between eighteenth-century novels such as *Moll Flanders* and *Jonathan Wild* and crime fiction of the late Victorian period and the twentieth century. (See John, Introduction to *The Newgate Novels*.) Bulwer Lytton adds to their interest by elaborating, in the foreword to the second edition of *Lucretia,* a theory of the novel that expresses a deeply Romantic sensibility, locating, like Wainewright, the source and value of art in the "soul" of the artist.

Lucretia is unusual among "Newgate novels" in not concentrating on low life—and much as it wants to understand criminal psychology, it cannot help deploring the failure of its well-born characters to honour their social position, and criticizing their extravagances (foppery and so on) as a sign of decadence. These prejudices inevitably spell trouble for Wainewright, in so far as the novel makes him the focus of its interest.

Bulwer Lytton admitted to using Wainewright as a source, and pored over relevant papers from the archive of the Eagle Insurance Company once he had devised his plot. Although the papers relating to Wainewright have long since vanished, part of the correspondence between the company's agent, Henry P. Smith, and Bulwer Lytton survives. (The chronology of the following quotations has been clarified by de Chantilly.) On 2 May 1849 Smith wrote from Westbourne Terrace in West London:

> I have just heard that Wainwright [*sic*] died recently in the Hospital at Hobarton [*sic*]. His latter days in the Sick ward were employed I am told in blaspheming to the Pious patients and in terrifying the timid. I think that he never lived to know the everlasting fame to which he has been damned in Lucretia.

Three years previously Smith had written to Bulwer Lytton:

> I will collect and send you all the Wainewright papers. There is no record of the forgery, that is, of the offence which sent him to Aus-

tralia, because my duties directed my enquiries solely to the insurances, that is—to the deaths.

This added to information that Smith had supplied still earlier:

In making a further search, I found a list of the contents of the forfeit trunks [brought back from France], and this led me to a second packet of papers and books which had escaped my first enquiries—I send them to you—& also our schedule . . . It will show you the books which the combination of his necessities & his tastes had left to him amid the general wreck. (You will see your own *Letter to a Cabinet Minister* was retained amongst his later treasures.) The drawings came out better than my memory had limned them to you. There is no proof of the nature of the poison used, but the general medical opinion of the time pronouned it to be strychnine . . . Mr. Thompson tells me that Wainewright confessed that he used strychnine and morphine, & you will gather more of his history from the additional briefs and notes now sent. (Curling, p. 313.)

It is impossible to tell from these remarks exactly what sort of confession, if any, Wainewright made in his papers—and the identity of "Mr. Thompson" is unknown (see chapter 15, note 7). Nor is *Lucretia* any help in this respect. Bulwer Lytton spreads his ideas about Wainewright across several characters rather than concentrating them in one; and while insisting in his Preface that "the crimes herein related took place within the last seventeen years," and "have their foundation in actual facts," there is nothing in the text to show when he is making a reliable report and when he is inventing. Wainewright, in other words, is less like the foundation of the book than its presiding spirit.

All this adds to the complications of an already complicated narrative, in which Gabriel Varney and Lucretia Clavering defraud a young heiress (named Helen) before poisoning her: "By the pressure of the hand, at the touch of a concealed spring, a barbed point flew forth steeped in venom, more deadly than the Indian extracts from the bag of the cobracapella,—a venom to which no antidote is known, which no test can detect." Eventually Lucretia and Varney are rumbled by a poor orphan boy, Beck (a prototype of Joe the crossing sweeper in *Bleak House*), who is also poisoned for his trouble, and turns out to be Lucretia's illegitimate son. (In the second edition,

Beck survives.) Lucretia promptly goes mad and Varney is transported, where he—"An Artist"—is "fastened" on a chain gang to "a gravestealer."

Lucretia mixes truth and lies about Wainewright, but contemporary readers soon stopped asking which was which. Never mind that the crimes it describes were part Borgia, part Wainewright. Never mind that some blame might attach to Eliza (Lucretia). Never mind that Wainewright had only been tried for forgery, not murder. The story it tells is concerned with an archetypal criminal, and offers proof of the evil that awaits those who live entirely by the senses (Varney), or by the intellect (Lucretia). It also, and just as bluntly, separates a life in crime from an interest in culture, as several of its original reviewers noticed. John Forster, for instance, was conventionally shocked by the idea that someone who had been (in Bulwer Lytton's words) "an artist, a musician, a critic, and a writer of liveliness and versatility" could indeed be a Janus. Forster condemned Wainewright as

the gaudy, violent, flaring artist; the insolent, bullying, double-voiced critic; the profane and extravagant entertainer; the shabby cheat; the swindler and forger; the unscrupulous and unsparing murderer; and, to the last, even when loaded with a felon's chains, the daring and impudent braggart.

Many of Bulwer Lytton's assumptions about Wainewright were shared by his friend Charles Dickens. Dickens had first seen Bulwer Lytton in the House of Commons, when one was a young reporter and the other an MP, and they were introduced during the 1830s. Bulwer Lytton encouraged Dickens at the start of his career, sharing his dandified tastes and his reforming zeal, and acknowledging his greater gifts; in the 1850s they worked together on the ill-fated Guild for Art and Literature.

Dickens went out of his way to collect information about Wainewright. He talked about him to Lady Blessington, whose niece's father had been drawn by Wainewright in Van Diemen's Land; he interviewed Dr. Locock—whom Forster flatly refers to as "that distinguished physician [who] had attended the poor girl, Miss Abercrombie, whose death by strychnine led to the exposure of Wainewright's murders"—over dinner in March and April 1849; and he corresponded during 1869 with Smith of the Eagle Insurance Company. (Smith became a good friend of Dickens, and godfather to two of his children.)

On the face of it, Dickens handles Wainewright in much the same way as Bulwer Lytton. His best-known treatment is the melodramatic short story

Hunted Down, which was commissioned by the *New York Ledger* in 1859 for the then record-breaking sum of £1,000, and first published in book form in America in 1861. (The fee was huge because when the *Ledger* first approached Dickens he was writing *Great Expectations,* and reluctant to turn aside unless the digression was made worthwhile. "Your proposal is so handsome," Dickens said, "that it changes my resolution, and I cannot refuse it. I will endeavour to be at work upon the tale while this note is on its way to you across the water.") In England, *Hunted Down* first appeared in *All the Year Round* in August 1860, then was published as a book by John Campden Hotten in 1870. Hotten made the connection with Wainewright explicit, writing a Preface which spiced up the accounts that had previously appeared in *The Spectator* and *Notes & Queries.* (The opinion of *Notes & Queries* that "the malignancy of his character seems to have been ingrained and ineradicable," for instance, becomes in Hotten: "He seemed to be possessed of an ingrained malignity of disposition which kept him constantly on the very confines of murder.")

Hunted Down accepts that its anti-hero must be able to fascinate people as well as commit crimes. The narrator—Sampson, "the Chief-Manager of a Life Assurance Office"—introduces Julius Slinkton as a man with a central parting which is as white and clear "as a gravel walk," and a "dainty white cravat and dainty linen altogether," who is grieving over the recent death of his "charming niece." His melancholy does not impede his sense of purpose. While telling all and sundry that he is on the point of taking Holy Orders, he is in fact planning an insurance fraud very similar to the one devised by Wainewright. His plots, however, are suspected by Meltham (a lover of the dead niece), who takes various disguises and tracks Slinkton to Scarborough, on the Yorkshire coast, where he exposes the crime. Slinkton tears his hair ("it was the end of the smooth walk") and poisons himself: a "fitting end."

It is difficult to see Dickens doing much in his story except make money. But there is one moment that suggests why he took such an interest in Wainewright—the moment at which the narrator says:

> There is no greater mistake than to suppose that a man who is a calculating criminal is, in any phase of his guilt, otherwise than true to himself and perfectly consistent with his whole character. Such a man commits murder, and murder is the natural culmination of his course; such a man has to outface murder, and he will do it with hardihood and effrontery.

This is the same judgement that Dickens applies to Jonas Chuzzlewit in *Martin Chuzzlewit* (1843/4) and to Rigaud (Blandois) in *Little Dorrit* (1855/7), both of whom are also to some extent modelled on Wainewright. Blandois is "Devoted to the destruction of a man" and uses fancy phrases to impress and deceive his fellows; Jonas (whose name obviously recalls Janus) is a stagy insurance crook and poisoner who resembles Wainewright in his dandified speech ("a-snorin'," etc.)—but not in his looks—and is prepared to go to any lengths to make a profit:

> The education of Mr. Jonas had been conducted from his cradle on the strictest principles of the main chance. The very first word he learned to spell was "gain," and the second (when he got to two syllables), was "money."

It is obvious from several other novels by Dickens that he had a deeply divided notion of criminal identity. In *Great Expectations,* for instance, by presenting Magwitch and Pip as he does, he fuses ideas of gentlemanliness with ideas of illegality. In this sense, both characters might be considered a transformed image of Wainewright—and to show that Dickens's manifest hostility to Wainewright is in fact a sign of complex fascination, rather than simple disapproval.

But as Slinkton, Jonas Chuzzlewit and Rigaud all demonstrate, Dickens was keen to keep these ambivalences out of sight in his work. In particular he wanted his audience to see that he was horrified by the thought that someone who had been "one of us"—an artist and a dandy—should have become "one of them"—a criminal and an outcast. The revulsion is unmistakable in the coda to Dickens's treatment of Wainewright: the mini-biography by Walter Thornbury that appeared in his magazine *All the Year Round* in January 1867 (information from de Chantilly). This essay, which conflates Talfourd's account with a careful reading of the trial reports, and uses the *Spectator* article of the previous year as well as information gathered from Locock and Bulwer Lytton, presents Wainewright as an "insufferable fop" whose "exulting egotism" and "coxcombical words" are proof of his voluptuous appetites:

> He is a fop and a dandy, but is clever, has a refined taste, and is the kindliest and most light-hearted creature in the world . . . His manner is most gallant, insinuating and winning. His face, however, is by no means that of the mere dandy. His head is massive, and widens at the

back. His eyes are deeply set in their sockets. His jaw is square and solid. He seldom looks the person he talks to full in the face. He has his hair curled every morning (a stray ringlet or so left free), and slightly stoops. His expression is at once repelling and fascinating.

The remainder of this essay recycles the murder stories of Waine-wright's friends and relations—including "the Norfolk gentleman"—as if they were certainly true, condemns him as "one of the most cruel, subtle and successful secret murderers since the time of the Borgias," and even adds that it is "well known that he wore a ring in which he always carried strychnine." Like *Lucretia*, it ends by finding Wainewright guilty—not as charged, but as suspected. In the process, it agrees with the man who did more than anyone to set the rumour-ball rolling:

Well says Mr. Serjeant Talfourd: "Surely no contrast presented in the wildest romance between a gay cavalier, fascinating Naples or Palermo, and the same hero detected as the bandit or demon of the forest, equals that which time has unveiled between what Mr. Wainewright seemed and what he was."

The last important nineteenth-century response to Wainewright's story was Oscar Wilde's essay "Pen, Pencil and Poison: A Study in Green," which appeared in the same year (1889) as his "The Decay of Lying." Wilde took the outline of Wainewright's story from various sources, including the Introduction to W. C. Hazlitt's edition of *Essays and Criticism* (1880), and de Quincey's essay "Charles Lamb." But he had first heard it when an undergraduate, and may also have spoken about it early in life with Sidney Colvin, with whom he was briefly in love as a young man.

Wilde's title, "Pen, Pencil and Poison," adapts a phrase used of Wainewright by Swinburne in his *Life of Blake* (1868). Wainewright, says Swinburne, was

admirable alike as a painter, a writer, and a murderer. In each pursuit, perhaps, there was a certain want of solid worth and fervour, which at times impeded or impaired the working of an excellent faculty; but in each it is evident there was a nobler sense of things fair and fit; a seemliness and shapeliness of execution, a sensitive relish of excellence, an exquisite aspiration after goodness of work, which cannot be overpraised. With pen, with palette, or with poison, his hand was never a mere craftsman's. The visible vulgarities and deficiencies of his style went hardly deeper than the surface. Excess of colour and levity of handling have not unjustly been charged against him; he does not seem to have used the material on hand, whether strychnine or mere ink, to the best purpose; his work has a certain crudity and violence of tone; his articles and his crimes are both too often wanting in the most delightful qualities of which finished art is capable, qualities which a more earnest man of lesser genius might have given them. The main object in both seems wrong, or at best insufficient; in the one case he looked less to achievement than to effect; in the other he aimed rather at money-getting than at enjoyment; which is the more deplorable, as a man so greatly gifted must have been in every way fitted to apprehend, to relish, and to realize all nobler and subtle pleasure in its more vigorous forms and in its more delicate sense ... On all accounts we may suppose that in days perhaps not remote a philosophic posterity, mindful that the harvest of art has few reapers worthy of their hire, and well aware that what is exalted must also be exceptional, will inscribe with due honour upon the list of men who have deserved well of mankind the name of Wainwright [sic].

Wilde's "Pen, Pencil and Poison" deals more generously with Wainewright's reputation, even though it continues to treat rumours about his life and personality as the truth. "To be suggestive for fiction," says Wilde, "is to be of more importance than a fact." The whole body of his essay, in fact, is a witty refutation of the standard Victorian line—and also, as one of Wilde's critics says, "a key to the crucial quality of the Aesthetic and Decadent sensibility of the 1890s ... a self-consciously precious and highly fastidious discrimination brought to bear on both Art and Life, a response beyond ordinary notions of Taste, beyond Fashion, and quite outside the dictates of Morality" (Calloway). For one thing, it tells the story of Wainewright's life without any of the heated moralizings that are so relished by his predecessors. Wilde accepts that "a young dandy sought to be somebody rather than do something," calls him "a forger of no mean or ordinary abilities" and "a subtle poisoner almost without rival in this or any age," and congratulates him on adopting masks ("A mask tells us more than a face"), and on trying "to revive style as a conscious tradition." This kind of judgement seemed like disgraceful flippancy to many contemporary readers; its effect, however, was to emphasize other aspects of Wainewright's achievement. His qualities as a critic, for instance. Wilde calls him "one of the first to recognize what is, indeed, the very keynote of aesthetic eclecticism, I mean the true harmony of all really beautiful things irrespective of age or place, or school or manner." Elsewhere, he reinforces this by concentrating on Wainewright's interest in prints, saying, "He never lost sight of the great truth that Art's first appeal is neither to the intellect nor to the emotions, but purely to the artistic temperament."

As Wilde extends his argument, he is careful to see off charges of unworldliness or self-regard. In fact he praises Wainewright in particular for his pragmatism and "technical" skill, sympathizing with his difficulties in evaluating contemporary work, and insisting, "The qualities that he sought for in a picture were composition, beauty and dignity of line, richness of colour, and imaginative power . . . He saw what our English school could gain from a study of Greek models, and never wearies of pointing out to the young student the artistic possibilities that lie dormant in Hellenic marbles and Hellenic methods of work." Wilde takes a similar attitude toward Wainewright as a writer. Where Bulwer Lytton, Dickens, and others look on his dandification as a proof of his insincerity, Wilde appreciates that the colours and contortions of the prose are signs of an attempt to present "his impressions of the work as an artistic whole, to give, as it were, the literary equivalent for the imaginative and mental effort."

There is a degree of identification here—and when Wilde later calls Wainewright "one of the first to develop what has been called the art-literature of the nineteenth century," and says "the conception of making a prose poem out of paint is excellent," it becomes explicit. "Much of the best modern literature springs from the same aims," he goes on, meaning to include such contemporaries as Pater and Symons to support his case, and also looking across the Channel to include Baudelaire and the Symbolists. (Mario Praz rightly calls Wainewright "a strange forerunner of Wilde" in *The Romantic Agony*.)

Wilde's belief that "in a very ugly and sensible age, the arts borrow, not from life, but from each other" is one foundation of his support for Wainewright. The other is more personal, and more complex. At several points in "Pen, Pencil and Poison," Wilde seems to anticipate his own arrest, his defence, and his experience as a convict (in detail, as well as in general: Wainewright never swept his cell; Wilde was "most inefficient" at the job). "Sin should be solitary," he says with a grave lightness, "and have no accomplices," before proceeding to give details of Wainewright's trial, regretting the verdict ("The sentence now passed on him was to a man of his culture a form of death"), and zooming in on the very question that Bulwer Lytton and Dickens failed to address: the relationship between Wainewright's high style and his low cunning.

This is the central subject of "Pen, Pencil and Poison," and it energizes all the other arguments in the essay. "The performance of personality," Wilde says, "is a very subtle metaphysical problem, and certainly the English law solves the question in an extremely rough-and-ready manner." What concerns Wilde is not the notion that people might change during the course of their life, but the idea that "there is no essential incongruity between crime and culture." He understands that moralists such as Bulwer Lytton and Dickens "rewrite the whole of history for the purpose of gratifying our moral sense of what should be" when faced with a figure like Wainewright. He also allows for the fact that "crime" might even have "an important effect" on a person's art, which does not therefore immediately become contaminated in the process. "The domestic virtues are not the true basis of art," Wilde says, "though they may serve as an excellent advertisement for second-rate artists." It is an idea that had already been put forward by Gilchrist, in his life of Blake, and it pinpoints Wainewright's importance for Wilde, and for succeeding generations of readers who are prepared to see him as a brilliant but flawed figure in the life of his times—one who illustrates the mood and quality of those times while also raising large questions about Romanticism, about the nature of the creative spirit, and about biography. "The truth of Art," Gilchrist says, "is as absolute as life itself, and demands a wholly independent verdict."

Select Bibliography

Books written or edited by Thomas Griffiths Wainewright

"Hero and Leander" by Christopher Marlowe, with unsigned Preface by Thomas Griffiths
    Wainewright (*Select Early English Poets*, No. VIII, 1820)
*Some Passages in the Life etc. of Egomet Bonmot Esq, edited by Mr. Mwaughmaim, and now first pub-
    lished by Me* (1825) [*Egomet Bonmot*]
Essays and Criticism by Thomas Griffiths Wainewright, edited by W. Carew Hazlitt (1882) [*Essays*]

Selected background reading

Ackroyd, Peter, *Dickens* (1990)
————*Blake* (1995)
Adamson, John William, *English Education 1789–1902* (1930)
Allport, Henry, *Early Art in Tasmania* (Hobart, 1931)
Anderson, Robert, *The Life of Tobias Smollett* (1806)
Angelo, Henry, *Angelo's Pic Nic* (1834)
Anon, *Literary Memoirs of Living Authors of Great Britain* (1798)
————*The Pictorial Guide to Greenwich* (1844)
————*Rules and Regulations for the First Stage of Convict Discipline in Van Diemen's Land* (1847)
————*Hobart General Hospital: Its Early History* (1921)
————*Colnaghi's 1760–1960* (1960)
————*Thomas Bock: Convict Engraver, Society Portraitist* (Canberra, 1991)
Antal, Frederick, *Fuseli Studies* (1956)
Armour, Richard, *Barry Cornwall* (Boston, 1935)
Barnett, George L., *Charles Lamb* (Boston, 1976)
Barton, Bernard, *Poems and Letters* (1849)
Bateman, Charles, *The Convict Ships 1789–1868* (Glasgow, 1959)
Bauer, Josephine, *The London Magazine 1820–1829* (Copenhagen, 1953)
Beattie, J. W., *Glimpses of the Lives and Times of the Early Tasmanian Governors* (Hobart, 1905)
Belmanno, Mary, *Pen and Pencil* (New York, 1858)
Beloe, William, *The Sexagenarian* (1817)
Bentley, G. E., *Blake Records* (Oxford, 1969)
————*Blake Books* (Oxford, 1977)
————*Blake Books Supplement* (Oxford, 1995)
Bindman, David, *John Flaxman* (1979)
Black, Ladbroke, *The Prince of Poisoners* (1932)
Blunden, Edmund, *Charles Lamb and his Contemporaries* (Cambridge, 1933)

————*Keats's Publisher: A Memoir of John Taylor* (1936)

Bolitho, Hector, and Mulgan, John, *The Emigrants* (1931)

Bolton, Arthur T., *Architectural Education a Century Ago* (1934)

Boswell, James, *Life of Johnson*, edited by R. W. Chapman (Oxford, 1970)

Branch-Johnson, W., *The English Prison Hulks* (1957)

Brand, Ian, *The Convict Probation System* (Hobart, 1990)

Breton, Lieut., *Excursions in New South Wales* (1833)

Broderip, Frances, *Memorials of Thomas Hood* (1869)

Brown, Charles, *Journal of a Voyage to New Zealand* (1842)

Browne, G. Latham, and C. G. Stewart, *Reports of Trials for Murder by Poisoning* (1883)

Browne, Max, *The Romantic Art of Theodore von Holst 1810–1844* (1994)

Browning, Colin Arnot, *The Convict Ships* (2nd edn, 1847)

Burnett, T. A. J., *The Rise and Fall of the Regency Dandy* (Oxford, 1981)

Burney, Revd C., *The Exposition of the Creed* (1810)

Buscombe, Eve, *Artists in Early Australia and their Portraits* (Sydney, 1978)

Calloway, Stephen, "The Dandyism of the Senses," *Studio International*, spring 1998

Carlyle, Thomas, *The Life of John Sterling* (1851)

Chancellor, E. Beresford, *Annals of the Strand* (1912)

Chesney, Kellow, *The Victorian Underworld* (Harmondsworth, 1970)

Chilcott, Tim, *A Publisher and his Circle* (1972)

Clare, John, *The Prose of John Clare*, edited by J. W. and Anne Tibble (1951)

————*Selected Letters*, edited by Mark Storey (Oxford, 1990)

Clarke, Marcus, *For the Term of His Natural Life* (1874)

Clayton, Timothy, *The English Print 1688–1802* (1998)

Clifford, James L., *From Puzzles to Portraits* (1970)

Cole, Hubert, *Beau Brummell* (1977)

Conrad, Peter, *Down Home* (1988)

Cooper, Thompson, *Lord Lytton: A Biography* (1873)

Crossland, Robert, *Wainewright in Tasmania* (Wellington, 1954)

Cunningham, Allan, *The Lives of the Most Eminent British Painters, Sculptors and Architects* (2nd edn, 1830)

Curling, Jonathan, *Janus Weathercock: The Life of Thomas Griffiths Wainewright* (1938)

De Quincey, Thomas, *Collected Writings*, edited by David Masson (1897)

Dickens, Charles, *Martin Chuzzlewit* (1844)

————*Great Expectations* (1861)

————*Hunted Down* (1870)

————*Dickens's Journalism*, edited by Michael Slater (1994)

Dobell, Bertram, *Sidelights on Charles Lamb* (1963)

Dutton, Dennis, *The Forger's Art* (Berkeley, 1983)

Dyson, Edward, *In the Roaring Fifties* (1960)

Ellis, Havelock, *The Criminal* (1890)

Ellis, Julian, *Fame and Failure* (1919)

Ellmann, Richard, *Oscar Wilde* (1987)

Emmett, E. T., *A Short History of Tasmania* (Sydney, 1937)

Emsley, Clive, *Crime and Society in England 1750–1900* (1987)

Evans, Robin, *The Fabrication of Virtue* (Cambridge, 1982)

Farwell, George, *Portrait of a Gentleman* (Sydney, 1946)

Faulkener, Thomas, *The History of Antiquities in Brentford, Ealing and Chiswick* (1845)

Fields, James T., *Barry Cornwall and His Friends* (Boston, 1882)

Select Bibliography

Finger, Charles, *Historic Crimes and Criminals* (Girard, 1922)

Forster, John, *The Life and Times of Oliver Goldsmith* (1848)

——*The Life of Charles Dickens* (1892 edn)

Fouqué, Friedrich de la Motte, *Undine: A Romance* (1818)

Francis, John, *Annals, Anecdotes and Legends of Life Insurance* (1853)

Fuseli, Henry, *The Collected English Letters,* edited by David H. Weinglass (1982)

Gilchrist, Alexander, *The Life of William Blake* (1880)

Goddard, Henry, *Memoirs of a Bow Street Runner* (1956)

Graham, Peter W., *Don Juan and Regency England* (Charlottesville, 1990)

Graham, Walter, *English Literary Periodicals* (New York, 1930)

Graves, Algernon, *The Royal Academy Exhibitors,* vol. VIII (1906)

Grieg, James (ed.), *The Farington Diary* (1926)

Griffiths, Anthony, *Landmarks in Print Collecting* (1996)

Griffiths, Ralph, *Ascanius, or The Young Adventurer* (1746)

Hackforth-Jones, Jocelyn, *The Convict Artists* (Sydney, 1977)

Hamilton, Olive and Nigel, *Royal Greenwich* (1969)

Hammond, Peter, *Thomas Griffiths Wainewright* (Brentford and Chiswick Local History Society Journal, No. 7, 1998)

Hart-Davis, Rupert (ed.), *More Letters of Oscar Wilde* (1985)

Hayden, John O., *The Romantic Reviewers* (1969)

Haywood, Ian, *Faking It* (1987)

Hazlitt, William, *The Complete Works,* edited by P. P. Howe, after edn by A. R. Waller and Arnold Glover, 21 vols (London and Toronto, 1930–34)

——*Selected Writings,* edited by Jon Cook (1991)

Healey, Edna, *Coutts and Co.* (1992)

Hollingsworth, Keith, *The Newgate Novel 1830–1847* (Detroit, 1963)

Hooper, W. Eden, *The History of Newgate* (1935)

Hopkins, Paul, "Thomas Griffiths Wainewright, his in-laws, and Wimbledon Manor" (forthcoming)

House, Humphrey, *All in Due Time* (1955)

Howe, P. P., *The Life of William Hazlitt* (1922)

Hughes, Robert, *The Fatal Shore* (1987)

Hunt, Leigh, *Autobiography* (1861)

Ignatieff, Michael, *A Just Measure of Pain* (1978)

Jack, Ian, *Keats and the Mirror of Art* (1967)

Jeffreys, Charles, *Van Diemen's Land* (1820)

John, Juliet (ed.), *The Newgate Novels: 1830–1847* (1998)

Jones, Leonidas M., *The Life of John Hamilton Reynolds* (1984)

Jones, Stanley, *Hazlitt: A Life* (Oxford, 1991)

Kenny, Tom, *Thomas Griffiths Wainewright in New South Wales* (Sydney, 1974)

——*Who Wrote the Pickwick Papers?* (Sydney, 1976)

Kerr, Joan (ed.), *Dictionary of Australian Artists* (Sydney, 1992)

King, Carolyn, *Henry Fuseli* (1974)

King, R. W., *Cary, the Translator of Dante* (1925)

Kirby, J. W., *Early Greenwich Schools* (Glasgow, 1938)

Knight, Charles, *Shadows of the Old Booksellers* (1927)

Kynaston, David, *The City of London* (1994)

Lamb, Charles, *Elia: Essays* (1828)

——*Complete Works,* edited by E. V. Lucas (1912)

——*Selected Prose,* edited by Adam Phillips (Harmondsworth, 1985)

Lanchester, John, *The Debt to Pleasure* (1996)

Lemprière, T. J., *The Penal Settlements of Early Van Diemen's Land* (Hobart, 1954)

Levey, Michael, *Sir Thomas Lawrence* (1976)

Lindop, Greville, *The Opium Eater* (Oxford, 1985)

Lindsey, John, *Suburban Gentleman* (1942)

Locke, John, *An Essay Concerning Human Understanding*, edited by David Campbell (1961)

London Magazine, January 1820–January 1823

Lonsdale, Roger, *Dr. Charles Burney* (Oxford, 1965)

Lucas, E. V., *The Life of Charles Lamb* (1905)

Lytton, Edward Bulwer, *Lucretia* (1846; 1853)

————family archives held in Hertfordshire County Record Office, Hatfield

Mackenzie, Kathleen, *The Great Sarah: The Life of Mrs. Siddons* (1968)

MacLaurin, C., *Thomas Griffiths Wainewright* (Art in Australia, 3rd Series, No. 7)

Macready, W. C., *Reminiscences* (1875)

Mason, Eudo C., *The Mind of Henry Fuseli* (1951)

Mason, Joseph, *Assigned Convict, 1831–1837*, edited by David Kent and Norma Townsend (1996)

Meteyard, Eliza, *The Life of Josiah Wedgwood* (1865)

Miller, Charlotte, *Thomas Phillips* (unpublished MA thesis, Courtauld Institute, May 1977)

Millgate, Michael, *Testamentary Acts* (Oxford, 1992)

Moore, James, *The Convicts of Van Diemen's Land 1840–1853* (Hobart, 1976)

Moore, William, *The Story of Australian Art* (Sydney, 1934)

Naugle, B. C., *The Monthly Review: First Series 1749–1789* (Oxford, 1934)

Newdick, Robert S., *The Life and Letters of Charles Lamb* (Columbus, 1935)

Nicholas, Stephen, *Convict Workers* (Cambridge, 1988)

Norman, Charles, *The Genteel Murderer* (New York, 1956)

Notes & Queries, 3rd Series

Palmer, Samuel, *Letters*, edited by Raymond Lister (Oxford, 1974)

Paston, George, *Sidelights on the Georgian Period* (1902)

Paulin, Tom, *The Day-Star of Liberty: Hazlitt's Radical Style* (1998)

Pearce, Cedric, and Ian Pearce, *Hobart Town Album 1804–1856* (Hobart, 1967)

Pearson, Hesketh, *The Life of Oscar Wilde* (1946)

Phillips, Thomas, *Lectures on the History and Principles of Painting* (1833)

Phillismore, W. P. W., and W. H. Whitear, *Historical Collections Relating to Chiswick* (1897)

Platts, Beryl, *A History of Greenwich* (1973)

Porter, Hal, *The Tilted Cross* (1961)

Porter, Roy, *English Society in the Eighteenth Century* (Harmondsworth, 1990)

Powell, Nicolas, *Drawings of Henry Fuseli* (1951)

Praz, Mario, *The Romantic Agony* (1951)

Procter, Bryan Waller, *An Autobiographical Fragment* (1877)

Quennell, Peter, *Janus Weathercock* (1952)

Redgrave, Samuel, *A Dictionary of Artists of the English School* (1874)

Rhodes, Henry, *Genius and Criminal* (1932)

Rhodes, T. F., *The Craft of Forgery* (1934)

Rimmer, W. G., *Portrait of a Hospital* (Hobart, 1981)

Robinson, Henry Crabb, *His Diary* (1872)

Rude, George, *Protest and Punishment* (Oxford, 1978)

Rule, John, *Albion's People: English Society 1714–1815* (1992)

Salwak, Dale, *The Literary Biography: Problems and Solutions* (1993)

Schenck, H. G., *The Mind of the European Romantics* (1979)

Select Bibliography

Schiff, Gert, *Fuseli* (1974)

Scholes, Percy A., *The Great Dr. Burney* (Oxford, 1948)

Seccombe, Thomas, *Twelve Bad Men* (1894)

Singer, Richard, *Notable Trials* (Auckland, n.d.)

Sitwell, Sacheverell, *Splendours and Miseries* (1943)

Smith, Bernard, *Place, Taste and Tradition* (1945)

Spectator (Melbourne), 14 July 1866

Spector, Robert, *English Literary Periodicals* (The Hague, 1966)

Stevenson, R. L., *The Strange Case of Dr. Jekyll and Mr. Hyde* (Harmondsworth, 1982)

Storey, Edward, *A Right to Song: The Life of John Clare* (1982)

Story, Alfred T., *The Life of John Linnell* (1892)

Sullivan, Alvin, *British Literary Magazines* (New Haven, 1983)

Swinburne, Algernon Charles, *William Blake* (1868)

Symons, A. J. A., *The Quest for Corvo* (1934)

Symons, Julian, *A. J. A. Symons: His Life and Speculations* (1950)

Talfourd, Thomas Noon, *Memoirs of Charles Lamb* (1842)

———*Final Memorials of Charles Lamb* (1848)

———*The Letters and Life of Charles Lamb* (rev. edn, 1908)

Taylor, A. S., *On Poisons in Relation to Medical Jurisprudence* (1875)

Taylor, Charles, *Sources of the Self* (Cambridge, 1984)

Thompson, C. J. S., *Poisons and Poisoners* (1931)

Thornbury, Walter, *Old Stories Re-told* (1879)

Todd, Ruthven, *Tracks in the Snow* (1946)

Tomalin, Claire, *The Life and Death of Mary Wollstonecraft* (1974)

Tomory, Peter, *The Life and Art of Henry Fuseli* (1972)

Vaughan, William, *German Romanticism and English Art* (1974)

Viscomi, Joseph, *Blake and the Idea of the Book* (Princeton, 1993)

Wainwright, Clive, *The Romantic Interior* (1989)

Waterhouse, Ellis, *Painting in Britain 1530–1790* (1953)

Webb, Peter, *The Erotic Arts* (1975)

Webster, F. A. M., *The History of the Fifth Battalion* (1930)

West, John, *The History of Tasmania* (Launceston, 1852)

Whitehead, John, *This Solemn Mockery* (1973)

Wilde, Oscar, "Pen, Pencil and Poison" (1891)

Wilson, Mona, *The Life of William Blake* (rev. edn, 1971)

Wright, Peter, *Erotica and the Enlightenment* (1991)

Index

A Note About the Author

Andrew Motion has written poetry and three biographies, and is presently head of the best-known British creative writing course, at the University of East Anglia. He is head of the Literature Panel of the Arts Council and frequently broadcasts on the BBC. He succeeded Ted Hughes as British Poet Laureate and is married to Jan Dalley, author of *Diana Mosley*. He lives in London.

A Note on the Type

This book was set in Fournier, a typeface named for Pierre Simon Fournier *fils* (1712–1768), a celebrated French type designer. Coming from a family of typefounders, Fournier was an extraordinarily prolific designer of typefaces and of typographic ornaments. He was also the author of the important *Manuel typographique* (1764–1766), in which he attempted to work out a system standardizing type measurement in points, a system that is still in use internationally. Fournier's type is considered transitional in that it drew its inspiration from the old style, yet was ingeniously innovational, providing for an elegant, legible appearance. In 1925 his type was revived by the Monotype Corporation of London.

Composed by NK Graphics,
Keene, New Hampshire

Printed and bound by Quebecor Martinsburg,
Martinsburg, West Virginia

Designed by Soonyoung Kwon

3/01

B
Wainewright
Motion
Wainewright : the poisoner